Talking out of School

by
Lexsana Pilewski-Carr

McClain Printing Company
Parsons, WV
www.mcclainprinting.com
2019

International Standard Book Number 0-87012-895-7
Library of Congress Control Number 2018911860
Printed in the United States of America
Copyright © 2019 by Lexsana Pilewski-Carr
Salem, WV
All Rights Reserved
2019

Cover art by Rachel E. Griffith

Talking out of School

Leo and Mary Kathleen Davis Pilewski pictured on their wedding day, November 23, 1948, the attractive, loving parents who produced Little Apple Head, a daughter with a saucy, sometimes seedy story with a S.T.E.M. (one of many self-labeling acronyms used in this essoir, this one standing for a "Slew of Teaching Experience Malfunctions"). It is an eyebrow-lifting story about a quick career work slide from golden and delicious to vinegary, a sometimes funny, unbelievable retelling of many embarrassing events pressed into remorse, redemption, and wonderful release the day that a retired teacher decided to purge her soul, share a little hard knocks wisdom, and do a bushel of talking out of school.

5/2019

Linda,

I've always considered librarians to be and puppy dogs to be the most dependable beings on the planet! I recently read a quote that said: "Librarians are search engines with heart." My best friends are librarians!

Hoping you find snippets in my book that speak to your heart, and perhaps inspire such a lovely person!

Happy Birthday!
Happy reading!

Letsana

Dedication

To former President George W. Bush, whose colorful word stock inspired my new blending of pre/post suffix-mixers, and other mispronounceables. I always wanted a nickname, and now, having written a book, I have one: "CompLexsana." It certainly defines other educators' perceptions of me! Mr. President, you and your unique wordbook would have been welcome in my accepting senior English class, where all ethnicities and languages were embraced! As a nonpartisan educator, and a fellow "Newlanger," I promise I would never have misunderestimated you. We could have been quite the unconventional grammarial dream team. God bless you and your talent as an artist, sir! And...malapropisms forever!

Table of Contents

Introduction   ix

Acknowledgements   xiii

Twenty-One Things Teachers Want to Say
    to Students Daily   xiv

A Subliminal Forward (Thinking Backward)   xvii

The Last Supper – A Prelude   1

The Cardinals vs. The Also-Rans, a Bird-Brained Story   6

The Vow Factor   27

My Father, the Pope   44

The Dorothy Belle Effect on Big Blonde   74

Mr. Berg's Bat, Mr. Cheese-It, a Poo Poo Wish,
    and One Hot Deputy Dawg   99

Lost Reports, Phallic Wind Sock Artists, Ron B. -Robbie,
    and Square-Headed Bathroom Humor   123

Tears at the Midpoint   136

Me and Mr. Lewinsky – Not a Love Story   153

I Wanna Be a Producer-r-r-r   163

How I Got Rooked – A "Humane Tail"   187

A Much Lesser-Known T.O.Y. Story   200

A Different Kind of Dinner for Schmucks   212

A Prom Rom-Com   220

West Side [Salem] Story and Revived Plants –
    A Teachable Moment   232

MRSA, MRSA Me! The Infectious Joys of Teaching!   243

Do the Right Thing – Students to the Rescue   260

A Note from the Teacher's Desk...   281

A Funeral Awakening – The Circle Closes   285

Epilogue   297

About the Author   303

A donation will be made for each book sold to the Harrison County, West Virginia, Humane Society.

Introduction

Dear Reader,

I was raised to believe confession is good for the soul. More recently, this confession business has gotten easier for me. Being raised a confessing Catholic helped. Talking into an empty booth of spray tan dimensions, feeding my soul's flaws into a semi-opaque screen order window to a priest thinking about Notre Dame's football team made my latter years more of a "speak easy." In effect, I learned to speak out easier. Confession was always my ritual and obligatory Saturday punishment for surviving yet another hellish week of unbelievable work. School--- meaning student, and later, surprise! teacher---(and I use my personal career title loosely) for me was subjugation and Cecil B. DeMille-grand disasters, flying chairs and administrative put-downs, kowtowing and trying to exercise any shred of saving creativity whenever I had the chance. Mine was never the sedentary, standardized classroom. And that's as descriptive as I care to be this late at night, because I wrote this introduction after the book, and frankly, I'm just too wrought with drain to rehash one more catastrophe. I feel tired.

The point is that as a non-traditional teacher, I held things in too much: retorts (they never came to me until nine years after the injustice had passed), regrets, secrets, urine, and my astute observations about all things educational. But...not...any...more.

For nearly three decades I survived, pressed on. As a retiree (it sounds so relieving and so aging all at once), I no longer hold anything in because for some basic biological reason, I cannot. The world does not care about my opinions, because as Mark Twain reminded me, "the world was here first."

Nonetheless, I have feelings and opinions anyway, and I intend to relate things, revealing things, favorite things, let them fly like drones on speed. All the thoughts that had been whirring above me like an angry, blonde-hating hornet, I could not swat away. So, I jotted down accidental missteps, my misgivings, and misadventures that somehow turned around. At some point, I'd grown as a true confessor and was freer to expose a smidgen of education's foibles that my working, check-receiving teacher friends cannot.

Like Miss Ponytail pictured proudly on her Warrior Cycle, I knew that I would someday pedal my innermost thoughts onto four separate computers, pay for publishing programs I could not even open or operate, and drive at least three computer techies into rehab of various sorts. Once all the chunks were gathered I began to dream of owning a "second spine" with my exotic-sounding name and appealing book title down the side of it, the kind of spine that turns heads over sharply to one side, admiring an unusual moniker, something as impressive-sounding as Conway Twitty, Sebastian Maniscalco, or Luciano Pavarotti.

What I'd wished for from my eighth birthday cake and candles blowout, I finally got. The dream took over a dozen years. It had to. I had to work *and* squeeze out every bad event in order to make my book attractive to the smart, curious public who love reading about other people's miseries and missteps. Calamity sells so well that a passionate author will throw *herself* under the bus if the hospital stay yields good material.

This book thing brings up a question I have always pondered: If we are what we eat, what are we, based on what we read? One big Pioneer Woman recipe card? A novel attorney? A King of horror things? Or, the one I could never be for long --- a woman of mysteries. I read almost half of the Nancy Drew books I got for gifts. Not once did I divulge how they ended. Where did I go wrong?

Why would I write a book shading the sanctity of teaching and say too much? Maybe too many teachers' meetings had erased my better judgment. Or maybe my mother reminded me over and over that I always divulged too much, yielding me uninteresting and perpetually single. I showed her! I got married! I was a mere fifty-eight and a half at the time!

Also, I needed to share out that some experiences should not be repeated twice. Teaching is one of them, and yet, I did just that. If a job is something so fulfilling you would do it happily for free, then doesn't this explain why so many happy, happy people teach? (I confess, as noted throughout the book, that sometimes there is a perception that I hyperbolize the truth by sometimes not telling it.)

So, know that the best-seller all the Americas have been pining for is at hand, as near as the John Grisham and J.K. Rowling sections of the bookstore in which you are currently standing!

I cannot undo my career choices, nor would I. I loved every miscreant I taught; yet, as I've stated, I might unintentionally lie a little, which I blame on advanced years and memory loss.

If you happen to be a teacher in training, please be mindful that "practice" and the actual "party" are two disparate things. Ask *many* questions during the school observation phase. No education course prepared me for my many mobocracy moments.

Any future teachers' college needs to round out its education course requirements with these curriculum considerations:

Purchasing Classroom Necessities/Snacks on a Shoestring Salary - "The Best Deals"

Group Counseling Without a License

Suze Orman's Armageddon Survival Kit in Airtight Portfolio - Teacher Disaster Edition

Dancing Down the Anger - Pop and Lock and Virginia Reel Basic Steps for Rival Gangs or Contentious Colleagues

Classroom Brawl Containment: Rapid Response Methodologies

The Healing Power of the Donut (Included: Donut Shop Locations and Hours of Weekday Operations, By State, for Early Ed Risers)

Keepin' it Holy-Real and Legal: The Power of Silent Prayer and Petitions - An Overview of Old Testament Fair and Impartial Means of Determining Discipline and Fitting Punishment

Afternoon Nappers and their Ringing iPhones: Muting the Disruptive "Sleeper" Cells in Your Class

Coarse content? Check! A bit raw? Affirmative! Redemption needed? Indubitably. Consider yourself disclaimer'd.

Perhaps you will embrace your mundane life more and tolerate your own career better after reading the slippery slope where mine traveled.

Enjoy my slide!!

Lexsana Pilewski-Carr

Acknowledgements

I wish to thank Joel Osteen for encouraging my dream each and every Sunday. Also, my husband who became an accidental editor, listening to passages and not holding back. Laura, Donna, and Gregg, the trifecta that kept me believing each day for several years that I could do the impossible, despite technology issues of all kinds. A big heap of gratitude to Marshall Tenney, computer store genius who cajoled my computer and printer into cooperating on my manuscript. Bless dear Mom and Dad, and Dorothy Belle Davis forever and ever. Amen. Special love to the awesome people at McClain Printing Company, especially Michelle Mullenax-McKinnie, who got my publishing party started. And to former student, Rachel Griffith, who never doubted that I really *had* written a book and needed a graphic designer. Special thanks to "The Trio." To Sarah, and all my students, whether you loved or disliked me, a thank you for giving me chapter material. I hope those creative writing students I so loved will write their own books someday, but hurry up! I'm getting old! Whoever said "The cemetery is full of unfulfilled hopes and dreams" -- Thank You. Now I understand it. And above all else, thank you to the most awesome-est Trinity: God, Jesus, and my hero, The Holy Spirit. Do you want to know something? God is faithful, and HE IS GOOD----all...the...time!

Twenty-one Things Teachers Have (or Want) to Say to Students Daily

21) Day One: Bring pencil and paper! I am not Walmart!
20) Day One Hundred: Bring pencil and paper! I haven't been to Walmart!
19) All Day Every Day: Put that phone away!
18) Pull up those pants! NOT telling you again tomorrow!
17) Pull up those pants! NOT telling you again tomorrow!
16) Yes, this quiz counts. One, two, three, four…
15) You were just joking about your acceptance letter from Al Qaeda, right?
14) Take out the gum and talk above a mumble!
13) Get your hands out of your pockets!
12) Get your hands out of your pants!
11) I'm not your mother! Think!
10) How many Christmas presents did it take to get you out of middle school?
9) No one is going to the bathroom! Use your backup bladder!
8) No, I did not know we were having a Code Red. And, no, I will not be your human shield!
7) I don't know what's for lunch. I hope it has serotonin in it.
6) Put your case of makeup away. There are no auditions today. Girls, likewise!
5) Do NOT curse! Stop lying to me! God still makes lightning strikes and I am standing too close to you right now!
4) You got an "F" because you earned that "F"!! Didn't I tell you? "F" is the new black ---- as in black hole.
3) Yes, as a matter of fact, I do own an iron. Would you like me to press your mouth?
2) No, we are not going outside to catch fly balls. Just sit there and sleep and catch flies your usual way.
1) Can the orthodontist tighten your braces *and* your mouth?

Teachers know that the lessons provided by time outshine our own best efforts. We inspire, but time matures and better teaches those we inspire. We must be tolerant, kind, patient, and respectful of time. It grows and completes us all.

Lexsana K. Pilewski-Carr

A Subliminal Forward (Thinking Backward)

Occasionally my husband and I act like we're important people (Republicans), like people in smoking jackets and rich brocade lady jackets (stained jeans and "West Virginia Cutie" T-shirts). We sip our finest tea (ice-cold Coke Zero in measuring cups when dishes are washing) and dive into (we don't swim) the minefield of education (Boom!) We recall rousing key events (hell-on-earth whole chapters) of productive moments (all students awake) in our own teaching careers. During one busy morning (of drooling nothingness), I decided to publish my "essoir" (essay parts morphed into a memoir). Husband's interest piqued (feigned).

"So, should I finish that book I started ten years ago? A memoir, maybe?" (begging the question), I asked him one evening as we ate smoked salmon at table (popcorn in our lounge chairs).

"A memoir? Of what, teaching? Do teachers do that? I don't think I ever read a memoir by a teacher," he reflected, deeply (never taking his transfixed eyes off a NASCAR race).

That was my epiphany about the profession both of us had just polished off like donuts (teachers' holy wafers). The inference from his teacher-author memoir question was that the reading public (some actually can read, and still read actual books), would resist parting with $17.95 to buy anything written by a teacher (profession with apparent zero side talent, but still manages to teach all the earth's other professions). The second inference was that teachers' supposed lackluster lives lack a life, because they are machines who never, ever veer from a forty-year daily grind. To paraphrase Lin Manuel Miranda (who knows about love of any kind and that mildly successful musical surrounding a ten-dollar bill on Broadway): "Teaching is teaching is teaching is teaching…."

We ruminated in the Hamptons one patriotic weekend (up on our hilltop mini patio, twirling sparklers), and let the juices flow (grilling hamburgers on a $19.99 WalMart lopsided charcoal grill).

"You'd better do the memoir while it's still all fresh in your head," hubby said (meaning, write it down NOW, before you ask me each morning why the Easter eggs are all dyed brown and hidden in an Eggland carton in the fridge).

"I intend to, and I am going to get started tomorrow!" said I (meaning in a future decade).

"Good, because no one else can tell your story but you." (silently repeating the earlier question, but only in his head: *Do teachers write memoirs, really? Well…better not quit my retirement job.*)

I had a rich story to tell (and private parts not to tell), something out-of-the-box, epic-like (marginally appealing, with that pity clap feel, destined never to become a major motion picture, like *The Bounce Castle* or *Thursdays with Sidney* or *Goodbye, Mr. Cheetos*).

In summer of 2016 I found one of those five-star NYC writing schools (online, with offices located outside the basement of Filene's Basement) and signed up for entry level courses (digital correspondence graded by passing subway commuters), instructed and hurtfully critiqued by a former cashier (prostitute) who wrote in-depth analyses per writing task (hated everything I wrote, even before I wrote it, the moment she found out I was a retired teacher). In one writing teacher-parody of a critique, she wrote that I should not sound so condescending in using phrases like "these people" and "Mairzy doats and dozy doats and little lambsy divey" (Al Trace---jivey!). Full confession here. I quit the class and wrote Academy Director Fleece-um (Filene's chief makeup artist), telling her exactly how I felt. I whined that my writing teacher (grim reaper composition-killing sarcasm churl) wrote me things that hurt like the Dickens (Charles). I heard no more from the underground academy without walls or sewage plant. (My Visa card was charged full tuition that summer, the minute I clicked on their kitchy website.) My writing career was kaput. (What writing career?) I put my head down on my no-good writer's writing desk for four weeks, lifting myself up only for life's barest necessities (carryout, TGIF spinach-artichoke dip and chips, and *America's Got Talent*).

But last fall, a friend from junior high, a sharp cookie I taught with before we both retired from the same high school (quite suddenly, for different but content reasons), purposely sent me two composition books, one with shih tzu puppies, the other, angora kitties, rendering me a blob of non-resistance to writing. My vow to keep my head down on my desk and count the braids in my living room runner was all over (ruined, actually, when Stripey Cat caught her claw in the runner loops and frantically pulled that full runner behind her like a second tail). I saved her. (She saved me.)

Since I didn't want to let my friend down, I wrote furiously in those composition books (the item numbers of every Isaac Mizrahi piece on QVC). Eventually, my writing paid off. (My Visa remained stout and immovable.)

Where would my inspiration come, that hook, the story arc that would propel the reader to keep exercising her/his right to read, and maybe resolve a deep conflict (between me and my wallet) and stir the reader to ask self-questions *(How many pages are in this thing anyway?)*.

So, I wrote the ending first. I remembered that when the essay/memoir/story starts either at the middle ("in medias res") or the end ("el fin"), it eventually leads back to the beginning, thus explaining the potential tale of woe in "full circle" (because that's how non-teacher screenwriters earn big bucks, writing in full circle airplane mode). I faintly recall that I used to teach this complicated story principle regarding the "full circle" of composition, holding out my left long-sleeved arm. (I forgot to depilatory it.) I had the perfect visual aid for the lesson, too! I was wearing my Joan Rivers oversized sunshine yellow faux-alligator watch (QVC, the "C" stands for cultivating composition), pointing at its big face (nearly big as my own), circling the full dial clockwise with my finger, naming story elements as I drew a circle from 12, down and around, back up to 12, illustrating to my captivated (yawning) students that this sophisticated demo was known in the writing industry as "circling the dial" (killing the last five minutes of class, keeping the natives from getting restless).

There were writers in that room! (desktop Bic pen cutters, always in bad moods, carving salty new common nouns into my desks). I listened to my own teaching, even taking notes for myself (grocery lists before the commute home) and decided that one day I would put my words where my mouth was. (I don't actually think that's possible.) I was overcome (tingly, picturing myself at a book signing, like Carrie Bradshaw), with a desire to share out my wisdom and perhaps spare some twenty-something a few deep-dug holes due to life and early career mistakes. (But, isn't that what therapy is for?) I also <u>celebrate myself</u> (unlike Walt Whitman's awful beard trimmer) and <u>sing myself</u> (shameful line plug from *Leaves of Grass*), in this book. This somewhat-like-a-memoir-written-by-a-six-year-old book is something I always dreamed of doing (because nobody cared to hear my tales of woe and hilarity for free). Now that it is finished, I can get back to my potholder loom and loop through the rest of next year's Christmas presents.

Thus, full-circle style, this story closes. (And so, it begins...)

A teachable moment for all...Rhonda (left) and Editor Becky encircle Miss Yearbook advisor. Their body language speaks for high school students everywhere who must take on the task of raising a good teacher. Their faith in my abilities was palpable. My blackboard was clean, for once as empty as my own apple head...Is that a phone on my desk? Without a receiver?? Clearly, if so, there was absolutely no talking out of school ---yet.

The Last Supper -- A Prelude

"You may just be the winner tonight, girl," I said out loud to the mirror. I was lying. I hated liars.

Still, my big honor moment might be coming, a mere two-hour drive from home, at the Charleston Marriott. If only George Clooney were already there, waiting for me. In the penthouse. With chilled Diet Sunkist Orange. And a board game. I could say screw the trophy.

I was dressing, putting on the whole armor of a winning warrior, ready for the statewide Teachers' Awards Battle, an annual September event in West Virginia teacherdom. I put on the bra lift of righteousness, the luminous makeup of vanity, my finest faux jewelry. And still, I was not feeling red-carpet ready. As in any other award nomination (totaling none), I was having flashbacks, misgivings. Was I really a potential winner of anything all-out grand, especially The West Virginia Teacher of the Year 2007? Based on my empty trophy case and my all-book book shelves, I was guessing…no.

There before me, the award warrior in the mirror, was an aura of memories: being called 'Pollack' by students and even more impressively, bosses who couldn't spell it; being told by a student I had the hands for a horror movie; taking amateur heckling from colleagues; being the grope-ee in my younger career years; getting stuck with every faculty assignment I really did and didn't want; surviving a real-life tornado; just being my martyr-y self.

What an impressive career bio staring back at me in that mirror, mirror! It was as speckled as the dried toothpaste dots dirtying the glass. Maybe, being a winner would win me back a little remuneration for my twenty-four years of real and imagined suffering. But, really, do losers ever win? Or choose to quit suffering? Or decide they have done anything remotely remarkable?

Suddenly I wasn't so excited about my slick pantsuit, designed by 1992 Miss West Virginia, Kim Parrish, now a celebrity and shopping channel mogul. Her titled name was significant; I was convinced the outfit from that lovely state native from Parkersburg would bring me luck.

"Take a raincoat, Lexsana, you need a 'wrap'!" (southern ebonics for outer wear). "It's going to rain. It's going to be dark soon and it calls for thunderstorms tonight."

...Yes, I lived with my mother. And, no, she was not a meteorologist. But she could make it rain. She made it rain on me every damned day, as if my spirits needed any additional dampening.

Nobody knew southern belle, Mary Kathleen Davis Pilewski, like I did. She was all steel, great skin, and low-tolerance for inferiority of any kind, especially regarding finesse. "Kitty" was already sick to death of hearing about the stupid awards banquet, sick of suffering along with me throughout the difficult application process. With fifty-five county contestant hopefuls, and one winner, she saw poor odds. I believe she'd already placed me with the sad-faced "majority divide."

Had my father still been alive, if Mom had intimated to him my predictable placement in the group-of-losers award outcome, I knew just what Dad would have said.

2

It would have sounded vaguely melodramatic, like the closing dialogue of a certain salacious dance movie, even if the original movie version did not have Daddy saying it: "Nobody puts baby in the [loser's] corner!"

"Now you know I can't go to that banquet, Lexsana. You know I can't walk and I will not use an ugly ol' cane! People would stare at me." Mom had a youth fixation. On herself.

People *had* stared at her when she was in her prime, a beauty who was ripe for Hollywood. Except she wanted Hollywood to come to her, having little encouragement to pursue her dreams. So she lived inside the glitzy pages of *Modern Screen* and *Photoplay* magazines. She knew the longitude and latitude to Hollywood. I knew every last one of Elizabeth Taylor's husbands in alphabetical order, plus the life-changing knowledge that Liz slept on silk sheets every night and every morning someone changed her bedding to new silk sheets. She supposedly had her favorite chili flown into whatever hangar was closest to her latest work. Mom considered this very important for me to know. It was. It made me hungry for chili.

Lately there had developed a teensy bit of Norma Desmond in my mom, minus that entire Halloween grimace thing; she preferred being frozen in time, immovable both physically and emotionally. And, ironically, that *Sunset Boulevard* Norma reference had extra meaning for me personally. It reminded me that I was Max, her dedicated, subservient butler. At times, I had the exact sullen, tortured face of Max---though in my movie, I was not her former husband.

"You need to stand up straighter. Put some Lancome blush on! Do you have on any mascara?" she asked Max. "Two coats," Max answered.

There was nothing wrong with Mom's eyesight. She wore expensive face creams and makeup (including high-dollar mascara) daily, and she could see a thread raveling on a floral skirt one county away. She only used cheaters for her favorite pastime, crosswords. Mom admired puzzles like Norma admired William Holden.

It was an unusual relationship between her and me. Kitty occasionally tossed out nice compliments with a subtle inference, the way I administered pills to my dogs, wrapping their nasty-tasting antibiotics in cheese. I served as her obedient fan base. Because for all her oddity, she had a Cracker Jack mind, elevated vocabulary, and spelling chops, a family-recognized dominance, plus a fancy pen, for which she did *New York Times* crosswords. "I like to do my puzzles in ink," she smiled, holding up the pen like George Burns' cigar, ready for an affirming compliment. She deserved one. I couldn't even understand most of the clues.

"I'm telling you one thing, Mom. Tonight, I am going to drive right past Charleston without my damned raincoat, and just keep going and going, me and my big, happy teaching career and life! HA! HA! HA! HA! HA!"

...Thought it, just never said it. But to appease her, the Salem branch of *The Weather Channel*, I would take the damned raincoat, knowing full well it wasn't going to rain. Not on my parade. Not tonight.

Of course, I would not drive *to* or *past* Charleston. There was no GPS in my Subaru yet, because I resisted all the latest technology on principle (meaning I could not even turn it on). I liked taking noble stands that always put me on the long track around the barn; therefore, tonight, if I drove more than one hour in any direction, I would be lost until Christmas. My brother, sister-in-law, and niece were taking me to the banquet. Clearly, for them it

4

might just be a total mercy mission. It made me feel even more…*directionless*, a highly significant term recurring throughout my career years.

Off we went, headed for Charleston. In no time, it was raining. I touched the hem of my raincoat, folded across my lap. Mom's words were drizzling right through the fabric, dampening my spirits. Dad nor Dorothy Belle would be there. I wondered if they could see me drowning in doubt, my two reasons for becoming an educator. I thought about the earlier bad teachers who moved me not to imitate them when I grew up enough to teach. *Had I grown up?* I wondered if *they* saw me drowning tonight and hoped my life raft had a valve issue.

What in hell did I know about deserved honor? I wasn't even sure I liked education yet, twenty-four years in.

How did I always end up in world bizarre? Why had I made things so hard on myself again, always working months and years for a single moment that had a consistently negative end? My relationships, my canceled wedding, my staying at home, directing plays with Armageddon events? What was so important about this paltry little contest that I pushed myself to walk the plank of slim odds once more? What did I think a title would rectify?

You set yourself up for loss, old girl, because you like it; you think that's what you deserve, I thought, looking through the back seat window at the moving blur. Trees were losing leaves, pointing bony fingers at me. The skies were frowning dismal gray. I was beginning to get a sinking feeling, another cold reality. Had the temperature dropped? I felt I needed to put on that raincoat. Over my head.

One more time, I was getting the test before the lesson, just like always. The real question seemed to be: Would I learn any lesson tonight about self-worth, or just keep failing my own damaged personality test of trying too hard?

5

The Cardinals vs. The Also-Rans, a Bird-Brained Story 🐑

Eight-year-olds in third grade (even those in other galaxies), learn quickly the subtleties of innuendo, of watching and learning subtext and other attempts by adults at coded subterfuge. I was in my **Three Stooges** *films phase with my dad and brother, enough to know what the flattering term "bird brain" meant when said to another human. There were three stooges in those shorts, and Moe was not the bird brain. In one plot, Curly's head was X-rayed, revealing a working cuckoo clock inside his shorn cranium. Would my head reveal similar intelligence? Third grade had me thinking so.*

At eight, I got my first exposure to one of the dirtier learning trends of the twentieth century. At the same time, that pecking-good thriller, *The Birds*, came out. It was 1963, apparently The Year of Odd Ornithology. There was something scary about all the bird talk, and it wasn't Alfred Hitchcock. One of those en vogue, up-the-ranks education brass decided there was a birdlike, cagy way to identify elementary reading levels -- just identify student ability under cover of bird species! The project was given the code name A.V.I.A.A.R.Y. for: "All Victims in ABC Land Are Reading Yutzes."

My grade school bought into the trend. Nobody would ever, ever suspect there was something fowl in play. And, obliging employee of the state that she was, my third-grade teacher picked out discreet code names that attempted to mask any similarities between human capability and birds' brains. I was just a kid, but I had an epiphany as to why ornithology and third grade didn't work for me. Simply stated, third grade reading circle was a grim party owl the time.

"Read this passage and identify the story arc, literary devices, and denouement," Mrs. Spider directed us. It was a tricky comprehension question, one I can barely answer today. We all had a bird name. There were three divisions: redbirds, bluebirds, and blackbirds. In other words, seeing red as royal, they went from greater, to lesser, to bird brains. Who knew Moe Howard was on point with cutting-edge reading education strategies?

Blackbirds seated against the far row of windows were not in a flattering category or room placement. Those windows were drafty. They were reading's undesirables. Bluebirds nested in the middle. Redbirds (West Virginia's regal state bird symbol), meant entitlement and extra attention. If your seat was home to the wooden blackboard on the warm, inner wall of the classroom, you had a little more "cock in your walk."

The Middle was my home initially; I had the blues. How bad was it that my dad was a teacher and I was his lukewarm-minded daughter, color-coded? (cuckoo! cuckoo!) I didn't even like blue. Blue was for skinny blondes. Thus, I busted my tuft to get promoted to red.

"Lexsana, move over one group," said teacher one day. "Which way?" I nearly said, but caught myself. It was the nicest thing she ever said to me. Success came, because I worked hard to get out of that nesting place. There was a portal to the elitist Reds, one group away, and I got to migrate, but I would have to bring my red game!

We were naively un-cynical back in the dawn of civilization, the feathered dinosaur age. No one spoke of color internment camps out on the playground. We were too happy seeing the light of day. But I was bothered, consumed by it. Reading bird categories had labeled us like rock, paper, scissors, as in, dumb as a rock, blank as a sheet of paper, and sharp as scissors. It was labeling. Is calling someone a blackbird ever a good thing? Is black ever flattering, except in a slimming formal wear sort of way? Were the black flock the type of kids to poop on cars on their walk home? What a hypocrite I was! It occurred to me that I had all this empathy for the lesser species, yet worked my tail feathers off to reach Red. I felt like a double agent with a conscience, a "bath of fire," as it would be labeled by a high school teacher later on.

I arrived in Cardinalville, exhausted because just getting out of my seat taxed me. I went home at night with nut, bolt, and screw imprints on the tops of my thick legs. I raised and lowered my eyebrows to wake up my brain as I tried to discreetly squeeze into this new nest, a smaller seat. Teacher was quick to see my facial tic, but soon was emulating me. No human can stand against the silent eyebrow challenge. No human wants to be a low brow. You raise your brows, they raise theirs. We kept eyebrow push-ups going for a while. It was all meant as a distraction tactic. But it wore off quickly.

Mrs. Teacher pitted us against each other's smarts. She was Merv Griffin, and we were her game show pilot.

Example: "Lexsana, what orbital path did John Glenn's craft take?" I looked at the passage, but I hadn't been listening during oral reading. My cheeks would burn with a chance to shine, mingled with the possibility of saying the wrong thing, causing our teacher to pull out portable oxygen from her private closet. I drew on my best friend, imagination, narrowing my eyes to look smarter.

"Well, John Glenn is from Ohio, our neighbor to the west, close to where My Aunt Patty and Uncle Mason live. I would guess a western world kind of orbit around the axis of power, with the chance of burn from re-entering orth's erbit."

I almost had her right there till the end. Then, the cardinal with brighter plumes, Lynn, corrected me. We did not have to scrape teacher off our county-issued moon glow-painted ceiling.

"God," I prayed, "let jumbo me be covered by my fast reading. Let me peck out the message and show those skinnies. And please don't let my stomach growl before lunch. Amen." It never did, because you can't starve a rhino, especially when Mom's cinnamon French toast was on the morning menu. I concentrated harder, using my ability to inflect when I read out loud ---as if my smarts would camouflage the whole side-of-beef of me.

But, I *did* know how to ask Teacher the probing questions. Boot licking smile required!

Example: "Teacher, can you explain to us red birds how to find our way at night, with the constellations as our only guide? And, as I was reading in *World Book* (smarts plug), is it true that certain gemstones helped sailors at sea find their way at night? What were the stones they used? That's exciting!"

I cannot recall her answers; she answered nonetheless, because she was an eagle, a category limited to high-flying teachers only.

My chair was way too small, even though it was the biggest model the janitor could drag in the room without herniating himself. It was as far away as teacher could put me without making me pass my papers in from the brick window ledge. By lunch, I was usually stuck in my chair. There was lots of leg squealing, "skeeking," and it mimicked the way athletes' sneakers would catch on gymnasium floors. When my sweaty flesh worked its way off that varnished seat, those closest to me either rolled their eyes or covered their ears to preserve their hearing. Both my not-so-birdie-legs had red wood burn.

"Miss Caufield will be here tomorrow for music time," Mrs. Spider announced.

OH MY GOD! N-O-O-O-O-O! I thought. *Not the red-headed devil!* I knew because I was so big, I would be an easy target. I would have to identify a sixteenth note and a scale note besides. I had to retain my red bird-bright status. Mom, the family's librarian, would find a noteworthy picture for me in our expensive alabaster and pine green and textured faux leather set of *World Book Encyclopedia.*

And in third grade, my hatred of all things acronym promptly began.

"PAY ATTENTION, CLASS!" Miss C harpied out to us. Her face was an oval of dry, white powdery spackle. Her eyebrows were the richly-painted-on kind, perhaps applied while driving her horse to my grade school. She knew how to torture the quaking inmates. "'F.A.C.E.' stands for notes on the spaces of the music scale, from bottom to top...**ARE YOU LISTEN-I-N-N-G?**" She held that "ING" out her thin, red-dyed lips like it was the last note in an opera where the ancient senorita with bumpy brows is startled by Barcelona sewer rats.

That frustrated old maiden treated the world like her poison pitch pipe. She put the fear of God in us fast when that mental equivalent of an eight-inch dental drill came out of her SOA---(saddlebag of agony). I knew she could eat that round pipe like the metal cookie it was. In her defense, I will say she treated everyone the same. We were all stupid turd-grade blackbirds with zero musical talent.

The Divine Miss C. stood over my desk. I am ready for YOU! I said inside my head.

"Lexsana, draw me a sixteenth note."

I would show her! I drew that black oval boat and vertical line with two ship flags sailing above it. TA-DAHHH!

*"NO! You haven't been **LISTEN-I-N-N-G!*** You drew the vertical line *on the wrong side of the note! It's backwards!"*

We were taught lots about things with scales. We were taught nothing that contributed to a child's self-esteem.

Our school health nurse was another pleasure. We anticipated her visits like childhood diseases. She knew her stuff, knew every name on the books. How did she keep all those names and matching slurs straight? "Pilewski, let's see your nails! Your handkerchief! Your tonsils!" The sight of my swollen throat-stored golf balls made her reel. "Yep, surgery's coming for you soon!" she said, tossing that wood tongue depressor into the garbage can with a loud TING! "Weight, elevated."

Then came the dreaded pencil and hair surfing for nits. I had to say, she barely looked for any in my pony tail. It was thick, too. Maybe she thought My Little Pony would swish my equine tail around and knock her on her health records.

Twenty-plus years later she was *still* the health nurse. I was teaching at my first high school. She still looked kind of the same. I did not.

"Well, Pilewski! You've lost some weight! Hm! You're bleaching your hair, too, I see!" I thought she might check my nails and hair and then order me to tear down then reassemble the old typewriter in my classroom while she timed me.

Red birds dutifully turned their seats into a semicircle, our backs to the rest of the class, as we read from coded workbooks, further delineating us from the rest of the flock. I held my own in that configuration, but every day, I glanced over my shoulder to the blank, sad faces. They sat there looking like oiled, orphaned birds with downturned beaks, left behind, on their own for survival. I saw that each knew exactly who and what he/she was, maybe a blackbird for life.

It was the Age of Exclusion in education---the inner circle of smarts was impenetrable, like a rich girls' sorority. Separationism was cool in a comprehension context and placement sort of way. Some teachers shamelessly pandered to those more postured students whose parents elevated their redbirds to snob status. The remaining class were handed worksheets and colored pencils. I grew to hate those sheets and I wasn't even receiving them. But they were accepting them like a Friday paycheck for cleaning toilets.

Secretly, I resented being accelerated, I had trouble concentrating around my semicircle seat wigglers, delirious with their own smarts. What I had worked for was not so wonderful. I realized that my big matriculation was bogus. Answers to Teacher's questions were spoken in brags. The classroom, at least mine, was little more than a game show for attention and prizes. I felt embarrassed by it. One would think that a teacher's attention, given only to a few, would have the remaining two groups plotting a blaze with those crisp worksheets. No sir. They were conditioned. Authority was cold, foreboding. My teacher's staccato, loud finger snaps and deep brown eyes kept everyone subdued.

"Stay on the blacktop!" the teachers barked to us at recess. After those four words, you were on your own.

I spent time at the silver pole parallel bars, pretending to be gymnast Bart Connor. I was partially shielded by the low-hung pine branches, trying to hoist myself into the air, lock my elbows and swing my feet. My socks were dusty every night because all I could do was shuffle my shoes on tiptoe, scuffing those black patent canoes through the dirt.

I had time by myself to spy on the two or three teachers gathered, their lacy sweaters caped over their shoulders, oblivious to the cruelties on the playground. When they laughed, I felt it was against the slow starters. When they nodded, I figured they were concurring that Hitler had the right idea about society's weaker elements. When they smiled, they were saying cruel one-liners like their student counterparts.

God! I hated school! I dreamed of a day when I would never have to see inside a school again. Did that prayer go out into space and infinity like some wayward flashlight beam? That misguided wish must have, because I spent forty-five bizarre years inside walls that sometimes revealed invisible bars.

In addition to the music supervisor, our teacher also had her own pitch pipe, shaped like a big, smashed Oreo and we heard it puffed at us over and over during our Caufield-less jam sessions, wails that made it hard to ever love harmonica tunes in later life. Teacher's gaunt cheeks swelled out like bubbles then burst and deflated.

Sometimes it was a sour note, a big "Waaaaaaaaaa," that sounded like an old train crying. It might not resemble the actual tune at all. She had written a parody for West Virginia's 100th Jubilee to the down tune of that Broadway standard, *O My Darling Clementine*, from the Broadway musical flop, *Make Mine Mining!* I remember those Sondheimian lyrics to this day:

> **West Virginia, West Virginia,**
> **Mountaineers are always free,**
> **Come and join our celebration---**
> **in this splendid mountain state...**

I sat near the brick ledge singing to myself: Come and join our celebration, *nineteen hundred sixty-three*, thus denoting the hundred years of statehood, 1863 – 1963, plus rhyming it together! Maybe I'd had an extra stack of pancakes that morning off the breakfast buffet at home. Maybe I had the syrup sweats. We put bright bird Lynn up to broaching the rhyme dilemma. She decided to use our suggestion!

One of the red birds happened to like me most of the time, for whatever reason, though two of her could stand inside my full-figured child-adult body. She was thin and had a proper nose and skin like softened French vanilla ice cream. I could have licked her face off like a quarter ice-cream cone. Her skin was that sweet-creamy. Her hair was always somewhere between Little Lulu and Orphan Annie. Hair was fixable. Fat was forever.

She tapped me on the left shoulder. "My mother said you are a big, fat cow, hee hee."

It was nothing to me, hearing it said. If I had no sharp, mean girl response, I had to take it, I figured. But it hurt.

14

"As it turns out, she's probably right." *Why* was I being so self-deprecating, just the way prissy people and bullies like it. I never defended myself. I let others pigeon hole me, mock me. I was their soft target.

My passivity was not my only reason for letting that classmate live. I could have bear hugged her into an irreversible coma in seconds.

She owned Barbies and Midge, and hunky Ken. She had the pink Austin Healey Barbie roadster, and she let me come over to gaze upon Barbie's Dream House. Walking into her tiny bedroom, seeing her bed laden with clowns and dolls in hand-crocheted cascading dresses was good, but her Barbie collection was so covetous I still want it today. I was in the presence of the pink side of Heaven----*Barbiedom!*

"You have the best dolls in the world!" I said to add more joy to her happiness collection. It was easy. Her mom had asked me to stay for supper. I smelled chicken frying! Yes! Toss that stick girl a compliment! For hot biscuits, I would find a second one.

So, yes, I took her taunt. I would be bovine, keep calm, and moo on so I could Barbie down.

Since she was obliging with her Mattel playthings, I had to be happy for her the same day each year, on Halloween. Real-life Barbie always took first prize for the school Halloween costume parade's "prettiest costume." The entire school went for "ugliest," knowing that taking on the pretty meant excommunication by the entire, Barbie-captivated faculty. In effect, we were doing some pigeonholing on ourselves, labeling our class, one pretty, majority ugly.

I remember the voluminous cloud of a princess dress she wore that year we were cardinals, perhaps

15

Cinderella Blue. Her mother had been adding chiffon underpinning by the yard since the day after the Christmas before. This gown was the one even fairy godmothers and magic mice couldn't sew. She swept into that room and that mile-wide dress literally parted us like the Red Sea, split us asunder in her spinning with the added air current of her swinging scepter-wand of Domination.

"You're the most beautiful Cinderella we've ever seen!" we screamed, like she was Paul McCartney in disguise, with diamonds. We barely got the princess wave back.

Grade school was like that. Oh hell, any school was like that. Every school had its Glinda Dress-up Girl. She already knew she would be on the Homecoming Court someday *and* drum majorette. She (Head Red Bird), was solely responsible for the heavy girl's distress (mine), resulting in the Salem Twinkies shortage of 1963 at Troy's General Store.

I would watch so many crime dramas maybe for inspiration, in case red birds ever got to read *Hardy Boy Mysteries* or *Nancy Drew* books. Perry Mason was my favorite detective, probably because Perry was on the plump side with eye puffs and dark circles. Every time a murder occurred and the police chalk artist drew around the deceased, the white chalk outline was always just *so bony*. This caught my attention. Not once was there a *fat* chalk outline because only the toothpicks of the world lacked the fiber and fatty tissue to survive. I never remember a fat corpse ever. I could only deduce that in order to stay alive, one must not be lean. "Skinny people are walking murder candidates!" I told my stuffed tiger, Stripe. "The thins are being killed off by jealous fat people!"

Although Stripe never answered, I was onto something. This was big! And, as if that weren't enough

16

to sweeten the pot, I heard my grandma remind my mom one day: "Remember: Feed a cold; starve a fever." I did some hypothesizing. If I got a cold, then I could feed it. This might require playing in snow with wet hair, without rubber boots, then later slipping Dad my grocery list of get-well goodies, which we could stash in his 48 Chevy!

Christmas. I was really hating school, the closer the holiday got. There were no new surprises for the holiday program. My budding acting skills would not get exercised yet again.

"Lexsana, you'll be the flying reindeer, powering Santa's sleigh!" Teacher announced with all the joy she couldn't contain.

Beauty surpassed my performance potential. Barbie got the lead. In outright disgust, I protested by refusing to exercise wherever, whenever. Barbie was the princess because she already had the costume, prepared (if the script called for it), to part the Red Sea all over again with that tulle bulldozer. Lexsana was going to be the big and tall reindeer, singlehoofedly able to pull Santa's heavy sleigh weight while Barbie Domination sat, helping direct us. This plot was precisely how Larry and Curly felt when Moe headed up the paint crew, the construction job, the plumbers' very wet basement repair, eating his foreman's snack.

Mothers were sent out notes announcing the cast and costume needs. I took my note home in my red book satchel, joyless, thinking how stupid I would look, just like The Wolfman with wavy antlers and a jingle bell. I opened the back door. There was Mom, bless her, making enough fudge and cookies to fill old Forbes Field and feed many hungry Pirates. I prayed for willpower. Instead, I got The Appetite of Anger. Oh, how I wish I still had that take home note. I'd read it once more, then eat it.

It might have read as follows:

Dear Parents of a Red Bird,

Our annual Christmas Pageant will be held in the school auditorium, two weeks from Friday at 7:00 in the evening. Please read all directives and appropriately costume your child according to his/her weight and height measurements. The entire class will be showcased according to that particular criteria and many damaging others! Above all, we want the whole holiday experience to be a positive one for your child.

Lexsana has been cast as the reindeer---a flying reindeer! If her costume seems like a big, expensive hardship, might I suggest dyeing several old bed sheets brown? Poster board would make lovely, floppy antlers, colored in with a brown crayon or your own Maybelline eyebrow pencil. Won't she look just so...won't she have fun? Go, red birds!!!! Fly, little-big reindeer!

Also, would you consider making one of those rich Hershey chocolate cakes Lexsana spends recess talking about to the playground squirrels? We need them for the refreshment table. I have a good idea that once you take one piece of that chocolatey rapture you just can't quit! Hmm.....

Thank you for supporting your child. That must be quite the task at times for so many reasons!

Mrs. Spider

Third Grade Teacher

When I married later (a mere fifty years later) I moved to the country, making it my place of healing. While packing up nearly sixty years of stuff accumulated by a five-member family, I was emptying out a bedroom chest of drawers. There in the bottom drawer under granny panties were the rumpled, faded reindeer sheets. I took them out and rubbed my hand over the stupid, waxy poster paper antlers. I sighed. I couldn't remember the pageant, but I believe my parents were not sitting in the front row.

My mother had the face of a young, starry-eyed Paulette Goddard in her single years. She was stunning. Her boucle coat buttoned down the side with oversized square buttons, trimmed in faux fur. She was looking at something there onstage that could never help her fulfill her deferred red lip dreams. They would stay packed away with the family-inherited fur coat in her Lane cedar chest, straight from her deep-South home. There sat my dad in his only black suit and string-thin black tie. He wasn't thinking about me the way Mom was. He was thinking deep down in his gut that his job as a teacher would never be enough to make his little girl the pink princess she deserved to be. My dad, the mayor, the councilman, the parish council member, the night school teacher, the private food bank for those in need, the daytime teacher, the principal, the county administrator, the laundromat owner, the gardener---all driven by his father's excessive old-world work ethic and borderline poverty. I believe by the time I hit junior high, Dad was completely exhausted and dreamless.

After an ending carol, *The Christmas Pageant of Not-Glad Tidings* was over. The thing about being a flying animal onstage for the holiday pageant is: No one can see beyond the big brown-dyed sheets how beautiful you know

19

you could look in that holiday velvet dress you will never own. Additionally, animals can actually hate themselves nearly as much as chunky children hate themselves.

At curtain call I stood upstage against the rear wall, imagining I was growing claws and giant teeth, looking upon my extensive Christmas buffet selections. After becoming carnivore reindeer, I would stand over the leftovers and say, "Sorry, kids, I have to eat and run-------no, fly! HA! HA! HA! HA! HA!"

My mother, while a tad uneasy with my weight, was clearly guilty of aiding and abetting my dress size. Dad was a little guilty, too, furnishing the extra A & P bag of just desserts not on the marketing list. When your ancestry is divided between Louisiana and Poland, the food flows: kielbasa, liverwurst, kraut, pierogies, cabbage rolls and kapusta on my paternal side. Buttery grits, fried chicken, bacon-grease-fried breaded okra, sweet cornbread, and three-layer cakes that gave me liver the shiver-me-timbers, on Mom's side. I ate it all like a badge, for I was saving some starving kid in China, where I hoped I might one day travel. I heard they made Chinese food called "carryout," and sweet and sour stuff, which I was used to, between Hershey cakes and homemade, carraway-seeded sauerkraut.

In May, with just weeks to go till summer break from school year three, a weather event occurred that would have our elementary school talking for years. We were in our usual bird formations. The reds were dutifully learning numbers in Spanish and someone overcome with disbelief on the blackbird end of the room forgot himself, his place, and squawked out, "Look outside! It's snowin'!!" He was quickly reprimanded for speaking---and speaking incorrectly. "Snow-**I-N-G**," (the dreaded

ING!) Mrs. Teacher corrected, acting all stern like she had ordered snow to make spring harder to enjoy. We were allowed to walk quietly to the window and see what Nature had wrought. Big fat flakes were wafting down, plopping on the Rhododendron and school sidewalks just as sure as I wore size 6x in first grade. What did all this falling white fluff mean? I thought quietly to myself.

It meant cold put-downs, the way Nature was putting down the snow, and the winter of my discontent was beginning in three and a half months. Fortunately, I couldn't see it coming.

I never remembered any other snow in May after that freaky squall. However, I remembered third grade more vividly when I was on the final leg of my own teaching journey, on the afternoon I found a hammer-packing elf for my "shelfs".

Fifty years saw positive changes in educational theory and practice. Nobody made learning distinctions blatant and birdlike any longer. Those defunct fossils were replaced by inclusion and supported by Individualized Educational Programs (IEPs.) There was support, encouragement for all learners. It wasn't a big deal to be less than genius, and we teachers were relieved, because we were not.

As my students were finishing up their assignment with a few free minutes to go, Carl, a crafty senior, came up to my desk. He was always smiling.

"Miss P., I saw the box back there for your new book shelves. Can I put them together for you?" His eyes were so genuine I could see that he really wanted to help me. That, and get out of fourth block. I thought maybe I saw ancient seeds of his father and grandfather in those eyes, the same kind of blackbird eyes that haunted me in third grade.

"You know, I am sure I could read the directions as a last resort and do it myself," I said.

"Well, no offense, Miss P., but where are your tools? Gotta have 'em," he said, twisting his face sideways, smiling even wider. I thought, Carl, you sure are smooth.

"You're absolutely right!" I said.

I had the tools right there in front of me, which sparked a bit of thinking.

"Okay, I'll write you a note just for today and this will be your project. How's that?" I asked him. It didn't matter what was happening in his fourth block. This was his moment. "But, you have to finish them today."

"Here ya go." He was back in a flash, note signed by teacher without question, because in another three years I would be marrying his fourth block teacher.

He separated out the parts, laid out his tool belt, and worked like a construction shelf elf with a new pay grade. His drive was admirable. This boy could aggressively picture and complete the finished product. All I could picture was the picture on the box.

Carl got the job done and my imitation wood shelves from Big Lots were ready to get loaded, with books. I watched him pack up tools I could not name, come over to my desk and thank me (here comes the best part), and walk down the hall. I watched him out of sight, his gait suggesting quite the conquering bad ass.

Recently, my husband was on the hunt for new tires. He parked the car. Nearby, he noticed the Clarksburg Water Board on high alert. Waiting for a backhoe to dig out an electric line, the team was standing by so it could get to a leaking water line. There onsite was Chip, one of the funniest humans on earth, one of my students at our final teaching post.

"I saw one of your favorite former students today," hubby said. "Yes sir, Chip was standing there patiently waiting on a backhoe to finish its job, all smiles, looking swag as always."

"I love that guy!" I gushed. "He's as funny as Chris Rock. He used to do and say anything until I laughed. He always said someday he wanted to go to film school. I hope he does."

"Well, based on your writing there, I'd say it's never too late," husband replied.

Chip had that desire to perform, playing the handsome Christian (and may I say tearing up the stage as the suave *Black Panther* version) in his class's read-aloud performance of *Cyrano de Bergerac*. Beau portrayed Cyrano and Courtney, the lovely Roxane. Those two later married and have lovely children. A good English teacher can make that happen. They fared far better than their stage counterparts, "Cyr. And Roxie." Both of them tragically died virgins.

"You know what?" Mr. Carr said. (I still called him that sometimes, for old-time's sake.) "To a lot of passing traffic, that job looked pretty menial. But I thought, *all* labor is good labor. Imagine if those guys hadn't been there. Having water in that spigot is pretty important."

"Well, yeah," I answered. "Like breathing normally, without COPD."

Husband continued. "I asked Chip how things were going." "Things are good," he said. Hubby noted something else. "He always says that when I see him." "And how's my favorite teacher?" Chip inquired.

"What did you tell him? Did you mention the book?" I asked eagerly.

"No, but I did tell him you were 'fine as frog's hair.'"

Such a trés amphibien reply.

Third grade taught me something that would be helpful when I eventually took the teacher plunge. All the BS about ranks and placements and holiday pageant typecasting only worked for a small percentage of educators whose heads were turned by status. That old flocked-up stuff was accepted back there in the E.E.L.O. (Early Education Labeling Olympics). Fortunately, that arena decayed, like Hitler's big Berlin Olympic stadium in the late thirties.

Labeling died out. Unfortunately, instructional jargon became the new learning benchmark. At eight through fifty-eight, I was on to those conundrum cats. I knew that those who wrote state guidelines with supercilious language usage (like the word supercilious), sometimes missed their calling as comedians. Many never visited a classroom, and still, they knew precisely what was best for both child and educator. "Hey, let's make it harder to understand what an educator's supposed to be doing!"

Why would they do this? Because they simply had to prove in their own minds that they were superior thinkers to teachers. Those folks knew that somewhere, maybe many places, some brave teacher in an interpretive conclave to discuss the hip new curriculum guidelines, would ask the burning question, "What does all this jargon mean? I don't understand this stuff."

The big shots had called it. Five-syllable words and more clever acronyms replaced three-syllable words and less-clever acronyms. Decimal points and broken numbers representing the life expectancy of the elephant ran rampant through the curriculum disciplines. D.A.T.T.A. (state acronym for "Disseminating Aggravating Technical Twaddle Absurdities") was in full circulation! *BOOOO!!* State curriculum framers could also surmise that as sure as they were composing geniuses, a startling chain reaction of interpretive bewilderment would start: state to superintendents, county superintendents to various directors, principals to teachers, and lastly a few disinterested students. One of those token, confused, irritated students would raise his hand and ask the exact question the irritated teacher had asked earlier: "What does all this jargon mean? I don't understand this stuff."* The jargon juggernauts figured slow-thinking teachers by this time, would have forgotten what all the new s&%+ means, rendering them lost and sputtering before their pupils.

Unbeknownst to those composing upgraders (that pride of smart state lions), their renovation of how teachers teach and reach had created a broad principle that would live forever, penned by a retired educator while cleaning out accumulated meeting packets, unnecessary materials in retirement. She had an epiphany that morphed into a little acronym tweaking herself. She called it the "F.U.N.K. Effect." meaning "Few Understand; Nobody Kares." At last, a truthful message, even if it did contain a misspelled word, which further illustrates that when curriculum objectives for English---silly basics like spelling, sentence diagramming, and parts of speech were suddenly deemed passé, society degenerates to the level of preschoolers who cannot spell c-a-t. But I digress.

* *"Stuff" would **not** be the first word choice for those irritated students, who would have preferred sharper, more street-indiscreet nouns over those formal, less in-school-suspension-sounding nouns.*

25

Insane expectations drafted in unknown tongues were as meaningless as 1960s bird calling. I wondered if some of those state-level administrators were likely red birds themselves.

Throughout third grade, I wrestled with my self-confidence, discovering how pathetically hard I would work for a puny little compliment. It was over half a year in coming. I knew then that teachers needed to *find something* to compliment a child about, at least twice a semester.

I started a spiral mental notebook of "fix-its" of how <u>not</u> to be as a teacher:

- *Don't wear bright red lipstick. It scares little kids.*
- *Burn any trace of a lace sweater. UGH!!!*
- *Don't let students turn their backs to other students. It's always wrong.*
- *Don't ever produce a pitch pipe!!! E-V-E-R!!!!*
- *Don't stress the "ING" of any word...E-V-E-R!!!!*
- *Don't have favorites!!! Be nice!!!*
- *Avoid talking about birds and/or Alfred Hitchcock!!!!*
- *And, should it ever snow in May, let students run outside and play!!!*

Home blotted out the unfairness at school, but I wish it had been a happier time. I shouldn't have been able to read right through that nutty, demeaning CORP (Captain Obvious Reading Plan) bird levels business. If only that era had been equality, instead of categories, for all. The policy makers deserved the categories.

I'm glad I never shared what I knew with my classmates about the labels... Oh, they knew anyway. Big deal, they thought. *Third grade words (or lack thereof), can't hurt me! Categorize THIS!*

26

The Vow Factor

Right before fourth grade started, in 1963, I was floating down a hallway on my backside watching ceiling tiles fly past. My father kept up as an old school, white-clad nurse wheeled me down that green mile towards the operating room. I was having an emergency tonsillectomy.

"She'll be fine," the nurse said over her shoulder to Dad. Older nurses were tough. They were unmoved by parental cataclysms.

"Liar!" I thought. It was my favorite word of condemnation, especially regarding myself.

I enjoyed carnival rides as much as the next kid, but this was creepy. Was I about to be catapulted off that bed into an Ohio corn field? The hallway was quiet, except for that squeaky gurney with maybe one bad caster. I had watched Dr. Kildare enough to know that once they paused at the final double doors, it was OR go time. I was going in and hopefully finding Richard Chamberlain there, masked up, gloves in the air like (I hoped) he cared! I would come back out about five ounces lighter. Weight loss, no matter how small, was good.

Cut away! I thought. I can take it! You can't scare me, doc! I watch you every week on-----TV? -----Hello?

But I saw no doctors, only nurses getting ready to knock me out into the Lathyrus odoratus (sweet peas).

Maybe the IV was kicking in, but I swore that tough nurse said, "Spell your big name backwards for me. It's a pip!"

It was summer, and I wished I had my bicycle. It would have provided my escape route out of Marietta Hospital before being put to sleep. My tonsils had locked in a blistery embrace and I could not swallow. Humans manufacture six whole cups of spit *a day*. It's got to go somewhere. Saliva had been pouring out of me with the near-force of Black Water Falls.*

Worse, my earthly pleasure, eating, had been shut down by the flaming dryer balls burning beyond my tongue. I was promised my weight in orange popsicles if I would be a big, brave girl and have surgery.

I was already big, because Mom replenished our dessert bar back home 24/7. Doctors said I looked exhausted. If I woke up in the middle of the night wanting pie, would I not have to go downstairs all by myself to the fridge to get it? The long trek back up those twelve creaky steps was Everest-like. Well, of course I looked exhausted! Doctors could be sooo dense!

Nobody was smarter than my daddy, the school teacher. With tonsil surgery, I had a golden opportunity to begin a diet: water, popsicles, air. Repeat.

Anesthesia sharpened my prophetic abilities. Instinctively, after coming to, I knew this would not be the worst thing that would ever happen in my life. Raw pain led to my first life declaration. I would <u>never</u> have surgery again. Further, I would <u>never</u> swallow again, so help me God. The cool blue popsicles canceled that vow three hours later.

We literature teachers call that shameless plug of a state's big tourist attraction (in this case, Black Water Falls), the author's use of "local color" to understand, enhance the native setting better, assuring the other forty-nine states that we have kick-ass beautiful places to visit, too!

"Honey, I'll be with you all night. I'm going to sleep over there in the corner."

"But Dad, there's no bed over there," I said and began to cry, still groggy from the drugs. "Ouch! It hurts to talk, Daddy…"

"Of course I'll have a bed! I'll just roll my jacket into a pillow and ask that nice nurse for a blanket. Now don't you worry. You just rest and don't talk for a while."

I opened up like a reservoir and let that spit pour on my pillow.

My throat had been removed, scored like an Easter ham, flattened with a throat-meat mallet, and put back in upside down by Doctors Moe, Larry, and Curly. Where were the bedside pain pumps I needed that did not exist yet?

The surgeon told my dad I would never again suffer strep throats or pneumonia.

"Your daughter will never again suffer strep throats or pneumonia." Additionally, that doctor warned my dad, I might walk with a limp for a while and talk in great detail about the Lost City of Atlantis.

Great news! Better health meant a financial windfall for my mother and dad! No more medical bills on their sickly second child!

The next spring I, Jean Dixon, had correctly predicted it. Worse calamities did arrive. I had pneumonia. On my birthday. Thank you, Doctor Nostradamus, for being so medically accurate when you assured my dad I could run naked at the South Pole and be well. I remembered that bold claim that I would be disease free the rest of my days. Not only did I have pneumonia, but I missed months of school. That turned out to be a plus.

My fourth-grade teacher had done the infecting, causing me the kind of sickening stress fatigue only seen in combat. She was trying to kill me, but alas, she only made me sick. My resistance to germs and teachers was low. I was her whipping girl, the reason she didn't retire. She riced me like boiled potatoes, comparing me on a regular basis to my smarter brother.

"Why can't you be smarter, like your brother?" she queried.

"Because I got the talent and the excess weight, you rip!" I never said that. But I felt she decoded it as I let the words speak through my trembling shut mouth and sweaty upper lip.

The clench of her alleged wooden teeth was always the punctuation after a subtle slur. Her Revolutionary War-styled yellow-white hair made her a ringer for the Father of Our Country. It formed a perfect trapezium (you can Google it just like I did), and turned me against the dollar bill forever. If her face were placed over Washington's on that particular currency, she would be the F.O.O.C. She could have singlehandedly stirred the economy. Consumers would have joyously spent out those ugly paper bills just so they wouldn't have to keep that face in multiples in their wallets. Today I would never say she looked like George Washington. That was too unpatriotic. She actually looked like an aged version of Alice in the *Dilbert* comic strip.

Before the pneumonia bout second semester came the mother of all horrible Black Fridays. It was November 22, 1963. Four short months after my tonsil popsicle opera, President Kennedy was assassinated.

The principal visited all classrooms. "Girls and boys…Our president has been shot. We don't know why this unfortunate thing happened or any details, but we are dismissing school early today. There will be no school Monday, either. Please go straight home."

Nobody could muster words. We just glanced at each other in our little class corn rows, shocked and joyless over the unexpected dark holiday. What had happened? Who would shoot another human being? Why was there no school on Monday? Our young minds had trouble processing that this day would rob us forever of our happy innocence. I was frightened to walk home. November 22, 1963, silenced us all. It was the mother of all murders, the eclipse of truth and trust in America.

I did not let my mother out of my sight. "Go next door and tell Yvonne the president was shot." I was afraid to leave the house, but I did what I was told. I rapped on the back door and Mrs. Burke, our renter, came over to watch television with us. I wanted my daddy, as always.

"I can't believe this happened in Dallas, of all places," Mrs. Burke cried. Both she and her husband were Texas natives, and she made the best sugar pie I ever ate. I loved Mrs. Burke and wanted to reach over and dry her tears.

The earth darkened morally that day and quaked from the physical shaking of about 189,241,798 scared Americans. We ran to the perilous safety of home and picked at meals in front of our black and white Motorolas, seeing a real-life murder, make that two...three, counting Officer J.D. Tippett. This was not an episode of *Mannix* or *Mission: Impossible*. This was our president. We only had the evening news and evening paper as social media. Therefore, our president was nearly savior status. We knew nothing of the man with more mistresses than cabinet and Supreme Court members combined. We trusted him because he let animals in the White House.

31

He was rich and handsome and common, and a war hero, all at once. His family was beautiful. In our limited scope, he was beloved by everyone around the entire world.

"My God, my God, why is this happening?" my mother cried. She did not cook much that evening. We watched a blood-spattered first lady stand helplessly by as her husband's casket was returned from Dallas, loaded into a waiting hearse. "That poor woman, and those children! What will happen to them now?" Mom bawled into a Kleenex.

My family sat motionless in a lopsided semicircle on our old turquoise sectional. I felt its texture like a lady's Persian lamb coat. I had bounced two springs out the back to music Mom played for me on the corner table's green RCA radio. Peeking beyond my mother's heaving breast I saw my father crying tenderly, crying along with Walter Cronkite and Dan Rather. It was something I never realized he could do. His jumbo tears scared me and through my own tears, his looked opaque to me, like bits broken off a boulder. They stalled a second in the crinkled corner ditches of his eyes. I could almost hear them fall on the throw rug under his tiny child's seat. He did not answer my mother, instead swallowing, not touching his face to reveal he was crying.

I felt extra bad, because November 23 was my parents' usually happy anniversary.

Dad sat in his undershirt apart from us on one of the two orange and white children's chairs my brother and I grew up using for our imaginary B & O train trips. Here was my dad, a strong principal, leaking out his humanity, not the face of control who'd slept on the floor while I recovered in the hospital. Today there was no toothpick dancing in the side of his lips, which typically signaled the start of evening TV watching after Mom's over-the-top suppers. That weekend, nobody wanted dessert at my house. We spent three days in front of a television set, every few hours producing more shocking news.

It was all too much for my excessive sensitivity --- the surgery, the assassination, Torturous George, pneumonia, and an impressive case of pityriasis. The flesh was weak from it, and so was my spirit. Raw, itchy, runny sores popped out on my knuckles. If I bent my fingers, the sores broke open and ran clear juice.

"Do you own a heat lamp?" the doctor asked. "You have pityriasis. There's no known cause or cure. But stress can make it worse." I wanted to tell him about my wonderful teacher, but maybe she was his third cousin. Why tempt the fates that way?

A question popped into my head. Why was school a dread, made worse by the person who was entrusted with caring for us, teaching us? Where was all that hopping-good learning fun time I watched on *Romper Room*? To counter Teacher's meanness I vowed, no, swore that I would bear the standard of empathctic teaching. I would cancel out some of the negativity.

"I will never, NEVER make any child feel the way I feel every single day," I said under my breath walking home, as that grade school shrank ever so slightly over my shoulder. She was already in my head, old Georgie Washington, in support hose and orthopedic lace-up cockroach stompers, in a real-life painting I called "Washington Crossing the Line."

PART II

I was used to Dad's pleasant dinner hour stories about happy teaching and the livelier teacher misfits who managed some teaching miracle daily. Fourth grade showed me that there were different kinds of teachers, some who did not self-fund classroom materials or treats, who heard no student problems on or off the clock.

My fourth-grade teacher was unhappy. She treated her charges like a bad marriage. Except she was a single for life. I believed that when she looked at me she saw herself buried somewhere under my skin, overweight, two pointy heads taller than her classmates, miserable, unwilling to excel, taunted to the point of resignation, a silent sufferer. "Me" was *she*!

"Why aren't you writing this down, Lexsana?" she chided. "You should have your pen ready all the time."

I think the blackbirds from our third-grade bird houses felt relief. They were no longer the "prime targets of scorn daily" (PTSD). Because now... I was. I had no spine or I would have told her what I was thinking. "You're right, Georgie W. I *should be* writing all these pleasantries down, because *some day*, years and years from now, not only will I surpass your skills in a week, but I will also spill every last slam you ever leveled at me---**IN MY BOOK!** HA! HA! HA! HA! **HA!**"

Teacher stood like an ancient lighthouse, thick and tall, narrowing at the top, a rapid blinker with eyes that had a far-flung yellowed cast like a beacon. With talent that unusual she could signal ships to safe harbor--- if she desired to be that magnanimous. How I wished her own ship would sail. To the Bermuda Triangle. To Atlantis, where that tonsil anesthesia had briefly taken me.

She perpetually stood at Parade Rest for balance, uncomfortable having her bony ankles touching. "You'll never be the student your brother was," she said leering above me more than once, her eyelids rolling independently like slot machine cherries. That positive reinforcement really helped out with the ethnic taunts I got before and after school. I was so much more than a Mary-loving dumb Pollack sauerkraut-eating lard bucket. On the inside was the real me, an actress, an author. When I suffered the most, I turned on the loud applause in my head. It drowned out the unacceptance.

I never asked one question that entire year. I kept quiet during the day and back home. Boomers did not tattle out of school, at any stage of learning. The rigid checks and balances and classroom cameras dangled over today's educators didn't exist that far back. Teachers in the sixties could freestyle all the contempt they desired.

Her most favorite classroom game was "Weight Chart Roulette," one that I had the distinction of inspiring.

"Today is Health Check Day. You will be weighed and measured," she said, as if delivering a news bulletin.

"Oh, God, no! Not today, *please* Lord," I whispered into my hand.

Teacher wore her blackest vestments on that special day. She was The Recorder, standing at the rear corner of the room by the windows to block the sun streaming in, thus bringing out her shadowy opaqueness. She carried her weight chart form on her clipboard, her favorite black Zaner-Blosser in hand. In the opposite corner of the room stood teacher's little pet, presiding over The Lighthouse's favorite weight scales. The Recorder sorted out her victims like tiny stones in navy beans and dutifully they got weighed for a little friendly bean counting. The tall charcoal and white scales were a big step up, requiring something to hold onto for balance. I watched fellow students scale those scales over and over, wondering how they made contact without tumbling backward. My heart raced like the athlete I would never be every time said pet called out said poundage to The Recorder. I felt the sweat of shame move from my developing breasts down into my underpants. My shaking hands left moist, ripple-y imprints on my workbook pages because I knew I would be pitted against the entire class, held back for her *grand finale*, preceded by the smallest peanut in the classroom for a shocking contrast to my adult-equivalent weight. Rules were rules.

Only a heavy child gets how deeply, horribly cut open it feels to be the fat entree at the table of disgrace. At nine going on ten, I was convinced that only grownups got prayers through to God. Kids didn't get wishes granted when they wanted to die, because maybe God intended them to grow up and eventually be blessed and happy. Besides, someone had to remain on earth and eat all the plenty He had provided.

"Lexsana," she called out, controlling her Christmas-like excitement.

The whispered bets commenced. "I'll guess two hundred!" Then another: "No! *Three* hundred!" The anticipation was tangible. She had eclipsed any shred of empathy from my classmates. Mild tittering was mingled with "coliseum eyes." My walk of weighted shame was a long one to those scales. It never occurred to a child of the sixties to just refuse to get up. I was about to get what dogs get when they dig out couch cushions. But for me, worse. *Why* me? My own heart was louder than any applause distraction I could create in my head. The tonsillectomy was only the prelude. The scales were now sudden death.

Step up, fatty girl!! Watch the needle dance wildly right to left. Weight for it........ "One hundred and forty-two pounds," scorekeeper called out.

The Recorder smiled slightly, head frozen, eyeballs fixed in a euphoric catatonia for several seconds. There I stood in my own *Twilight Zone* episode. Then she took her good time writing down my three-digit weight, giving the class exactly what they wanted---extra time to make fun of the saddest little elephant at the zoo.

The groans, the "*Wh-o-o-a-s!*" and the pretend fainting in seats commenced as the laughing swelled. Never once did The Recorder stop them. I did not yet know that Jesus was the lifter of my head. I stayed low, and I knew every scuff mark made by her ugly black shoes, down where my eyes stayed.

Why weren't my parents storming the principal's office with a petition? My mother could show her pointy reckoning if one of her children was unfairly hurt. Dad had an Olde World temper. Once he held an Army recruit up by the ankles and used him to mop the barracks after being called what I was being called. Would Dad have visited the brick school's second floor and performed the same janitorial feat with her Washingtonian head? I wanted to think so. But where there is no snitching there is no action, and better for me, no guaranteed retribution.

Did Teacher see this transparent fear in me and feed her hatred from it? Or was she a marvelous woman, sweet as Judy Jetson, who just had a life-threatening allergy to human kindness?

Another's wheezing and humiliation was one teacher's oxygen. She breathed on greedily. If I walked up the stairs too fast to stand in line after a restroom break, she made me come back down to the bottom and walk back up.

"Lexsana, you're running. Get back down here and WALK up those steps!" *Running?* All one hundred and forty-two pounds of me? I couldn't even see my feet and fear of bouncing like a Bumble on the ugly brown staircase kept me under the speed limit. She meant well, making me her Jack Lalanne's Biggest Loser project, figuring extra time on the manual step machine would work off a few M & M's I got from the quarter candy dispenser. It didn't work. I just got hotter, because heavier people are warmer-blooded than their stick figure comrades. I never went home without being some degree of damp.

Shortly after the stair stepper workouts, I got a visit from "The Dot." One day, there was a pain, an underwear stain, and the right to remain silent. I knew a period in one context, and it was grammatical. No one had told me about cycles and "obaries." I mispronounced them out of ignorance, the way presidential debate politicians mispronounce the names of foreign leaders they haven't met or want to. Frightened and speechless, I prepared for my own demise. I assumed I was leaking to death.

Mom discovered my early womanhood stigma on laundry day. Her generic explanation made me writhe with subtle discomfort. If I had been a betting woman-child at ten, I would have put down odds that no other girl in our class knew what I knew. I looked around my classroom at the female innocents. I felt older than they were, discovering right then that I was two girls: 1) the early developer and 2) the best secret keeper, next to the dead. Why be the messenger? Sometimes, silence isn't golden, it's pure platinum covered in rich rhodium.

But in March, I had the weight sweats even on a non-weight day, chills, too. If I missed one day, the return would be predictably worse than the yellowish-brown phlegm I was suddenly coughing. I started hacking. My chest rattled and vibrated. My lips burned hot. Sickness would be a cure all, a vacation from Tortureville.

While Mom registered my high fever, I was practically biting the mercury out of that thermometer, fighting to breathe through my stuffy nose with my mouth clamped around that glassy sucker stick.

"She's really sick, Leo. I'm calling Dr. Ritter," my mother said.

"Go do it now before we miss him or he's eating supper." Dad and I understood that food was always the ruling issue. He didn't want to interrupt another man's meal. He stuck his head in my room. "You're going to be okay, baby daughter, but you're not going to school for a while." I knew he would sleep on the floor by my bed again if I asked him. He did, with his head not far from the "steamer," as I called it.

It wasn't just the era of black and white TV. It was also the unbelievable era of doctor visits *to the home*. No long car trip and no need for the patient to shower first. Just lay in wait. With black alligator satchel in tow, he was a traveling hospital encased by two leather handles. My doctor came bounding up our creaky steps. He was always well dressed, older, with glasses and gray-brown thick hair.

"What's wrong with you, young lady?" the good doctor asked me. "I feel bad, Dr. Ritter," I said, wanting to cry so he would hold my hand. He sat his satchel bag on the bed corner. He opened the top like a tackle box and pulled out little shelves. So many compartments! That cold stethoscope on my hot back made me jerk. Doc debriefed my parents in the next room. "It's pneumonia, but only in the right lung." I heard my mother's breath catch as she intoned her usual "Oh, dear." No hospital stay? That surprised and delighted me! My parents put great faith in Doc Ritter. Mom loved him because he owned a coppery cocker spaniel she coveted. Dad liked his forthrightness. I loved him for his chic satchel, because it was a metaphor for my eventual triumph over disease, meaning Teacher.

Dad went to Woodruff's Drug Store and got me an industrial-strength vaporizer made of thick glass with a black lid hat. I called it my steamer. It chugged like the Chessie System over the tracks behind our 1910 white house. My breathing aid puffed out Vicks VapoRub steam day and night like an old locomotive's coal furnace. I got several white tablets daily, tasty as ear wax, pure penicillin. I was startled by the loud crackles produced whenever I coughed.

"Spit that out!" Mom would yell up from downstairs. Though she had a hearing loss, she heard every sound emitted from her children. My cough was a timpani roll. Why would I *not* spit that thick-as-chewing-gum stinking crud out of my mouth? Boxes of tissues outlined my legs like runway lights, me, the landing strip for disease and debasement.

One night while I was especially weak and generously medicated, I think I dreamed my class was on an end-of-year picnic near a local dam. Classes actually went there for year-end fun. It was Disney World to a nine-year-old. In my dream we were roasting wienies with safety caps on the ends of twigs, compliments of my bib aproned mother. In her spare time away from the kitchen she had received a patent on her safer-style roasting twig end caps Every poppy eye of childhood would be safe. There on the grill of fatty meat, next to my mom's free dessert bar, was the one hot dog with my name on it, crisping and sputtering out high C sizzles over the hot flames. And inside was Teacher, shrunken down to bun length, her terrified blackened cheeks, toothpick arms, and bony ankles kicking and flailing through the wiener casing. I reached for (as we called them back then) a frankfurter roll.

"I'll be good," she cried, rolling downhill on my Dixie picnic plate, dripping out a little fatty guilt. "Honest, I'll be good!"

"Oh, yes, yes you will," I answered through drool, drowning her in French's. "You will be very good," I taunted, laying down the chili, unhinging my mouth and opening wide for my Anaconda-style lunch.

My return to school was unheralded. Mom had to threaten me to get me to walk that sidewalk plank one block down to the place I most dreaded. "If you don't go back to school, you won't get to go to fifth grade. No more pie, either!" Enough said. I bolted out that old white curtained front door of ours lickety-split.

Though my homework assignments were all caught up, I still failed to please her. Coming to see me would never have entered Georgie's white hair. I was too tired to be as appalled as I once was. The May countdown to my release date was on. I was about to be loosed from the calaboose. No one in my grade seemed sad.

41

But first, I was accused of copying a homework assignment, one for which a classmate had begged to see *my* paper.

"Come over here, Lexsana," the F.O.O.C. said. *Tap! Tap! Tap!* went that Zaner-Blosser on my homework, putting inky dots all over my answers. "Why is Marlene's paper identical to your own?" The lighthouse beam seared into my head. I was temporarily blinded, unable to move for a few moments.

I needed friends! "Marlene" had come to my house after school and copied the homework like a greenhorn, verbatim. But no confession followed from either of us and Teacher let it drop. What a loyal, mum government agent I could be someday! But it wasn't in the cards. I had more important things to accomplish than always keeping my mouth closed.

The last Weight Roulette was recorded, done. She was a deflating dirigible. Her party was over. How would she fill the summer void with no chub to cut up? Maybe there was a beach blanket somewhere with her name on it and she could swim with the crabs. Maybe she had a summertime wall poster of Herman's Hermits for sinister dart games. Maybe she would go on safari for a little hunting of tame, undeserving animals. I just couldn't be sure. Or maybe she would retire. (She did not.)

"Have a nice summer," she said to us on the last day of school, shifting down hard on those smile muscles to produce an audible suggestion of pleasure. Clearly, her face had creaky manual gears tucked somewhere inside, perpetually in low. The wish was just sincere enough that I felt my heart stretch ever so little. Even in disgust and resentment, I wanted to be like Anne Frank and find a small bite of tasty good in everyone.

"You, too-o-o," some of us whined back forcibly in singsong style as we raced the hell out of there. There was no looking back, because I knew what happened to Lot's wife. My grandma loved telling that sodium-laced Bible story and I wasn't feeling like becoming the frozen chick on the Morton's Salt box. As I exited, I *did* vow something under the threshold of that dark place. "I *will* teach in the name of every dark horse and bottom dog limping along my career pathway. I won't be like you, either, sister!"

Looking up on that "Oh Happy Day" release revealed Wedgwood sky, citrine sun, and chirping topaz blue birds. Though I hadn't lost a pound, I felt weightless...almost. NEVER would I allow myself to become the second lookalike for the snowy-flaxen Father of my Country. Further, I believed one day I would lose the weight, too.

I believed that because one of Dad's visiting sisters, SISTER Mary Julianne, a Felician nun/teacher, monitored our fridge: "Oh, Lexsana! Is that a Klondike in your hand? Remember: Momentarily on the lips, forever on the hips!" Her 85 pounds in a habit made me feel like George "The Animal" Steele, a big pro wrestler of the day. Was that my destiny? To be a hairy-chested body slammer? Worse ---- *he was a high school teacher!*

My vow to be the teacher I deserved in the fourth grade stuck. I would never become Georgie Washington, a teaching (or flying) nun, or a biting wrestler! Instead, Patty Duke became my role model, because she was thin, she had her own show, playing identical cousins; and she had the best flipped-up hairdo on network television!

My Father, the Pope

I walked up the center aisle of Immaculate Conception Church in Clarksburg, wishing my stroll was for a friend's wedding, for a baptism, not for a funeral---my dad's funeral. I was a little tipsy from the Valium prescription Mom and I had taken earlier. My cousin, Mark, held my elbow tightly. I was sure at the final "Amen" I was going to drop on that red carpeted marble floor and die, too. The pain in my chest was the Almighty's surgical removal of my life support. My world was wherever Dad was. My world was now removed from my body. I wanted nothing more than to return to the spring earth with him. "And I will ra-aise him up, and I will ra-aise him up, and I will ra-a-a-i-se him u-up on the la-ast day," the little lady's choir sang. Bless their hearts! It was their standard hymn during all Catholic funeral masses. Making final arrangements on the phone, I had requested the priest to have the ladies sing Dad's favorite, telling hymn, Amazing Grace. "They don't sing that hymn for funerals," he said too casually. "They will tomorrow," I answered. "It was my father's favorite hymn. I am guaranteeing they'll sing it. You tell them they are," I said. My epiphany? Grief can make one instantly impious, a dissident.

When I was born Dad was ecstatic, mostly over my "round little apple head," apparently the distinctive head shape of the day. Dad cooed so much about it the nurse holding Baby McIntosh up for him to inspect began to snicker, as he tells it, in "tee-hee-hees."

After hearing all that happy applesauce a dozen years, I started to wonder just what special shape my

44

brother's head was when he was born. I also began to make a correlation between the baby fruit head story and the career Dad had picked out for me, moments after I crowned into existence. "Follow my lead," he was saying, holding me. "Apple heads are a sign! Teachers get apples. Your daddy loves getting apples! They're free, so it's a job perk. You'll be a teacher with apple pie for life!"

But, when all the predicting came to fruit-ition, I deduced there was an apple shortage, because I could count the total number of apples on my career desk on one hand. One of them may have had a row of toy gun caps sticking out the bottom.

The pictorial says it all, but for the reader's clarification, I must state that I am the one on the left. I would not reach Leo's height and weight till fourth grade.

Just turn on *The Lawrence Welk Show* and Dad and his little "sobowtor" (twin) were ready to polka! Every day at 4:30 there we sat (minus Mom, busy making apple pies) howling to *The Three Stooges*. If there was any kind of a monkey involved in a plot line, Dad's feet came off the ground laughing. That was the life for me---monkeys and *weightless* laughing.

45

In spring, when the horse manure ripened right around planting time, there was a friend of Dad's with an old buckboard and two work horses who plowed up our garden plot. All that pungent fragrance yielded food, so I was right there. I loved animals and felt it an honor to pet those beautiful fertilizing machines.

"Why do you have to get *all that horse poop*, Leo?" Mom asked, putting cotton balls soaked in McCormick vanilla flavoring all over the house's affected areas until at least two rooms looked like the cotton boll field from her childhood home in Louisiana.

"Because it's spring, and it's free, and we'll have the best of everything in the garden this year, Momma," he said, cajoling her while stating fact.

Leo J. Pilewski was mayor of Salem for a term and shook things up. It was no secret that abandoned, decaying properties were getting torn down or burned. Salem got a sweeping out. A new water plant was constructed, plus a Bell Telephone Operations building. He had close buddies like Howard Flint and Gary McCallister who had his back at council meetings.

When folks placed emergency calls to the city building for needful things like a holiday fowl or a prescription refill, if no one else were available, Dad offered home deliveries for those items himself, happy to help. He knew the citizenry well, which families were lacking. Mayor Pilewski told us a special holiday edition story each November of buying and delivering a surprise Thanksgiving bird to a family who needed a little help.

"I climbed the hill to the tilted back porch, knocked, and the father opened that kitchen door. I said hello and handed him his main holiday course. My heart felt a little glad, doing what the Bible says we should. That poor guy looked in that A & P bag and said with all the gratitude he could muster, *"This turkey ain't cooked!"*

Dad's laugh could go up one octave if the Berosini Chimps were on *The Ed Sullivan Show*. His overflowing generosity pulled me in and for a time, I thought Dad was a green grocer, except no cabbage exchanged hands, meaning money. He bagged the best of carrots, lettuce, onions, dill, peppers, and a couple ears of corn for select folks waiting on their clothes to dry at Leo's Laundromat. "First fruits," as he called them with Biblical homage. His open wallet seemed not to have a shut-off valve.

At church, Leo had two duties: usher-offertory collections, and free infant pacifying. He was The Baby Whisperer. Moms would literally pass their fussy babies back four rows into the sturdy hands of LJP and by the count of ten, they were calm, if not making baby snore sounds and releasing little baby gases. Dad loved children even more than apple pie. I watched him stare at those little ones, swaddled in his arms. He was sizing up their head shapes and prophesying correlating careers for each little sleeping one of them. Fortunately, there was never one banana in the bunch.

Dad had a wily way of circumventing things around my mom. She liked to dip into his stash of twenties in what looked like a thick money sandwich wrapped in foil under the mattress. "I need shopping money," she'd say if I caught her doing it. He strategized never to say anything about the twenty-dollar drain, because I guess he figured if he were not calling her out, she would leave him alone when he opened that cash-on-hand charity bundle to help a cause greater than shopping.

She said to no one (meaning me), one day: "Your father takes every last dollar and puts it into *that* Catholic Church!" ("That" was an adjective of disdain often repeated by Mom because she was Protestant and critical by faith.) "I found a receipt where he bought a copy machine for the rectory! Of all the idea! Why, I don't even have a dishwasher! Or a ruby, and I have a July birthday, too!" She could make her eyebrows slant downward in an almost-believable angle of hurtful injustice. To which I said under my apple-laced breath, "Oh, Mom, grow up. Let Dad be Dad. He's freer than free when he gives." *Translation: There are other charities than just Kitty Pilewski* (though Mom earned far more than she withdrew).

Once a young teacher, Betty H., went wailing to the principal's office and told Dad in teary terms that a certain young man (the only one in her room at the time), had allegedly lifted a twenty out of her purse. "I know it was Mr. J. Sheetz," she said. "I turned my back for just a couple seconds to erase the board." Dad leaned back in his chair, paused, and flashed that charitable smile, responding, "Well, Betty…consider the joy of it! You just donated twenty dollars to the United Sheetz Fund!" Even Betty stopped sniffling and laughed.

That same young man named Jimmy based his junior high career on the cafeteria menu. When there was cornbread, cake, or pizza, he was all in. "What's for dinna, Mistuh Piliski?" he'd ask on the phone. Efficient secretary, Becky S., had orders to patch calls from Jimmy straight through the pipeline. She did so, because she loved my dad like her own father, so much so that she bought our entire family amazing Christmas presents every year.

Dad would look on the menu and rattle it off to his favorite student. "Homemade vegetable soup, crackers or cornbread, apples, and oatmeal cookies, Jimmy. Now I want you to get on that bicycle of yours and pump those pedals and get a speeding ticket."

Jimmy would come at lunchtime, sweep a little of the cafeteria floor, then head for the principal's office, where blocks of yellow cornbread with butter packets were waiting, wrapped in lunch napkins, with a couple half-pints of milk.

Dad probably never got quite a full belly back home with seven others vying for the last of the boiled potatoes. The eventual *No Child Left Behind* legislation may have flopped, but Dad's one school rule flourished, for he left *no child hungry*. It was stupidly simple and would be poo poo'd now by the state and nation, but Leo's simple truth was that a child with an empty belly could not feed it on curriculum only. Those were different times, when every crumb was not counted by county administrators following state directives, and extra food was not lawfully required to be thrown in the garbage. Dad shared the surplus. "Someday, God is going to pay us back for all the sin of waste in this country," he cautioned.

Always the natty dresser, my father demanded that men teachers always wear ties. He believed that educators needed to dress the part. Dad never wore a pair of blue jeans in his life. One hot, sweltering May day, Coach Ritter was melting from the heat. He took off his clip-on tie and clipped it onto his pants pocket. Principal Pilewski stopped him in the hallway.

"Coach Ritter," he said, smiling, "I suppose when I told men teachers to wear ties, I didn't say exactly *where* they should wear them."

Dad led by example, and his style influenced mine. He loved his two-tone wing tips and cashmere-infused dress hats. His suits were meticulous, topped off with silk ties. I know this, because eventually, my teacher checks bought all the above for him (though he begged me not to). I did it to be more like him, and doing it made me "Dad glad."

As I grew older, I watched my dad grow also into being a better father, and most surprisingly, mingling old gospel religion with his strict, pure, untainted Catholic upbringing. He died a satisfied man, unafraid and spiritually, a Samson. But in between those markers on his lifeline were our times at home and magically, abroad.

In early June '79, I was covering my Room 11 book shelves for the summer with the ever-expendable sports section, mopping away sweat during the end-of-year close of school, thinking and smiling. The door opened and it was Laura Richards, with whom I shared that classroom.

"Guess what, Miss Richards! I saved money and I'm taking my father to Poland this summer!" I must have sounded five years old to her!

Biology teacher Laura was an angel on earth, always encouraging. "Well that is wonderful, Miss Pilewski! I know it will be the trip of a lifetime for both of you. You're a good daughter," she said, walking past me with her signature scent, Youth Dew, pleasantly masking the stale classroom odors of another year of teaming germs.

My big summer surprise for Dad was hidden in an envelope at home----Pan Am Airline tickets for a visit to Poland. Dad had a ticket to ride, back to his roots and maybe, to find a few relatives. I knew that for all his altruism he had little savings and no money for something so frivolous as a life-changing journey. It took more than one lifetime to save that many thousands of pennies. If he opened that envelope and did not jump up and down like a *Price is Right* contestant, I would be crushed to the bone.

"Oh, baby daughter," he said smiling, a little choked up, holding that prize ticket to the ceiling light for a better look. "What a nice thing to do for your dad. And the time is just right."

I did not realize that "the time is just right" meant he was living his final five years, and he certainly wasn't telling me. Someone who looked so much like a pope might have that mortality insight. I was worried when he insisted I take a friend so he would not hold me back from running all over Warsaw. How could he hold me back? I never questioned Dad, instead going wherever he guided. My friend and colleague, Martha, accompanied us that summer. I was glad she would do that for us. It wasn't exactly an invitation to go grab a burger

"Will you be alright, Momma?" he asked Kitty at supper.

"I'll be alright. I've got Mom here," she said, indicating my grandma, Leticia Mae (Beaird) Davis. "We'll be alright."

I pinched my thigh to assure myself I had heard her straight. The fact that she would even permit such a bold jaunt from her two life support systems was a sign we should make the journey fast. She feared being left alone. She could never have handled the single career life. It was not part of the southern belle culture of her day.

I had traveled to Forbes Field, Newport, Ohio, and Cape Cod, my first sight of a body of water bigger than our bath tub. I had never flown, much less crossed an ocean.

When our flight left Pittsburgh, I held Dad's hand until the "Fasten Seat Belt" sign dinged off and my stomach returned to the upright position. Leo's sizeable hand felt like the touch of God, the ultimate safe place.

Dad knew how to help me drown my fears. When I was younger, he simply took me grocery shopping with him. Teacher me required a greater distraction.

"Tell me a good school story," he said.

What a guy! keeping me performing so I wouldn't have time to be afraid. Or, was he grading my storytelling skills every time in his mind, comparing my style with his? I reached down into my little reserve of humor and shared my favorite awful story. And there were many.

"So, no matter whether I was at school or sick at home, there was always trouble brewing in Room 11, my room, you know, Dad?" He shook his head, smiling. "I was so happy to be sick that Friday and get a three-day release from teacher internment camp I didn't care what happened. My sub that day was a sweet, retired lady of very small stature. Gary Gould, my teaching pal and owner of the Paul Newman-bluest eyes in education, told me the whole story on Monday morning."

"A senior boy asked that sub if he could go to the restroom about ten minutes before the dismissal bell. He timed his business out and decided to create a little excitement for that poor, innocent sub. While out of the room, he applied a generous helping of Crazy Glue to the door, injecting it generously into the keyhole, knob, and bolt. It locked up tighter than a bank vault after 4:00 p.m.," Gary said. "Newman had sealed that class's fate securely."

Gould said, "I was passing by Room 11, like always, happy to get out of Dodge. And there on tippy-toe, her face hardly visible, was that sub tapping a tiny fingernail on that eight-inch glass panel in the door, barely tall enough for me to read her lips. 'Help me!' she mouthed, eyes filled with fear, twenty-something seniors wild-eyed behind her."

Dad's eyes were crinkling. He had these hooded eyelids, the same aging flaw that sends supermodels straight to *Nip/Tuck*. He laughed a chesty laugh, shaking his head, picturing all those captives' big eyes looking to ol' Blue Eyes standing there, outside in the crowded hallway.

"All those eyes of seniors pressing in behind her, desperate to be let out for weekend leave," Gould said to me on Monday. "I nodded to the frightened sub and reported the unlucky hostages to the office. This is the worst part. County maintenance had to come from Gore -- as you know, a good half hour away, and take the hinges off your door to get the class and teacher out."

"Some poor soul had lots of explaining to do when those kids all missed their buses," my dad, the ex-principal said, coughing after laughing.

Raconteuring was becoming a verbal competition between us, and I liked it.

"Did the teacher ever sub for you again?" Dad asked.

"I'm wondering if she lived long enough to sub again," I said.

Leo found the humor in school, not the ugly. He was creating that talent in me.

"Would you like me to tell you about the joys of having class in another teacher's room? I had a football player pour a whole can of Ajax into the heater during my h-u-u-u-ge journalism class. I must have been working with another group and didn't see it happen. It was the germaphobe teacher's room who everyone said nipped a little at noon, the same one who Saran-wrapped her lunch tray before walking back to eat in her sterile classroom.

"When the heat finally came on, that Ajax spewed up like magician's dust, at least four feet high. Maybe a genie would appear. I should be so lucky! I doubt Mrs. --- ate her lunch in there that day." I grinned. "The janitorial staff had a dust storm to clean up later. Between the chalk dust and the cleaning products, I should get white lung benefits down the road. I bet the whole faculty will have a pep rally when I leave there someday, Dad."

Dad's wise brown eyes smiled and I saw my reflection there, the apple head of his eye.

LJP loved my brother every bit as much as he did me, except in me he saw his little chubby miniature all grown up now, perhaps too much like himself. Now he had someone to tell *him* the funny school stories, at dinnertime and beyond. Leo may well have been thinking of his own career experiences, minus all my drama. But for certain, he was wondering how I got into such predicaments, and even more incredibly, how I was always able to extricate myself from them. Leo saw me becoming independent and confident in my own abilities. Nothing kept me down for long. Perhaps Dad was seeing me as a peer, an adult with the two survival skills every teacher needs to succeed: a lot of inner strength and a big self-deprecating sense of humor.

"I know it isn't easy as it used to be," he often reminded me. "It's a tough job. But, even on the worst days when everything goes wrong, you just smile and think about that upcoming paycheck and say, 'piss on it!'"

We landed in West Germany unexpectedly, when an altimeter malfunctioned. That little gauge turned into a six-hour ordeal, spent at the airport. Three hot dogs set Dad back nine bucks, and this was 1979! That sneaky hot dog vendor looked at me, smiling. I knew what he was thinking: "Stupid Americans! You blow your money on designer jeans, so you can do the same with my wieners. So, 'Auffressen' (meaning, "eat up!") to you Capitalists!"

Finally, our destination was nearer as that jumbo Pan Am approached Warsaw International and started down through the cloud cover. Below the underbelly of the grey sky were what looked like chess pieces in uniforms, a sea of foreboding drab objects without movement. We landed delicately in Warsaw, right on its pre-Solidarity timeline, in the city Lech Walesa would soon govern. For now, there were dour, uniformed Russian soldiers everywhere, forming a spreading oval around the disembarking passengers.

"Dad, look. Every single one of those guards is wearing some kind of military sash of honor!"

"Ssssh! Those aren't sashes---they're ammunition belts. They have their fingers right on the triggers behind their backs. Don't look at them!" he whispered. Obedient baby bird, I became aware of danger. He was a veteran, no stranger to war and happy trigger fingers. I could not think one of these men would perforate a blonde in half right there on the tarmac. These blonde and blue-eyed hotties were handsome men! I sneaked a long peek out the side of my Foster Grants. There was enough metal and bullets out on that runway to melt and make Sputniks 2 and 3. How sexy it all was!

What kind of greeting is this? I thought to myself, sniffing European air for the first time. Poland smelled oppressed and industrial, like wet army blankets and black factory smoke. This was not the trip I'd dreamed of taking with my father. There was no jet ramp, no excited travel reunions, no laughter or sounds, except the soles of our shoes occasionally crunching a loud pebble into the paved area where we walked like soldiers.

An expressionless Russian woman, the type you would never want babysitting your super-spoiled child, rummaged roughly through every item in my luggage. I wondered how clean her hands were. She touched every pair of underwear I owned.

The winds of Warsaw in August bit at our backs. We had not packed the right clothing. I would wind up doing exactly what Dad said, running around our corner of Warsaw looking for cable-knit sweaters and socks. "Lut?" I asked in the hotel, thinking I was asking for ice, instead of the correct term, "lod," for ice and a concierge hailed me a cab! My Polish was off-the-chart that bad. Europeans are cool cats with no need for ice-cooled drinks. Their formal demeanor lowers the temperature in liquids *for them*.

Our hotel rooms seemed a little hospital-like and the beds had sheets with circular cutouts that fitted over crimson blankets. The front desk staff advised us to say nothing against the government, except for topics like lazy American capitalists and the impeccable quality of American education and discipline reflected in *Welcome Back, Kotter*.

Dad leaned in as the gentleman behind the front counter spoke low in spotty English, "Never leave passport a second. Don't lay down. They will be gone. Passports they are prime for thieves. Hide them or you cannot leave this country."

I watched the natives differently after that, amazed at their ability to remain cool in their own country under Soviet occupation. Russians had control of their homeland and those Poles were as squared and normal-seeming as my safe and secure friends back home, living in an unappreciated democracy.

"Dad! Are we being watched?"

"I believe my friend at the desk. We probably are,"

he answered as we entered our rooms.

If they kept us, we had no choice. I would ask if I could please sign up to teach those tarmac Russians a few key English phrases, like "I like the sausages here"and "Would you meet me halfway in Pittsburgh?" "Duzo szczescia" (good luck) with that map quest!

"Where is the meat, the produce?" Dad asked a hole-in-the-wall grocer.

"Raised here and sent to Russia, with most everything else," the slouched store owner answered with no expression, in Polish.

The elderly man was accepting of the three bags or so of items on his scanty shelves. That worried Leo Pilewski. He went to bed every night and prayed the whole world would have enough food and clean water.*

Our tour started with Warsaw Square where stood granite homage to King Sigismund. He moved the capital from Krakow to Warsaw. The pedestal beneath the statue, plus the king, looked at least seven or eight stories high. I put King Dad at a similar height.

The Winter Palace of Kings and the Warsaw Ghetto made me too full of sad contrasts---the grandeur and inspired beauty just steps away from the flame-throwing Hitler troops who incinerated the resistance fighters. Were our descendants now ghosts in that city's burned bunkers?

Our bus tour guide was bilingual. Lucky for me, because a story he shared in a museum was the second most inspirational point of the entire visit.

"After the bombing of Warsaw during World War II," the guide said, "survivors climbed out of the leveled

*He prayed that selfless petition while kneeling at the side of that old cherry bed that doubled as Mom's debit card. In the banking realm, Kitty was ahead of her time, though Dad was ahead in answers to prayer.

portions of their beloved city. Survivors glued the building crumbs back together into bricks, then rebuilt the city exactly as it was." He pointed to two old, framed photographs, depicting the original buildings pre-war, then the rebuilt crumb buildings, post-bombing. "These two pictures look identical," he told our tour group. "Only a Polish historian could detect the tiny differences." He smiled, ending the tour saying, "And that, ladies and gentlemen, is the enduring spirit of the Polish people."

I drew so close to those old pictures I could hear the explosions, the reconstruction hammers. His story reaffirmed to me that ethnic jokes were not funny and further, were told in ignorance by unlearned lips. How many people in the world could restore crumbs to bricks to buildings?

My God! I couldn't even teach the use of apostrophes to Americans, ironically, the spoiled people who *owned everything*, according to foreigners. It seemed a sacrilege to own nice things and not even be able to punctuate possessives correctly with apostrophes, as in "The foxes pelt made me a beautiful coat, but I wanted a lynx' one, Daddy." Societal grammar, which is so rich it needs no rules, and love of furry objects as outerwear proved us spoiled capitalists unawares.

It was humbling being in a place that held some of your DNA. I wondered how many of us Pilewskis were teachers. Many, that was my guess. Hearing Dad speak in two languages made me appreciate my heritage and even better, this adventure with him. Multiple languages are not easy to know. Dad spoke German well also, growing up in a stew pot of an ethnic neighborhood, there in Oil City, Pennsylvania.

We boarded a cattle-friendly passenger train, the overflow passengers standing shoulder to shoulder. When you stand with your backside so close you know the sex of each stranger pressing in on you, that is telling in an awkward, unmarried sort of way.

"Honey, I have got to have a drink of water or soda...anything," Dad said. We three were sweating profusely, gripping overhead straps.

I carried my zlotys in my fist tightly, passing through cars of weathered, stony faces. The last train car before the dining car was stuffed with Russian soldiers, drinking and frisky, attracted to my blonde hair. "Jesus, save me," I prayed, and I thought about Dorothy Belle for a moment and was less afraid. I'd go through any army to get Dad what he needed. Teaching had toughened me. Those soldiers were *spiffed*, singing off-key drinking songs, some swinging their steins at me.

The man in the dining car took the three bottled drinks I selected and picking the zlotys out of my hand, smiled, and left a couple. "Dziekuje," (thank you), he smiled. Those sodas were "powerful good," as the older mountaineers said back home.

We were hot and thirsty because of the heavy, stale air in those speeding cattle cars. No bathrooms. I imagined myself on one of the death trains, going over the same routes to one of many "final solution" camps. I would have urinated down my leg many times. However, fear cannot be fully measured until one meets the particular threat face to face. My hands were sweating.

"Dad?" I asked, as I tried to get my soda safely to my mouth. "Would you want to fly to southern Poland? Visit Krakow maybe?"

"No, honey, I couldn't." He gave no reason, but I knew standing in that hallowed hell ground at the southern town of Oswiecim (the Germans made it their own, renaming it Auschwitz) would drop him. I did not persist. We let the train trestles do the talking for a while as the train thundered and clacked along the jumping rails.

Dad made inquiries in the city of Poznan and found a female first cousin, Michaelina. We could not believe our luck! I have forgotten most of their two-hours-long reunion, but there was joy on both of their faces, the exact way DNA testing reunites families today. Dad managed to do the same thing his way, without so much as a spit. His cousin was a plump lady, close to Dad's age, already smiling, hugging us.

"Dad," I prompted, "ask our relative if she is happy to see you. Tell her this is a moment in our lifetime."

"Chwile w naszym zyciu," he relayed to his happy cousin. He would remember that day the rest of his life. He offered her money but she refused, just excited we had come (and a little too proud for any charity). This was their history time when questions got answered during an unexpected, found common thread of DNA.

We should have stayed there in Poznan longer. I should have questioned more, recorded on tape my only foreign living history lesson. Family is supposed to plant a tree that stands forever. I was proud Dad helped his grow a bit more that day. I still have the picture of their smiling faces. If I was smiling, imagine what God was doing up there, seeing His plan unfold, uniting them.

Later, at an inn where the three of us finally got to relieve ourselves and eat fish with the head and scales still attached, I had to say the obvious to my father. Our relative lived small. "Her house is not very big, Dad. But she seems so happy."

Dad was sawing away the head and telltale eye of the fish before him. He looked at me. "I'll tell you exactly how happy she is. That's a converted chicken coop she lives in, and she's the happiest person I know." Dad had a way of summing it all up, the way a conductor makes colossal, opposing circles with abrupt finality to end a grand symphony.

Wherever we went in Poland, Dad got "the look" of mistaken identity. Pope John Paul II had been elected pontiff the previous year, the first non-Italian pope since 1523. Their heritage, their builds, the white hair, wide foreheads, and peaceable faces were virtually interchangeable. There was no language barrier as I interpreted expressions on faces at stop lights: *Is the pope here in an American suit and wingtips? ---- With a BLONDE? And a BRUNETTE?*

"Dad," I said as I nudged him on the street, "I think we could do a Faux Pope World Tour. You're really getting the eye!" Pope Leo smiled and frowned together, for Dad was not a boaster.

"You have to be prepared to prove all you say you are," he told me once. That was advice I would tuck away discreetly and use later, like the cases of Bounty and Charmin (so old they were in original packages and colors of peach, green, and yellow) that he stockpiled in our Herman Munster Basement shelves along its damp concrete walls.

On the return trip, I walked in pain with zlotys in my shoe. How stupid was I?

"You didn't keep any currency, did you?" Dad asked as we approached New York.

"Well, just the coins in my shoe," I admitted.

No comment from Dad. Had I been frisked, I might have been carted off for stealing from that controlled country. When we touched down at JFK Airport and were asked if we had anything to declare, I said, "Yes! God bless America forever!"

The landing had been rough, forcing our stomachs against the seat belts, lunging us forward until it hurt. When we reached the bottom of the plane stairs, Dad turned to me. "I see why the pope kisses the ground when he lands. I thought the pilot was going to flip that jet."

Part II

By 1980 I had travel wanderlust all over again. It came by accident, in the form of a shirty challenge at school. Someone in the teacher's lounge asked me a loaded question after hearing me say I had a sponsored child in Brazil through Christian Children's Fund.

"You think that kid actually gets that money you send? Chh!" he said critically as his faithless end point.

That night I drove home feeling like a total dumb ass, picturing the Boys from Brazil cashing my monthly checks off their bogus CCF organization. Two hundred and forty dollars a year donated, with love, to South American swindlers. "Obrigado, Americano!" (thank you, [dumb blonde] American)!

"Two teachers told me today I was stupid if I thought Adriano was getting the money I send to CCF," I said to Dad after supper. The minute my whining was out, I felt like an adult two-year-old, tattling. Still being with your parents can unlock immature regression. Once a colleague walked up to me, looked at a new skirt set I

62

was wearing and said, "It must be nice to still sponge off the old man." I tottered between deserving that and letting my fist educate her un-wise wisdom teeth.

Dad was in thought mode. I would wait for the brilliant reply from my own at-home education therapist, something deep and substantive from Father Leo, alias The Pope Double. He would explain to me the smallness of criticism, the tests of teasing, the spiritual blessings of forgiveness---

"I'll go with you," he said out of the blue, with a bit of papal authority. I wanted to kneel and kiss his ring. Good fathers with pontiff-like faces naturally create that kind of venerated reaction.

One summer after Poland, we were again airborne, headed for northeast Brazil, Fortaleza.

This trip was the tipping point. Air travel had tired Dad, but the trip into the Fortaleza foothills would exhaust him. CCF workers met us at our hotel to prepare us for our visit with Adriano.

The terrain was rough and it felt as if the Jeep were being bounced on a rock-filled trampoline. This trip was a mistake. The sights of villagers with swollen limbs (encephalitis, according to our guides), raw sewage, and adobe dwellings without windows overpowered my travel companion. I saw him turn his head away. It was the most emotion he'd shown since JFK's assassination. Why had I opened my mouth and boohooed to my father about ignorant remarks? He was not always going to be available to dry my tears with time, money, or a Fig Newton.

Abruptly the Jeep slammed to a stop. Small children came belching out of their tiny houses on baby bird thin legs. "Ola, criancas!" (Hello, children) our guides greeted the children in Portuguese. Out of the circle's center stepped a smiling mother holding the hand of Adriano. I recognized him instantly from photos. He smiled shyly and took my hand, not letting go of his mother's hand. My heart literally moved towards him, and I felt as though I were meeting a little one up for adoption, except he was not that child. His mother told the translator he had been waiting on our visit for days.

"Adriano, I'm Lexsana, the lady in America who writes to you!" I said, smiling, waiting for our guide to translate that into Portuguese, a language more difficult to understand than men. His eyes were like small black checkers, little wisps of black curls fringing his beautiful broad face. "Ola," he said, pulling back, in a step of security, a little closer to his mother.

What was he thinking? Moreover, what would come after this visit? Would it be singular, like a moment carved out of history, never to return again? Like Poznan?

Visiting Fortaleza: CCF worker, Adriano, Lexsana (amazingly able to squat deeply), and Adriano's mother.

64

As we walked in a little group around the dust and chickens, something happened. People came out of houses, beginning to run toward us, shouting things in Portuguese. We froze on the spot, determined to keep smiling for whatever was next. As they grew clearer across the flat parched earth we could see some clutching rosaries, some blessing themselves, some extending their arms. I could not close my mouth and it suddenly had dirt in it, this crowd raising the crumbled earth.

"What are they saying?" I asked our guides, wishing I could spit. "Are they angry or happy? I can't tell."

One of our guides answered, "They are saying 'Il papa.' That means 'the pope.' They think your father is Pope John Paul II! Look at their faces!"

I turned to relay the message to Dad, but the crowd was already upon him.

"No, no. No 'Il papa,'" he said, motioning in a kind of negative jazz hands way. I could see he was embarrassed. Clearly, he felt it a mortal sin to impersonate a pontiff without wearing so much as a white cassock. Just the same, I was never so proud, like a daughter accompanying her movie actor father to the Academy Awards.

Had I been the popish one, I would have shamefully started making the sign of the cross. Acting was my forte.

Their sun-browned arms were extended toward him. They wanted a blessing from perhaps the palest face they'd ever seen, convinced that this pope owned light green slacks and a light green knit sport shirt, not to mention a daughter. These would be his unwanted fifteen minutes of fame, his penultimate moment. Children put their arms around his knees. And as he had done with countless school kids who never saw much candy, he reached those fatherly hands into his pockets and began separating out

Life Savers and sticks of Juicy Fruit, distributing them like plentiful loaves and fishes. Just by being his charismatic self, he made that moment last a lifetime (like he had for his Poznan cousin) for that excited circle of lovely people we would never meet again.

I was honored to have witnessed this all, especially seeing some of Dad's strength and color come back, if only for a short time. Because somewhere over the Amazon River, our plane dropped about a quarter mile *straight down*. "Oh God! Jesus! Help us!" I said loudly. That plane began to vibrate with gusto. I heard pockets of screams. Dad gripped my hand tighter, praying *The Lord's Prayer*. This devil drop made me do fast thinking. My saddest thought was that my mother would have to plan our funerals and since she seldom left the house, I pictured her putting typed sheets of instructions under our front door, out to the mortician's lily-white understanding hands.

Suddenly, we were tethered on the end of one big bungee. We stopped falling, took a midair bounce, and proceeded to gain back altitude. Eventually the pilot was revived enough to announce to us seat-wetters that we had just gone through "significant turbulence." I wondered what his final grade was in Intercom Reassurance 2.0.

I had the evidentiary support gathered for the lounge lizards, though having it did not bring me joy. These weren't court exhibits. I didn't need to plead my case. We left our friends a half-world away, just as we found them, and I envied that what they had was all they needed.

I had taken my last sentimental journey with my father, the pope, one that was emotional and risky. It was the last time I would ever feel completely safe and loved, the way we feel when someone embraces all sides of us.

Before Leo died, I took family emergency leave. Kitty had fallen and broken her arm in two places. I was the parental unit of two physically helpless parents, running atop a floating log, trying not to fall off and drown. With school as the added bonus, plus a laundromat to run, I was overwhelmed.

In the mail one day in early spring 1984 was a letter addressed to Dad in an intentional faux-child scrawl. I opened it. On the typing paper page, printed vertically down the sheet was the word, "RETIRE. RETIRE. RETIRE. RETIRE. RETIRE..."

"You dirty bastard," I said quietly, ripping the letter to shreds. Somebody wanted his job. I believe the rat still lives. My consolation is that God knows that person *by name.*

Dad was slipping away from us. I had already pre-planned his funeral a few days before Christmas, 1983. I sat in the old Davis Funeral Home listening to iron bells caroling in a church tower nearby, thinking a little while about how Dad's career choices may have helped melt his health down. We had all done our part to save him, but God was preparing a place for him and we had to accept that. The director walked in with notebooks of samples. I felt like I was ordering wallpaper for a foyer.

"There are many grades of vaults," he said, after I selected a bronze casket.

"I want the one that will be most waterproof. That is important to me," I replied.

For a devoted daughter, there is no greater betrayal making burial plans for the unsuspecting father, especially at Christmas. I was the apple of his eye. No. I was nothing but a traitor, proving my own deep lack of faith in miracles.

Leo Pilewski died in the hospital April 28, 1984. I was there.

At least seven other bodies lay in state at the same time, and Dad ended up on the top floor of the funeral home, where the casket display normally was. I was not happy.

"Can't I just stay here tonight? I can sleep on the floor, I don't want to leave him," I cried. Clearly the grief period was underway, full-on extreme. The fact I would be surrounded by dead bodies bothered me not at all. I had never left Dad alone. When I was ill, he never left my side.

"No, no, we all need to go home," one of the employees said, as if I were five, quite put out with me. I wanted to shove his ass into one of the more costly and secure casket models and slam the lid.

Dad was moved downstairs the next evening. Staff had put a kneeler by the coffin, because the service would be Catholic.

"Why is that kneeler there?" a relative asked, a bit angrily.

"Because he was raised a Catholic and his friends are Catholic. It isn't going to hurt anything by allowing the people who knew him to kneel and pray."

The kneeler stayed.

Every day, for months after his funeral, I visited the gravesite. Sometimes, I walked around the grounds. If it started to rain, I held my umbrella over the plot, protecting his remains. On sunny days, I would stretch out alongside the freshly-turned earth and stare into the Heavens, as though his face would appear. I was a mess, talking to the sod, but it was the first and most painful death in my family. I was finding my way through my new school of loss.

"I know you aren't here, Dad, but the physical father part of you is, and it's all I've got now." Every holiday was hell, a new occasion to feel that absence more. I hung out at the cemetery because my mother spent every day crying.

"Your mother needs professional help," my aunt said on the phone from Ohio. Her own sister! Why was it that every family criticism always had to be submitted to me, Ms. Fix-It, like a work order? Maybe I needed help. I wanted to leave my life behind, but I had waited far too long. I was Mom's giant tear blotter, her Dad fill-in.

I could never fill those shoes in any capacity.

It was years after his passing before I unlocked the door to Dad's flaws. It felt illegal, like a thief digging up martyrs' bones from a holy altar. I knew those shortcomings were there all along. I realized something big about loving a relative. There is no such thing as true love. True love requires admitting the smudges and defects of the person. I loved Dad in hero mode, which masks all spots and blemishes. I could not find those cracks and fissures in his life. I'm sure there were a few unselfish pundits who would have happily pointed them out---students, teachers, community, maybe, perhaps family.

I closed my eyes to the undesirable side. He had a temper. He was no businessman, because a giving heart limits profit margins. He had zero cover skills when he disliked someone. He had a bit of prejudice which manifested in an occasional bad word choice. Once upon a time he believed that only Catholics met the criteria to be excellent people. "Marge is such a good Catholic woman," he would say. I never contested it, but I am sure there were other things that additionally made Marge better and also best as a woman. In simple terms, he was human. But because he loved me, always called me "baby daughter," and thought my head a fruity masterpiece, I gave him exclusive deity status even before I ever knew he was doubling for an honest-to-God pope.

This is not healthy. Girls who find no flaws in their fathers find no flaws in potential mates. My dating record proved this. What an animal reserve that whole mess was. It seemed I would always look for Dad Perfect in a male. No one could be that. I needed my father to protect me from wild beasties. He could not protect me from anything. He was gone. I was not part of Dad. He was all of me.

"Don't be mad at God, Momma," I heard him tell his confused, morose wife one cold rainy day in late March. In weeks he would never be available again to help us understand anything. Those two were sitting at the old kitchen table, where all major decisions were made, all important documents were drawn up, where the Bible was read, son-in-law to mother-in-law. "If I hadn't gotten this sick, I wouldn't know Him like I do," Dad said to Mom. I don't think she heard him at first. But seconds later, she was weeping, her head down on the table. Dad brought up a frail hand out of that wine-colored velour bathrobe sleeve, the one I'd gotten him for Christmas. It hung on his shrunken body, his emaciated hand stretching forth like the Ghost of Christmas Future, touching Mom, showing her what was to come but trying to save her from perishing with him. That was as much final days preparation as I could take.

I wished he'd said that to *me*. Maybe I wouldn't have stayed mad, very mad, furious at God for years. After firing myself during a heated county office phone call, I floundered. I tried my hand at a craft shop, The Country Cove. Nice things, wrong location. I wanted to work at a florist, but the owner never needed my help.

Finally, a job came up at Salem College for an alumni and publications coordinator. I knew people, so they hired me. That job lasted three years, but the president knew we disliked him. He loved to torture tall women. Nothing we did pleased him, not the lady dean, not the feature writers, not the registrar. Still, we were a family, and we enjoyed our work. Best of all, I got to be an assistant to the charming Senator Jennings Randolph when he visited his alma mater. We had quite the pen-to-paper correspondence. Jennings was legend, responsible for the twenty-first amendment, giving eighteen-year-olds the right to vote. But it all ended when our fearless leader sold the college to a foreign entity. Our jobs went bye bye.

Again, I was cleaning out a desk. I slammed myself down into my office chair late that night in June. Where was I going now? And further (thank you for the song, Diana Ross), did I like the things that life was showing me? How had I spent the last five years? I could barely remember. Was this the pattern for the rest of my life, selecting a career of the month, then picking up my tent a few months/years later, ambling on?

One day five lost years later, that brief, last kitchen conversation Leo had with Mom came back to me, confronting me. I walked in our big kitchen and stared at the chair where Dad had sat consoling Kitty, trying to prepare her in an odd orientation session for life without father. He knew she would want to die with him. He realized the weight I would carry later. That weight had petrified my heart to stone. How stupid I felt, dying to grief like that.

Hearing Dad again, telling my mother, "Don't be mad at God" was transforming after being so mad and a little bit bad. His words shook my heart like a reprimand. It was a teaching lesson. It melted me. That was my five-word awakening. If God had turned His back on me, I forgave Him. (Wasn't that big of me?) At last, I felt something again and the hurt fell away. I woke up.

I had stood in the Unemployment line for the last time. I would avoid going places no longer. My journey, now past the halfway point on the circle, was heading left and upward, back to the beginning of things. I was moving forward, going back to my career roots. I believed my courage to try other things made me one of the "can-dos." Here were all my crumbs taking form again, like the bombed-out Warsaw buildings glued back together during World War II. I would go back and grovel if I absolutely had to. There were worse things than reenlisting for another tour. I could take it; I had sturdy genes. I'd been through worse. Dad didn't raise no pansy!*

*Actually, Dad did raise pansies and they were big-faced, resilient, and bloomed until snow fell, even after. You can learn a lot from a seemingly mild-mannered flower bed, lovingly cultivated by an unyielding WWII Army staff sergeant.

Deciding to go on for Dad, one of the truly great educators, I would do a few extra-credit assignments for God while paying homage to my father. Many former students had written Dad the kindest notes about how he taught them life skills, how he treated them in high school, thanking him for all the letters of recommendation. He always found time to help someone. I would forget myself, and get lost in caring for others the way Dad had.

It had been a long time since I'd felt that way. Whatever should happen, I would teach my butt off, keep my heart open and pliable, knowing that nothing would please Leo Pilewski more. Nothing.

The Dorothy Belle Effect on Big Blonde

I knew again at thirteen, and the urge was stronger. It wasn't pubescence. I got that old feeling back about teaching. I was going to teach English, the world's most fulfilling job. It was my "teacher mitzvah" moment of becoming a young careerist. Never mind I was neither Jewish or a good judge of good-paying professions. I was headed for the classroom because of one inimitable woman---Dorothy Belle Upton Davis, author, columnist, speaker, director, and upper division English teacher of local renown. If I'd already elevated her to a literary lesser god, then where might she elevate me someday? I was tingling to find out. Dorothy was floating every day, on a saggy, public classroom stage right over my head.

In eighth grade at Salem High, I could not wait to experience the "Hiroshima Effect" of Dorothy Belle. She taught junior and senior English, an atom-splitting explosion of an educator. I imagined that busy blackboard of hers as a silver screen, the celluloid backdrop on which she performed her heart out. Standing outside her door, a stalker (I) might believe they heard a Broadway recording of *Macbeth*, but it was merely Dorothy doing all the cast voices. If I could but touch the hem of her self-made New York wool Vogue-patterned dress, I would be made a whole teacher, achieving the impossible, even with the most unwilling English students. I would be rid of anything rotten that had ever been done or said to me, vetted, respected, and intellect-ed. I would teach

English because right brain was all I had. My left brain was destroyed by Mrs. Goldchien's Jack the Ripper-esque penchant for slicing open living things.

It was 1968. Teachers were making under $7,000, which explained why those adults educating us were so cranky. I was sitting in science class and we were dissecting frogs. I could not bear it or the endless drone of terms rattled off by a teacher who talked like someone being choked. One floor up, directly over my head, was herself, The Legend in the flesh, reading and floating to her own unique choreography. She was above me, dancing across that squeaky wooden floor, slicing open her students' heads, pouring in a solution of life and new thoughts mixed from a beaker of authors' words.

"Now folks, with your forceps, pull back the skin, thus exposing the duodenum. Pay attention! Now I want you to pin back...."

-----*Shut up, shut up, strangled lady! How can I hear my idol upstairs if you're down here talking about frog parts? Your cruelty is appalling------Was that a cartwheel upstairs? Oh, why can't I be a junior now, NOW!*

Dear God, I said, allowing my lips to move, let the ceiling open and take me, take me up----but only as far as Mrs. Davis's English class!

Two and a half more years would pass before I could be mentally irradiated with her brilliance. Perpetual Christmas would come for me, eventually.

Dorothy Belle did not suffer fools in her English work camps. By stepping one foot across her threshold, you were signing away your safety and stupidity to her drills and rigorous maneuvers. No lesson plan critiques, bell ringers, technology objectives, or one single walk-through by any brave-enough administrator would have made her more perfect. No educator specialist alive today would have debriefed or improved her. You had to be one of her students to be part of the elite group who got what DB was. She had the gift of full-body intimidation. Her eyes were so piercing she could count the hairs on the back of your head. She was just that rare, just that cobra-like. Instant bruises to the tibia were her trademark for nodding off, even for a nanosecond.

"Ssssh!" she cautioned our class one morning, her power finger to her lips as Mr. Swag, class clown Billy Matthey, slept head down like the dead.

Bill was Will Rogers and Don Rickles rolled into one continual floor show, edgy and sometimes cruel. Even if he made fun of your best friend, it was hard not to smile. Bill was the only one of us brave enough to play literary critic to Genius Geoffrey Chaucer.

"The little darling needs his rest," she whispered, monster-creeping up to his seat. An alligator was about to take him from us. The lot of us slowly leaned towards him, trying to send powerful mental signals.

As she came within arm's length of his head we all screamed silently, **WAKE UP, BILLY! HOLY GOD! SAVE YOURSELF!** She cocked that hammer leg back and shot him one in the shin bone with her low pump. We believed it was steel-toed. It sounded like pig skin getting punted through two goal posts. He rared up like a wild Mustang and his lips retracted as he sucked in air, exposing big clenched teeth, tight as our frightened asses.

She could make us *feel* things, painful things, which is the mark of true acting and old-school teaching. If Billy ever wanted to return fire then beat a hasty retreat, he never once considered it, for DBUD could outrun most any car, new or used, on Route 50 between Salem and Clarksburg.

Poe's *The Bells* was her golden gramophone nod. I'd never seen it paced to a horror gymnastics routine. Even in mid-spin Dorothy never dropped that beefy textbook laying helplessly in her narrow but strong, lengthy palm. I watched her Edgar Allen face contort like heated Silly Putty in overly-zealous enunciating. There was a particular look she got when she said Poe's created word, "tintinnabulation" that was the identical face my dogs made when I fed them spoons of peanut butter. Watching it, I realized I'd pulled both my cheeks together with my own tremoring hand. I was attempting to keep my own facial parts where they belonged, heeding Mom's warning: "Never screw your face into any expression you can't live with until death." I heard that threat ringing in my head, along with the screaming of *The Bell-l-l-l-l-s*. Dorothy *Belle* reading *The Bells*. It just made sense. But for a teaching Pilewski, it would be tough finding that same-name poem for my trophy piece.

She loved each one of us, even those for whom the shoe flew. Her heart was abundant. A fellow member of the class of 1972 told me at a recent reunion lunch, that "Dorothy quietly offered to pay one of our classmate's college tuition. All four years."

DB hid her generosity in the same seam pocket as her compassion and tissue. She kept her eyes on Biblical principles and did her good works in the dark. All students respected her, even if she was not their own North Star.

When we read Moby Dick, she said something random, but I never forgot it.

"Given a choice between losing a limb, always choose an arm. I know soldiers who lost legs in the war and never were able to accommodate artificial limbs. That very singular pain is hell; it's always there."

No teacher I ever had said that. How could we know what things were about if someone was not allowing us passage there, stirring our young empathy, revealing the unpleasantness of life? My imaginings were about her handmade dresses and accessories. The fabrics were smart, with varied textures. One day, a skirt that was like braided horse's mane, coarse and textured; another day, a jacket, with oversized tortoise buttons, smooth and slimming. Even so (and those Vogue dresses were form-fitting), she could face us and do a clean Rockette kick like an exclamation point for a selection from *A Tale of Two Cities*, whether that shocking punctuation belonged there or not. That Naturalizer shot straight up, sole facing the ceiling, and she would laugh unashamedly, gauging our reaction to being flashed. She liked us to look shocked. She jumped off her desk decades before Robin Williams was directed to do so as Professor Keating in *Dead Poets Society*.

"Get up and leave!" she'd crescendo in her monk-like library sepulcher because she was also the book warden. If you talked one word in Dorothy's library, you got bounced. She hoofed it to school every morning so she could unlock that research prison promptly at 7:00 a.m., regardless how deep the snow was. In the event of a tsunami, DBUD would have surfed her own black and white composition book down main and right up High School Hill, arriving bone dry. She was fearless, never sick. Colds and misfortune tiptoed around her.

When Mike Underwood invited me to Salem High's Homecoming dance in tenth grade, I had my talented Aunt Patty work a little doppelganger dress magic.

78

"Make me a sheath dress from a Vogue pattern," I ordered up. "Plaid wool. It has to have long sleeves, and a bateau collar."

It was an exact replica! The wine and taupe plaid wool under my neckline scratched like briers. Dorothy Belle never saw her red-necked, itchy-skinned Vogue clone. She wasn't a dance chaperone type, instead working at home writing a book or column, making cheese, sewing more dresses, making Christmas cards with wildflowers she'd pressed over the summer. My belief that she never slept made her even more heroic.

Inside that intense room of learning English were no accelerated or slow learners. We all kept up at the same speed. She scared us into succeeding, no matter our love level for English. She would have pecked the eyes out of that grade school teacher who gave us bird brain names. Cliff Notes were not a smart way to wheedle out of reading *Animal Farm*, *The Scarlet Letter* or *Return of The Native*. She memorized them and knew fudging when she read it on an essay test. Every class she ever taught memorized Macbeth's soliloquy in Act V, Scene V, without any mandated modifications for special needs. As we faced the class, her penned hand rested over each name for a grade. Every word had to be precise. She watched the audience. If anyone distracted us, that idiot got an "auto F."

"Tomorrow, and tomorrow, and tomorrow, creeps into this petty pace from day to day to the last syllable of recorded time. And all our yesterdays have lighted fools the way to dusty death…[Life] is a tale told by an idiot, full of sound and fury, signifying nothing."

There was a reason I could still recite (and gesticulate) the entire Shakespearean passage flawlessly to my seniors, thirty-five years later. Somehow, saying those words made me youthful though depressed all in one. My classes had no electricity in them, at least the kind that should have been generated by me. It wasn't for lack of trying. Maybe I wanted to show them the old girl still had it, meaning me, not Dorothy. For another, I wanted them to get that part about life meaning nothing, being told by an idiot. My life was a brass imitation of Dorothy's gold teaching; when I finished with the final words, "signifying nothing," I wasn't acting. Imitation may be flattering in a live performance, but it only enlarged my feelings of inadequacy and failure. Instead of rapt attention and wonderment and applause, which is banquet food for timorous egos, I got girls twisting tresses and guys with stoned pupils dreaming about tractor pulls and pulls of all kind.

I realized then that I was the poor player Will I. Am Shakespeare was writing to, the frustrated actor with a teaching certificate who "struts and frets his hour upon the stage, then is heard of no more."

It was my senior year, and DBUD was announcing the big reveal, our senior class play selection. Dorothy directed all high school productions, two per year, paid zero per annum. Her plays were legend. What student would be idiot enough to accept a role then ignore her brilliant direction? In 1972, one such mistake-maker surfaced.

"We will be doing Mary Chase's comedy, *Harvey*, this April," she proclaimed.

We didn't know who the hell Harvey even was, but we didn't care. We were her acting saps with an after-school chance to be further postured and sharply directed by her.

During rehearsal, an unexpected storm and ensuing explosion blew up that was not weather or explosives related. My sometimes boyfriend, Richard, had not memorized his lines or brought a pencil for director's notes. As the lead, Elwood P. Dowd (the famous Jimmy Stewart role), he had many lines.

"You'd better read over your part. If you don't know your lines, she'll kill you!" I whispered to him in the ancient auditorium that would soon become the Roman Coliseum, complete with a roaring lion.

Richard shrugged. "I don't care," he said.

And those were the last three words he spoke. For a clinically long time.

I was sitting there in one of the old wooden theater seats about four rows back when the atomic blast happened. Richard stood onstage inert, like a dead battery, arms limp, staring at the tops of his brown Sperry Top Siders.

"Line!" DB called to the play prompter. A second instance of silence from Richard. "LINE!" she yelled. I could hear my classmate whispering the dialogue to him. My knees clattered as I gripped the black wrought iron under the arm rests. On the third **"L-I-I-I-N-E!!!"** the stage curtain began quaking under duress of the hidden, terrified prompter.

WHAM! went the director's copy onto the floor and down that center aisle she tore in stomps each the length of a Volkswagen. Her nylon slip swished against the lined wool until there was a faint burning smell. Fission passed right beside me and I couldn't stop it.

Jesus, save him, I said in a near-audible whisper, but first, save *me*!

Up those four stage steps she bounded without words, toward Richard. Would she go for the throat?

81

"General George S. Patton" began to glow, softly at first, ending in a mushroom blast. The general shook him violently the way stage managers once shook metal sheets to create thunder sounds onstage. We could see his hair and bobble head jerking free style. Then came the awful **ping! ping! ping! ping! ping!** *What was that?* Loose change from his pockets? Teeth? What a throttling! The bowed stage floor was bouncing. Our mouths fell open wide enough to comfortably fit hockey pucks, and we noticed his pin-striped Oxford shirt open to the waist flapping like two shutters in an Okie twister.

When the bright flash was over, we saw it was the pearl shirt buttons doing the pinging, flashing in the footlights, rolling away from the ruckus, afraid of getting stomped. Finally, she let go of Elwood P. Dowd. Harvey, the invisible rabbit/pooka, had abruptly left the stage. **I saw him!** My private parts were even trembling and I squeezed my thighs together even tighter, creating my own little fission reaction.

"I will be in the L-i-i-i-brary," she roared. "If you can conduct yourselves enough to pull this mess together, you can knock on the door!"

There stood my grade school frenemy, Cinderella herself, Dorothy's student director. She was the appointee to brave the actual knock upon the door. If she still had that big ol' princess sea-parter Halloween ball gown she could just knock the door in with her skirt!

Our cast had boldly wasted her donated time. We avoided looking at Poor Richard. I feared he would shake inside like a maraca with two floating kidneys the rest of his life. After DB disappeared, I did wonder if she went to the library, stage left, mad as hell, or instead flopped in a chair and laughed till her flat belly hurt. She knew we were out there preparing to grovel, crawling around like frantic worms looking for the late Elwood P. Dowd's shirt buttons and incisors, mopping up our own excretions. Rehearsal was *o-v-e-r*.

"How was play practice?" Mom asked. "Hunky dory," I said, charging up the creaky staircase. My ears were ringing. Sweat was dripping inside my hands and underwear. In my room, I turned on my Webcor record player and tried to listen to Neil Diamond: "*Song sung blue, everybody knows one...*" I replayed what had happened. I can't be her, I thought, because she was The Red Devil tonight. For certain, it was the honeymoon-ender.

She had shown me her darkest colors. Was she "demon"-strating how to bring the hammer down for best effect? Could I ever become The Blonde Devil? How far would I go to teach that contact sport life lesson to a student---the harsh example that erases stupidity and laziness but requires orthodonture and button sewing, not to mention job interviews?

Nope, I couldn't go there. Not *that* far. I wouldn't count my teaching accomplishments someday and have "incarceration" among them.

And therein was my own future lesson in hypocrisy, about judging an angry teacher, one I would remember every time I found my screaming voice and my silent desire to choke the life out of a nonproductive, rude seventeen-year-old.

Richard's parents were both teachers, but no call was ever placed to the principal about that rehearsal. Neither cast or crew ever spoke of the incident, because telling our parents would have ensured "backfire revenge." Somehow, if we ratted out the Button Popper we would get the punishment. We'd be told that we had done something to bring on the German Blitzkrieg. It would all be on us; thus, the cast's code of silence held. No backfire. Our parents always sided with the teacher; therefore, nothing good came from talking out of school. Just the same, Elwood was loaded for bear by the next rehearsal, spitting those lines out with eyes wide open, through a full set of spared teeth.

My best friend, Wegie, and I were Dorothy's library assistants. It was quite an honor for the two of us nonconformists. We dusted those book spines and yellowed cellophane protectors, and stamped dates due with a vengeance.

One day Mrs. Davis was grading term papers at her desk and looked up at me over those readers that matched her hair.

"Lexsana, if you should become a teacher, you will both love and despise it. Because of your sensitivity, you will experience a bath of fire the rest of your life."

Here was the vinegar poured over my happiness waffle. *What did it me-e-e-e-an?* I wouldn't dare ask, because maybe she was just Dorothy-ing me. Was a bath of fire a real thing? At seventeen, I dismissed it, because she surely meant I would need a professional plumber to install and set the temperature on any future-purchase hot water tank later, when I lived alone. Evidently, she was worried I might scald myself in my old maiden-ness, trying to bathe three-legged dogs and a blind cat.

But the writer in me analyzed things differently. Maybe she knew I would never let go of the boarding gate so I could fly off and be the actress I wanted to be. I think she thought I overthought, over-felt those things requiring decisions. Either way, I would prove her wrong. I would show her I was fire-retardant in the tub or out.

Salem College had the best English/drama professors: Jean Christie, Carolyn Tallman, C. James Kelley, Ed Spatafore, Billie Freeland, Pat McHugh. My third year in college lovely English and creative writing professor, Jean Christie, had our creative writing class do a big end-of-semester project. Jean was cool beans. She let me cough out every creative thought I ever had. In a parody piece I wrote a Tammy Faye Baker-style skit about a minister obsessed with money. I wore a robe and had back-up choir. We sang jubilantly:

Amazing work, how sweet the sound
That saved a jerk like me
I once was broke, but cash I've found
It's making a millionaire out of me.........

When I looked down at the audience from my little sermonette, there sat Dorothy Belle waving her arms, a spirit-filled congregant. Dorothy also made time to see my Art Center performances, particularly my role as Flo in *Picnic*. The congratulatory note was a keeper.

Harvey and Richard's shirtless wonder rehearsal came back to me every spring when I did a little limited-capacity closet thinning. Every time I pulled out the dress DB had sewn, the elegant one I'd worn as Veta Louise in *Harvey*, I got that old feeling. I'd see my director foaming at the mouth for a few seconds up there on stage, then I'd hear applause from reaping Dorothy's direction. I ceremoniously held my arms around the dress in the mirror and strummed those suture-like metallic gold and silver cocktail threads across my fingertips, quoting some Veta Louise dialogue about an orderly at Chumley's Rest being a white slaver because of his trademark "close-set eyes." I touched the hem of her beautiful garment often, like I'd dreamed about in junior high school.

"I want you to have this dress," she had said backstage on closing night, with a half-smile, then walked away in those yard stick strides.

"Oh, Mrs. Davis, you're *giving* it to me?" I asked.

"I am," she said, still walking. "It belongs to you now."

I always wondered what she was thinking as she passed that symbol over. She disappeared up the empty aisle of the old theater in Salem College's administrative building, the very place I would work someday when I took my soul-searching sabbatical from teaching. Did the Vogue gift of a moment that she'd made to wear to a New York theater premiere affirm that I had a bit of acting chops? Or was she just advancing me a tip, an example of how to pay it forward when future teacher me directed?

"Make haste slowly," she admonished the cast between show scenes. I wanted to scream out "Juxtaposition, and maybe an oxymoron!" but I did not want to make my inferiors feel inferior. I decided to choose my career that way, by making haste slowly with my decision. I just wasn't slow enough, looking back. The dress is still mine, though it is a bit too tight. Clearly, it shrank with the fiery bath passage of time.

That yes-to-the-dress moment was my West Virginia Lottery win, twelve years before the lottery even existed.

Part II   Do You Have the Map?

I was in my second post as an adult education teacher when the phone rang one Easter break…

"Ehhhhh, Lexsana! Dorothy Davis here." (She always began with "ehhh," the thinker's version of "ummmm." Or "duhhhh".)

I held that princess phone with both hands. "Well hello, Mrs. Davis! What a surprise!" I said, shaking, peeing a little.

"Oh, call me Dorothy...I'm hosting a luncheon for a few friends on Tuesday, and I want you to come."

What? Now wait, am I a guest or a server? She knows I could handle those big, heavy casseroles. "Okay," I said prematurely. She gave me the guest list: a doctor's widow, a college librarian, and a concert pianist. And me? What did I have to offer that Algonquin Round Table discussion group? Dorothy Belle would become Dorothy Parker. Either Dorothy could be tough. Parker once said to her celebrity elitists at that big New York table of famous sarcasm: "You can lead a horticulture, but you can't make her drink." There seemed to be murderous teeth in Parker's mouth and pen point.

So, I was sunk. I picked out a goofy outfit for the Algonquin gathering, with ugly sensible shoes and, just in case, I put two oven mitts inside my purse.

Driving to the widow Davis's house, I thought about how starstruck she'd always made me. I recalled a story she had told about hearing Helen Keller speak during a tour. "She spoke in a strident, high register because, naturally, she could not hear how she sounded." I remember thinking, *Helen has nothing on you, Miss Dorothy Belle.*

I held my own during lunch and did not lift a finger, because DB had that spread all under control: iced tea, salmon loaf with mustard sauce, spinach casserole and lemon chiffon pie for dessert with real, perked coffee and cream in fancy crystal and sterling pieces. Was I surprised it was delicious? The conversation flowed like the coffee poured from her silver pot. I was feeling so good I kicked off my shoes under that fancy table. Gripping the carpet with my toes was relaxing. Had I known things would take a bad turn, I would have kept those ugly white teacher flats on my briefly-relaxed feet.

All was going swimmingly when she suddenly leaned into me, invading my face space, tilting her head and narrowing her owl eyes. *(Gulp)* "I have lived in Salem decades, but never have I seen your mother out. Anywhere. Does she like living 'in isolato' so much? That isn't healthy."

There was that trademark **WHAM!** The lemon chiffon suddenly had the faint taste of pickle juice. Of course, she was right. My mom rarely left the house, except to walk our dogs early or under cover of darkness. My God! Maybe neighbors thought Kitty was a government agent! I rubbed the rest of my lip gloss onto that white linen napkin and gingerly put my shoes back on under the table. Time to go.

"Well, she used to go out. She was a homeroom mother for years, but all those cupcakes just wore her down." More owl-staring and owl head turning. "No," I let out a little tense breath, "she never left the house, except for surgeries."

That was the stupidest response I'd ever vocalized to another human. Clearing my throat to prevent choking, I finished off any chance of ever coming back there. I was always explaining my family to someone, and I was fairly sure, they were doing likewise. *Thank you, Emily Dickinson/Kitty Pilewski, for being my mother. I hope you have to spend eternity in a Michael Jackson concert. Onstage. As his opening act.*

I returned many times for lunch and sometimes it was just us two. I took advantage of those times to ask her advice on teaching things. Her answers were never complicated. Even her advice had literary elements: characters, rising action, conflict, and most importantly, outcome. I tried what she told me. She never over advised. If only I could point myself at the world like a weapon, without ever once measuring the depth of the wound.

One day as we drank our coffee on her porch I said, "You have a lot going on and a pretty big piece of realty to run by yourself. Your son is in New York. It's a long way to come fix the plumbing. Who helps you then?"

"My students are my family here. When I need help, I call upon the family."

Her answer had the profoundest effect on me. She knew she had given all and for the dedicated teacher, there would always be that payback appreciation from former students. I decided to keep on putting school ahead of myself so someday when I retired, there might be that short list of student phone numbers on my refrigerator, a checkless Social Security bonus.

I didn't hear from her for a while. Then one summer day, Dorothy phoned again.

89

"Ehhhh, Lexsana? Dorothy Davis. I called with an invitation. You and I are going on holiday. The trip's on me. We will be going to a wedding in Pennsylvania and the reception is at a country club. Can you go? We'll spend the night there next weekend and leisurely make our way back Sunday. I'm sending you the invitation and the map with directions."

"Okay," I said, wondering if she'd drawn a line through every other student non-family family member on her list. Was I the only one who didn't have an excuse or another holiday trip on tap? Oh well, what the hell. I was in.

Late Friday night I packed. What would she wear? I would take two dresses and a checklist of things not to say or do. The list was all in my head like a memorized soliloquy:

1) No BM's. I would hold in all four meals and two hunks of wedding cake and wait till I was safely home.
2) No big vocabulary words I could not spell, define, unscramble, identify the part of speech, and use in a sentence.
3) No seeking school advice. We were on holiday.
4) No fast driving. I had precious cargo.
5) No onions, meaning no after-hours flatulence.
7) No nightshirts with stupid slogans. I would wear a sweat suit to bed out of modesty.
8) No overeating. She was a wooden spoon. I would draw a mental line down my plate and eat exactly half of whatever.
9) No swearing or coarseness or gossip. And no mention of "that play when Elwood forgot his lines."
10) No forgetting anything! This was Dorothy, for God's sake. I was sure she could still split atoms.

That Saturday morning, I was late. I'd overslept. I never looked back when I sped out the back door. If I had, I'd have broken my jaw on the door frame. I pulled up Dorothy's driveway and saw her slender form growing

90

taller, more ominous. She, the tree, was throwing vast shade. Her belongings were at the loading dock end of her sidewalk. I jumped into her long shadow. My Lumina was not fully in park.

"You're *late!*" she barked. "I despise tardiness." I crammed those bags into my trunk right on top of my carefully-positioned wedding wear. Jesus save me! I had just been Dorothy Belle-d.

Right past the West Virginia border, she turned that auburn head and asked, "Do you have the map I sent you?"---- *A test!*

I felt every artery and organ shutting down. I saw dead people. *Me!*

"Ehhhh-mmmmm, I believe I packed it in my suitcase," I lied through my chattering teeth.

"Liar!" she said through her eyes, her dark pupil daggers pulsing to fly out.

I wouldn't admit to anything. I prayed my heart out until the sweat on my forehead had color to it.

Somehow, we still arrived in that quaint Pennsylvania community, found our hotel, and unpacked in our room. As I was opening my old blue suitcase, I looked over at her bed and out of nowhere there was a virtual buffet. She had prepared homemade chicken salad with crisp lettuce on homemade bread in pre-sliced diagonals, her own bread and butter pickles in a new pint jar, jumbo fresh-baked cookies and a chilled thermos of lemonade, and service for two, all on a beautiful table cloth. My mouth watered at that trademark spread of hers, but I was committed to eating like a bird.

After lunch, she had that banquet broken down in seconds, all packed away in a piece of luggage I had assumed was a portable sewing machine with fabric to build a complete outfit, including her infamous punter pumps. I felt so relaxed, so happy, because those cookies rocked.

"When Lyndon Johnson was president," she said, brushing a few crumbs off her bedspread, "he wrote in his autobiography about the importance of afternoon naps. Naps must be taken in pajamas after brushing teeth. Preparing for sleep is key to comfort and relaxing."

I went over to the sink to wash my hands. When I turned back around her hands were crossed over the front hem of her New England fisherman knit sweater and whoosh! went that sweater, over her head, revealing bare wood with two drooping downturned candy canes. Immediately, a mental picture of Lyndon B. Johnson in his union suit was hastily replaced. I pivoted on my dry heel so fast I pulled out a carpet loop. The sink became my stage prop, and I rinsed my hands repeatedly to "Throw Out the Lifeline" with good reason, refusing to look in the mirror. I counted to thirty slowly and turned around carefully to find her in a full-length flannel gown, applying white socks. She was ready for her Lyndon nap. "You can go down to the pool and read," she said.

She didn't have to say it, because I already was nervously grabbing for the door knob, trying to will it open. Down the outer steps I bounded, some two at a time, thinking *why does she do these things?*

"Idiot," I answered myself poolside. Maybe people were watching the dazed blonde talking to herself, wringing her hands."She's the Shock Doctor and today, you're the test group!"

For one split second, I considered just running until I hit an Amish farm, joining up, like Harrison Ford did in *Witness*. "You can resteth here," the women would say, pointing to a hay loft, feeding me shoo-fly pie and buttermilk left from a barn raising. The elders would pray over me. My conversion might involve growing a beard, to delineate me as an import and not a native, but hay fever would always mark me first.

I tried to read at the pool, but instead thought about what the rest of the day-into-evening might hold. I hoped to God I hadn't inherited my father's weak heart.

At 3:30, burnt to red, dripping sweat, I tiptoed back to the room, where I prayed she would still be sleeping. I'd take the world's quickest shower and---

---She was sitting on her neat bedspread, dressed in a beautiful cream silk dress, ready to roll. I was a sweat hog with no time to shower. I grabbed whatever clothes my hands hit first, fearing another lecture about being late. Out I came in some dress, one skirt side clinging high up on my wet hip not yet dry from water splashes, hairbrush in hand, brushing furiously into the mirror. She was standing between beds now, inching closer, and I was creating a bald spot near my right temple. My arm pits were fully wet. In the mirror, standing behind me, her hands were raised like Eva Peron speaking to her adoring Argentinians.

"*Big Blonde!*" she boldly proclaimed, announcing it with the same pride the county fair judge awards "Best in Pork" over a 4-H'er's prize sow. "O-Okay," I replied, wondering what was in that fresh-squeezed lemonade.

Had she just made fun of my size? Damn it! She'd better not say---,

"Dorothy Parker!" she cried, almost ready to do a back flip. And there it was, the name of funny hypodermic needling.

I knew she'd bring up that blustery Algonquin witch! I knew it!

"Big, beautiful blonde zaftig! That's you---*Big Blonde!*"

Wow, really? Did she have to say "big"? I got that it was some short story by Ms. Parker, but I'd never heard of it, or the word "zaftig," which, it turns out, is Yiddish for "juicy," which in my big blonde-ness, I definitely was---juicy wet with chauffeur's prewedding sweat--- because I had *no map*.

As we walked to the parking lot, I saw an older couple dressed up in semi-formal attire. I beat a hasty retreat to them and on the QT, whispered, "Would you happen to be going to the Davis wedding?"

"Why, yes we are," the man smiled. "Would you like to follow?" "You have no idea!" I answered, thanking them. My relief was obvious as we entered country club country.

Our navigators *were* wedding guests and not two serial killers. Now I could relax and enjoy whatever the rest of the night hurled at me or my wary eyes, still in a light state of stare fixation. The overhead lighting bothered my still-dilated pupils. My damp dress stuck to me like a drunken wedding date. All evening.

That night I checked off every one of my "Don't Do" list items, though Number 10 was clearly off the table. I'd forgotten the map, but now, I wished to forget an image that I should have seen coming.

Someday this will all be in a book, I promised myself silently on the drive home.

"You bet it shall," I heard her say without words. *How did she do that?*

The last time we lunched together I remember two things from the visit.

"I want to live long enough to experience the New Millenium," she said at her dining table, "just to see how nutty-crazy people will get." It scared me that she was no longer directing the world. She'd had a pig's valve put into her chest years earlier. It turns out those valves have limits, like vintage automobiles.

The last story, my favorite, was about another holiday.

"Bond and I were on holiday with another couple in New York. We were getting out of a cab, dressed to the nines, ready for the theater. I noticed people staring, whispering. Soon more gathered. A man said, 'Hey! You're Jimmy Stewart!' (I remembered Bond and he *did* look like Mr. Stewart.) 'No, I assure you, sir, I am not James Stewart,' Bond explained, smiling calmly. 'Yes, you are!' the agitated fan fired back. A small crowd was gathering. Someone wanted Bond to sign autographs. I looked down at my watch. Sign the damned autographs, Jimmy, we're going to miss the opening curtain. And he signed them: *Best Wishes! Jimmy Stewart.*"

Our meetings and luncheons faded with time. School became a test for me. Now I was the one doing school plays, exploding on a smaller scale, sitting in her seat at a different high school theater in a different era. There were transitions, challenges we both faced, but hers were more finite.

She told me once how the county office had called her in, supervisors sweating bullets, drawing straws to see who would inform her she would no longer be a substitute teacher at seventy. She laughed hysterically, almost witchy. "They said I was scaring the little darlings."

Of course, she was. The remnants of old school honor and strong expectations exited with her first retirement. Students of a new generation couldn't relate to her great expectations; further, they couldn't even relate to Charles Dickens writing about them, and both Chuck D. and DBUD were spurned among the teenage literati.

Teachers were becoming too tenderized (including myself), and because of it, students were becoming soft. The twenty-first-century teacher, with all his teacher workshop training, was the educational GMO (genetically modernized oracle) expected to sift through the mental mind field of troubled teens and make everyone a college graduate with all the right stuff. If this included saying, "There, there, my wonderful student, you can achieve brilliance, and you can do whatever you want to, whenever you want to do it" ---then, shamefully we did it.

Dorothy's hands, feet, mind, and mouth were taped shut. The last time she subbed and told students they were all mollycoddled, some probably told their parents to call the superintendent because they were pretty sure some old bat had sexually harassed them.

DB lived into the early twenty-first century, just as she willed, but not on her terms. I could hardly bear stories about her decline. What I had loved about her I had so weakly emulated, and in pursuing that end of trying to be her and failing at it, I left her behind. "A mentor," it's written, "can be someone whose hindsight can become your foresight." I got that in a fortune cookie and taped it inside my journal because whoever wrote that experienced a strong neutron star like I did. I could not keep literary vaudeville alive. I let go of trying. Old school was as lost as silent films.

Dorothy died and was cremated. There was a memorial, but I could not complete this final assignment by attending. Was I really hedging because I had written a tribute and might not get to say it? Or, was I thinking about her the way I thought about wonderful Christmas---if I didn't put all the good candles and snowmen away, then it would still be Christmas? Sitting on the bed in my slip, looking in the mirror, I didn't like myself a bit more than I had the past three decades. Why had I allowed myself to get that lost in the 200 Dewey Decimal Mythology of her legendary life? Who would ever inspire me again? I had lost my two compasses, my father first, then my mentor. She was right to keep asking me, *"do you have the map?"*

The full-blown service went just fine without me. I wondered what DB would have thought of all that hoopla bath of tribute from her grateful students. "Hogwash!" she would have said if

Dorothy and the infamous fisherman's sweater with Pilgrim's [dowdy] Progress

she saw them spitting their words like memorization for a grade. Instead, her request would have been: "Take a walk in the woods. Nature owns wisdom. Pluck up some Jack-in-the-Pulpit for me."

Once we were sitting on her porch and I told her I wanted nothing more in life than to be a success with a Dorothy brand. "You're already a success," she corrected. "You're thinking the wrong way." I even talked to her about a failed engagement to a younger man. "You couldn't marry a baby," she said. "How would life be wedded to Peter Pan?"

Our relationship had grown from student and teacher to young teacher forever without master teacher. I wanted her to see what I might become when I finally grew up, because *I* was the real Peter Pan. Maybe a book someday, like herself, the author.

…..... My heart stayed sad, rent in two like Elwood P. Dowd's striped Oxford shirt.

Mr. Berg's Bat, Mr. Cheese-It, a Poo Poo Wish, and One Hot Deputy Dawg 🐑

In my many years as a child, totaling sixty-four now, I have made bad decisions and suffered through severely awkward moments. This chapter might be your opportunity to feel less stupid about your own poor decisions, a chance to kiss the shoes of whoever deflected you from becoming a school teacher. After hearing I had facial whiskers; a limp; falsies; a few extra thigh pounds; and personal class pets; the inability to teach anything; and was gay, I perfected my reaction. I just stood there, in the presence of my enemy, and tried to throw shade with my red face. It was always my shellfish allergy imitation face: wild-eyed, tear-swollen, and tongue-slurred partial utterances. They were the only game I had because verbal cruelty paralyzed me like bad sushi.

These are a few of my favorite [embarrassing teacher] things that caused my eventual work tic and the optical illusion of one of my ears appearing higher than the other after I started wearing readers.

It was a new semester. I was inching towards the twilight years of teaching, the same way athletes start being called "gramps" at thirty. I looked over the roll for third block. There in the B's was the name, "Berg, Matt." How odd, I thought, because I had taught another fellow with that same name when I was but a tenderfoot freshman at my first misguided teaching post. Could this lad be a time traveler, or was I seeing old student faces on younger bodies, reading double? "Matt Berg," I called and he said "Here." Yep, I saw the resemblance. "Did your father happen to go to another high school down the pike?" "Yes, he did," he said. "Do you know him?" "I taught him. And I have no bad recollections, so that means he was okay. Let's hope you are," I said, smiling.

He was okay, as were ninety-eight percent of the entire sea of faces I'd tried to teach over time. But one day during an activity based on the poem by Lewis Carroll, *Jabberwocky*, MB interrupted me. "Are you a bat?" he asked me quite abruptly, putting the kibosh on groups creating their own language and composing poems, like Carroll had done. I felt my shellfish allergy red face starting on my sternum. He was sitting in the second row, last seat, closest to my extensively-long dry eraser board. Several students turned to him, probably to give him a wink and a mental fist bump, though a few looked a little miffed at him bothering such a chic-in-progress teacher.

I was mortified! It was a semi-regular state of being over my surprisingly-long "misadventurous" career.

"What did you just say?" I asked in "uffish thought," stupidly, because any potential heckler worth the salt in his insult would repeat it. "I asked if you were a bat," he said again. Well, there went the "mimsy" out of *my* "borogoves."* I felt red start rising from the edge of my pima cotton top (under a really nice blazer with an

Hallucinogenic terms invented by Lewis Carroll, made-up words that Bible scholars often refer to as "an unknown tongue." "Mimsy," a somewhat noun, is Carroll's Oedipal term for his mother. "Borogoves" is always an interrogative statement, as in, "Might I borrow goves from you?"

expensive Isaac Mizrahi floral accent neck scarf). I "galumphed" off the stool behind my lectern, ready to fish for a Form 9 Discipline Report, "Teacher Name-Calling Edition." Of course, they were not where they were supposed to be. "Where they were supposed to be" was my Kryptonite. NOTHING was ever in that physical file. I would have to take this one on, singlehandedly. The conversation didn't need much prodding.

"I went home last night and mentioned your name to my dad," Matt began. "And he said you had been his teacher back in the day. My God, woman! I looked you up in his old yearbook. You haven't changed! You look the same!" he said, astonished, and I wanted to think it was authentic, not a lie to cover his not-so-tactful, odd-laud question.

I sat back down on my stool, and I refused to lower my face from that moment on. I had a compliment! Lowering one's older face over the teacher's edition could create a jowly appearance. I would review that Clairol Periodic Color Elements chart more often, too. And further, after he left, I would take my blue pen and in the grade book I would write beside his name, "2 EC" (two points extra credit). I wasn't proud of it, but I felt a little old-school frisky!

Years later, Matt was attending college. I knew this because he was a server at Ruby Tuesday, and he made a specific point of telling me he was attending college. Maybe it was a matter of too many desserts left at the close of the day, but as my husband and I finished our meal, here came Matt with two generous slices of thick cheesecake with fruity toppings.

"Wow! What's this?"

"Cheesecake," Matt said. "Complimentary." But I wondered if he was saying in his mind, finishing that sentence with: "Eat up, my darling bat. It'll be midnight soon and you can work off the calories flying around homes of sleeping villagers, unsuspecting of exactly what is to come."

Now, it's out there. I admit it. Everyone will know my *real* beauty secret, immortality! HA! HA! HA!

I was about seven years shy of retiring from the most noble of professions, the one that paid West Virginia educators as number 48 in national teacher salaries.

I was also dating the vocational-agriculture teacher three hallways down and things were looking up for me, because he was nearly a half-foot taller with the neatest, best-trimmed nose hairs I'd ever seen.

That long, tall drink of coffee was outside my door, knocking. First block class was underway as I read a short story aloud. I went to the door. Mr. C (the aforementioned Vo-Ag teacher), stood smiling, carrying that morning's school breakfast grab-and-go entree, the cheery cherry churro. "Don't want to interrupt, but I knew you were hungry on the way to work. Carry on," he said softly with a wave. With his carryout delivery completed, he was gone. Nobody admired a good ol' farm boy better than a gal who had a gentleman farmer for a father!

I laid the wrapped chewy churro on my chock-full chalk tray. Charming of him, I thought to myself.

Two narrative sentences later, a girl, Elise (not her real name), interrupted my impressive "multi-characterizationisms."

"Are you pregnant or something?" she asked, clearly churlish and perhaps a little hangry.

"Excuse you," I said, with my own dissed/pissed voice. That shellfish lobster-red shade swam all over my face. I felt my left eye protruding outward in a show of what I hoped looked like anger, if not one mean Bette Davis eye. "What did you just ask me?"

Of course, she repeated it, sighing like a grandchild who has to rub poor old grandma's crooked feet. She incorrectly assumed my Bel-Tones needed batteries. **"Are. You. *PREG-NANT?*"**

I was pushed off the cliff of normalcy, unprepared as always. No comeback. How cheesy of her! Plus, there was that lingering echo of her big say-over. But I knew where I would plant her for the next couple days. ABC-ya later! She was going to dance herself down to ISS. *WHUMP!* went the disciplinary form on my lectern. SWISH! STROKE! SWISH! DOT! DOT! went my Bic and my beginning tic. Anger deepened the red on my cherry cheeks. The smashing of the paper down on the wood had made a little grease spot from the cherry --------

----- *"Pregnant?"* That word was never spoken in my house, along with the disgusting word, fart. I knew to use the acceptable alternative, "flatulence," before I was three. A woman was simply "going to have a baby." Maybe I found it less gestating, less connected to "the act" resulting in a human being. That word was never spoken over me in a doctor's office. I had nothing female to work with. All of it was a tilted mess and a string of three horrible surgeries, the third Hoovering me out but good, as good as the Holland Tunnel during a terror threat.

Wait, I thought, still so mad I could not remember Miss Smug's last name requested on said form. After she slammed my door, I had an epiphany.* I had epiphanies often, and they were the only regular, always humbling constant in my stub-toe years walking about as a teacher.

I use my favorite word of all time zones, "epiphany," a total of two hundred times in this tome, nearly as many times as I've stepped in doggie presents while scooping our fenced-in backyard.

At fifty-three and decayed as Dad's 48 Chevy spark plugs, "pregnant" was a freaking accolade to my skin care regimen. If I looked like child bearing age, I should take her surliness as flattery. Still, deciphering when a student was being half-sincere, not playing, was never my strong point. The result? She wrote an apology essay, ending with "I don't know why I was forced to even write this. I didn't do anything..." Imagine asking your teacher that question, especially if you've lived a long time. It just wouldn't have happened. Because our revered teachers didn't even use the bathroom, much less....

There was only one thing to say to the rest of the class to salvage that short story.

"Okay, and we're back. Now, where was I?" Plus, this: "Who wants snack?"

That embarrassment was an easy coast compared to other mortifications. The mother of all embarrassments had happened years earlier, involving two officers in separate humiliations.

My debate unit for senior English class seemed like a fine idea at the time. With only a few years' experience, many things seemed like a fine idea at the time. One positive among young educators is their willingness to try more hands-on things in the classroom.

That is, before the older, more cynical educators react, like snarly Pod People from *Invasion of the Body Snatchers* with teaching degrees. Young teachers are typically appalled by the skepticism some older faculty exhibit. I knew one thing from my first-year teaching: Cynics either squash all your good ideas, making you into a Pod, or you guard your heart and your good ideas and say to them, to hell with you. Some of the teachers were so indoctrinated with structure, I wondered if they came out of the womb quoting Mussolini.

Mentioning special projects before career colleagues sometimes resulted in the rotten-cabbage-still-in-the-fridge face. I didn't care for the stank face, because I got it often. *How misjudged could I be?* I motored on. It did not occur to me to suck up their facial rebukes and seek out one of the less critical, less-stanked faculty faces with a law enforcement background.

On the project due date, there was a major altercation that involved several seniors in the cafeteria at lunchtime. At least one faculty member on the second floor was oblivious, hiding in her room cramming down a peanut butter and grape jelly sandwich. I had lesson plan outcomes on my mind, a good way to gain points in the office with a principal almost lovingly nicknamed "Groundhog."

My principal could be biased, for he had directly used two surprising racial slurs on me. One was "chocolate boy," regarding a Black student teacher who just "didn't fit in." The other reference regarded my own self, aka "Pollack," but he said it in such a friendly manner I did not get that angry. I realized it was part of his vernacular/culture. After observing me that second year, he was busily taking notes in the back of my classroom. I hoped he wasn't writing "dum dum" down the page. After the change class bell rang, he lumbered up to me. Whatever he was poised to say, I had no choice or tenure. So, I would become the quiet Electrolux and suck that up, too.

"Please, just put a tack there," he tapped on the front corner of my desk, "to remind yourself not to lean on the edge of your desk."

"O-Okay," I said, and that was all I would say. *W-h-a-a-t?* Meeting over. He was out the door. But, after a quick minute, I thought that was small potatoes for what I could have heard. I did what I was told!

The debate project would be fifth period, right after lunch. While I was arranging chairs for the debate, the fisticuffs were flying on the first floor, rearranging tables in the lunch room. With bodies. I thought their senior steps were louder than usual as they ran up to my room.

"Wow! You guys must be ready for debates!" I said with the usual cluelessness.

I saw the hurry up in their eyes. At last, my projects were paying off. *Yes sir*, I smiled to myself, *nothing has more benefit than student-guided, hands-on learning.* This was going to be a good class, one for which my colleagues would go home a little guilty, always believing me to be a step away from a cliff dive.

The first topic was up. The teams were ready. Really ready. The class was quieter than quiet. I took evaluation sheets out of my folder, and that was the only sound heard in the room. Unbelievable! This was a first. There was this feeling, an energy like heated air before a lightning strike. If the other groups were that focused, this would be the day a young teacher always remembers.

"Class, I just want to say before we begin, that I feel you've done your homework and you're ready for this, so thanks for that." *Oh, they were ready alright.*

Right after the "Pro-Life" team spokesperson addressed the class, the opposition "Pro-Abortion" spokesperson broke from the format, loudly announcing, "Abortion is not murder!"

And then, the masterstroke happened.

"I hope that baby **DIES** inside of you!" Pro-Abortion speaker said. I think. My head about snapped off. "You have no right to---"

That sentence never got finished from the girl's mouth, because a senior boy Pro-Lifer dove for her.

"NOT IN THE DEBATE RULES!!!" I screamed, as growls, and fists, and chairs flew. I was sitting in the middle of a bar brawl and I was getting educated from all sides.

"Jesus!" I yelled. **"Stop! STOP IT!"** I screamed to no one, for those with a shred of a conscience were busy pulling the football player away from killing the hater on the opposing team. How could I have known the pre-class fight downstairs involved a senior couple, a baby, and another angry gir!, and all of them would be in my English class? I didn't care about the particulars just then. I ran for the intercom box, slapping the wall to make contact, watching chairs tipping. *Push it, idiot, push!!*

"EMERGENCY!!! FIGHT IN ROOM 11!! NEED HELP NOW! REPEAT! NEED HELP N-O-O-O-O-W!" For once, it was I, not the secretary, doing the screaming.

The principal was panting from running up those stairs. **"STOP NOW!"** he screamed, his little wildlife nose twitching. I hoped it would not get broken as he jumped into that whole frenzy. The angry fists slowed, then finally stopped beating. Everyone was wide-eyed and gasping, having just survived a three-point-five earthquake. How highly entertained a teacher at that location one floor under must have been, assigning workbook pages in order to get a press release out.

As predicted, that was *the* Friday class period to remember, and an even better weekend starter. My phone rang off the hook, so my mother turned off the ringer. I described all the angles of the mayhem to my empathetic dad while my mother worked on supper. Food prep was therapy for her tonight.

"God, Dad! I've never seen anything like that before, except in a musical. I mean it was the Wild, Wild West! Girls were screaming, chairs flying, guys diving over guys. Prize fights with bad choregraphy."

Suddenly Dad laughed, inappropriately. *Not the right time, Dad!* This took the gloss off my heart-wrenching retell.

"Sounds like there was some ass-over-tin-cup time in your class!" he said.

I never understood what his favorite saying even meant, but I concurred with deep head nodding and an expected return laugh. But it wasn't that funny to me right then. A strict business and typing instructor, he listened, but I doubted he empathized completely. He never knew what a class brawl was because he did not say to me, "I had the *same thing* happen in my shorthand class in the 1950s, and I suffered three broken ribs and a shattered brow bone. Those girls were Sumo wrestlers!"

I felt responsible for all of it. But, in a few more moments he revealed his super dad cape a little when he ended the discussion swiftly with "I'll take care of this."

Looking back, I realize parents never change. They always want to protect their children from harm and vicious lawsuits. I bet Justin Beiber's mom tells him those same five words wrapped in a hug, at least three times a week.

Monday morning, praying unceasingly for a calm day, I had faith that God would calm the seas. The intercom immediately interrupted me during first period. It was the secretary. "MISS PILEWSKI, I NEED YOU TO COME TO THE OFFICE RIGHT NOW!" she said. I couldn't discern if there was a little vocal glee, a little urgency, but the volume was on point as always.

"Oooo, bet this is about last Friday." Then, "Can we go watch?" And, "Well, goodbye, Miss P. At least you tried." Finally, "Give her a break, people. *Nobody died!*"

Someone watched my class. Brave soul! I walked down the steps and felt the mantle of felon fall on me. The feeling intensified when I saw the reason for the hurried giddy up.

"Are you Miss Pilewski?" the sheriff's deputy asked.

"I am," I answered. He was tall and good looking and that made it all the more deliciously humiliating. I dropped my head, but I was really looking for a ring. I could see my blondie blonde hair in his black patent county-issued shoes. I would have gladly shined them.

"I have a subpoena for you. You have been named as a character witness for one of the young men involved in last Friday's altercation in your classroom, Mr. (Name) (Name). You must appear at the noted time."

"Oh, dear God!" I said with my head still down. I hoped he might consider my full head of permed long blonde hair and twice-mascara'd eyelashes and show some mercy. *Contrite face!* I directed myself. Nothing! Worse, I knew that newsy juice would make its way from floor to floor, flowing like a flooded storm sewer. And even worse, I perceived there would be a slight, buoyant tittering among the ranks as one of the upstairs crew would put my future arrest picture on the cafeteria bulletin board of good news, alongside the other vulgar drawings and filth. I brought the sense of euphoria back to my new alma mater. My co-workers were so happy not being green like me.

"And if I don't come?" I asked, quite out of character, but adrenaline gives me what I've always described as hot courage where a sexy man in uniform is present.

"Then I will find you and escort you there." If this guy wasn't married, I would have gladly forced his hand.

"I will appear," I said, with the red burning into my face and chest and head, like the scorch from standing too close to a structure fire you may or may not have set.

Twain said we worry about horrible things and most of them never even happen. Twain knew his stuff. Nothing did happen. Dad, not the county, escorted me to that hearing. The attending deputy came out to where my father and brother and I were. My sweating hands had created a glue reaction on the wooden chair arms.

"You have been excused by the judge, with his apologies that you were involved in this. You are free to go," the court worker said. I waited till I got to the car, then I let go and squealed with glee once the car doors were all locked.

Although my brother and I were never close, I can count a few times he stood up for his sister. This was one of them.

And here was what I learned through that classroom rodeo. There were no further debates, ever, in my classes, just a mock trial or two, based on the poetry of Robert Browning and the works of Shakespeare. Debates went the way of leisure suits, so popular and so wrong, back there in the seventies.

In that same school I lived through another standout memory that was both a disparaging moment and a tipping point, coming on the anticipated last day of school, when everyone is sick of everyone else and students just want to promote themselves right out the exit doors.

"I had fifty-eight leaves on that rubber plant when I left my room, Miss Pilewski!" she snapped, her drooping jowls and glasses shaking with every head-popping punctuation. I brought the best out in my colleagues.

Last period of the day for me (which should have been Hallelujah time), was in Room 8, run tightly by the old maid junior English teacher on staff. She loved the school, the entire football team, and her nieces and nephews. Me, she hated. All year we had tangles over her potted flora. "Your students are plucking those plants!" Or this: "Come over here!" (tap! tap! tap!) "See this desk top? The word 'ass' was NOT on this desk when I left it before seventh period! Your student, if you even know who sat there, carved that into my undeserving desk. I certainly don't allow students to write on my desks!" I almost lied and said, "Maybe I did it." Apple head vs. Miss Crabby Appleton, but *she* knew how to *core*.

When the last day for my eighth-grade students in Room 8 came that year, their fond farewell from me was my tough semester English 8 exam, all one hundred pieces of it. I watched them like the proverbial hawk (because that was the school mascot, after all), allowing my lower eyelid to blink upwards, keeping my head tilted and constantly moving, watching for cheaters, my intended prey.

"Okay, class, five minutes till bell and summer break. Let's finish up!" I said.

One particular Alfalfa-looking kid finished hurriedly but was not turning in his test. Two minutes to bell and he was still sitting with his folded exam. He walked to my desk and put his test *under* several other tests. As he strolled back to his seat, flopping his bangs repeatedly over to the side, I snatched up that paper like a danish. There on the last page, at the bottom where I had five fill-in-the-blank lines drawn, vertically stacked for grammar answers, he had penned his summer wishes to me. They read, and I quote:

1)   EAT
2)   Some
3)   SHIT
4)   POLL-
5)   ACK!!!

I was *livid*! His answers insulted me, a lady. But what put the nasty anchovies on my cheese pizza was his flagrant disregard for what had been taught him. How could he screw up hyphenation that way? Had he learned NOTHING about dividing between double consonants!?

As the bell rang, I made a directive, handing off the folded test like a track runner's baton. "Sue, go get the principal. NOW!" Sue flew, paper-baton pounding up and down in her hasty grasp. I jumped in front of my well-wisher. He wasn't officially on break yet, but he would be soon, following a little year-end rear end business.

Up came the principal twitching his endearing little face, my defender and my strangely de facto hero. In his mitts was a supersized paddle, drilled (compliments of the shop department), with extra-wide holes to make the experience more exhilarating and memorable, an aerodynamic feeling never to be duplicated, not even at Six Flags or Disney.

He told my good grammar student, "Grip your teacher's desk and lean forward. Spread those feet." I had to stay and be the witness.

This man had unleashed game. He swung that paddle around like it was a driver sending it straight up into Heaven and then down, down and made contact with that young teen's unpadded bottom. By swing two, I knew this principal was not the joke the students thought, especially the student leaning over my desk. What stamina! By swing three the boy might have tears forming and I no longer wanted to be part of it. I felt not a drop of restitution, thinking I saw a teardrop hit my tests on swing number four. Was this one more thing in an ocean of things that somehow seemed to be my fault? That sting of punishment would never happen in my room again. I would figure out on my own some alternative to corporal punishment, say a Yanni concert. Maybe a Slim Whitman vocal impersonation by the offender in front of the entire student body. Yeah, I could be tough.

"She can get *real tough*!" said no one in that hawkish high school, particularly the football players, who took journalism just to eat up all the free samples salesmen brought to the class as fundraising possibilities.

One such milquetoast fundraiser salesperson stupidly passed out several mini crocks of various-flavored soft cheeses as visual aids with his five-color brochures. "Please don't open the crocks," he requested weakly, possibly scared by the breadth of the football team's shoulders. I said nothing, but even I knew soft cheese and dirty fingers played nicely together.

"What flavor's this one?" the quarterback asked, smirking.

"Uh," he gulped, speaking a half octave higher, "that particular flavor is port wine cheddar with a hint of smoky bacon." He salesman'd on, sharing a spiffy flow chart he'd had printed at the Cheesy Fundraiser Printing Company. The football players started soft growling like stray dogs when one of them finds old hamburger in a garbage can.

When the demo wrapped and the handshake extended to me were both weakly finished, he was *gone*, his tie flapping over his shoulder from beating a hasty retreat before an athlete could Frisbee him straight out my row of borrowed windows.

One minute later, a feeble knock came on my door. It might be the regular teacher whose room I used that first year I got stuck with producing the yearbook. Once one of those players lit a desk on fire. They made her room a shambles. I believe my free classroom rental may have driven her to drink.

I opened the door to Mr Cheese-It. He cleared his throat. "Uh, pardon me, Miss Peloski, but I seem to have misplaced a half case of mini crocks. I need that cheese back as my samples, you know."

Lord! I knew they were gone as movie musicals. "Well! Let's see," I said, knowing damned well the crocks were history, probably stuffed down strategically into pants for " bigger effect" on the girls at lunchtime.

"Okay class! Has anyone seen our salesman's crocks? He says he's missing some." And, as predicted, Crisco or soft cheese wouldn't melt in any one of those mouths, or other body parts.

"I am so, so sorry Mr. Cheese-It," I said. "You know hungry football players," I giggled awkwardly. If he thought I was going to have a showdown with all that muscle sitting in the rear of that borrowed room, then his crock head was also made of soft cheese. He left. Never to return.

I learned something from those two of many tens of similar experiences: **Lesson #1**: People really do need others' help. I asked for that, and I got that, via the principal wielding his paddle on that eighth grader. However, running for manly assistance that afternoon reversed itself from reprisal into regretting the whole unfortunate occurrence.

My principal was doing his job, doing what was part of the discipline code at the time. It was what I thought should be done, too---for a brief time. That individual did not return to school in the fall, something I never forgot, feeling that short-lived rush of getting even. And, **Lesson # 2**: Soft cheese in a crock would have been the double fall of mankind if Eve had been offered a forbidden apple *and* Port Wine Soft from Mr. Cheese- It's case of many flavors. Soft cheese on bad-nasty apple would have cancelled the world before it even began!

On the wings of Mr. Cheese-It I had a great shred of a story to tell my dad over dinner. But I would make sure he was not drinking his iced tea during the punchline while I was being Leo Jr, Apprentice Raconteur.

As a New Millenium dawned, I was now teaching adult learners, close to that original proximity of cheese thieves and desk burners. It was yuletide, that time of year when people, especially homework-laden female teachers, put up last-minute trees with hand-thrown unbreakable decorations and icicles and buy half-priced, leftover treats from a choir bake sale outside, say, Southern States maybe.

But before hitting the sugary sale's leftovers, I made a quick stop at the doctors' building near a local hospital. The appointment went quickly and I ran back to my car hoping to run off a few extra calories. I had red and green M & M's at home, so whatever smashed treats I could nail at the bake sale, I would make semi-formal with those candies. It was the biggest problem I had for about three minutes.

There in my silver Lumina was my seven-and-a half-foot long needle faux Noble Fir tree I'd used at school as seasonal decoration. It was going home and get lit up, though I was not. The air was crisp with hope and joy and peace. I thought of even more seasonal abstract nouns as I put my car in drive, ready to start up the slight incline to the narrow road's intersection: *love, forgiveness, warmth, Black Friday sales, joy...*

As I got to the mouth of that side road, still rattling off my Christmas nouns ("*...wonderment,* tenseness, *yuletide...*"), high with holiday spirit, a huge tank of an older sedan made a tractor trailer-wide turn in. I laid on the horn. Before I could shift into reverse or ask Jesus to save me yet again, **WHAM**! He hit me, knocking my car backwards. He kept right on coming, like something I'd seen *The A-Team* do with a Sherman tank. I was screaming as I watched my holiday hood do the "Kris Krinkle." Frankie Yankovic and his Yanks could play a polka on the front end of my Chevy, like an accordion. When I came to rest, I looked back at half the big tree all over the back seat and the other half, undoubtedly scrambled in my trunk.

Diving out my car, seeing the now-vertical smoosh of a grill, I rapped my knuckles hard against the man's car window. "What the hell just happened? I want you to get out of your car and see what you did to mine."

"I can't," he said. So, he did not. This infuriated me and I repeated my invitation, glancing to see where his hands were. I never spoke up for myself, but I was changing all that, right stinking *now!* ----*What?* The hands weren't there----but there were *hand controls.* I noticed a factory-issued steering wheel and to the right, two controls for accelerating, braking. The man was paralyzed. He could not accept my irate challenge. I experienced what I call an Axis Shift. Instantaneously, my ire expired, taking with it my sense of dignity. Who could ever teach me exactly how to pick my battles? Luckily, these were pre-road rage days and its being Christmas, he seemed forgiving, a decent, nice-looking sort.

The folks next door where Hospice was then located, came out and asked me to step inside. They'd seen my Whoop Dance of Anger and wanted to cuff me for a BP count.

"Come inside," a caregiver pleaded. Her mouth was saying that, but she was thinking, "Definitely a school teacher! No patience, snapping fingers, flailing arms, closeup eye contact with the irritant. And, above all that, the Whoop Dance of Anger."

While I was having that measurement read, someone moved our cars. I knew this was not good and not in the accident play book.

When the driver's father came, I recognized him as a member of the state house of delegates. He proceeded to kick my tires.

"Do you know who I am?" he asked. "Not a clue," I answered, "but I bet you're going to pay for this."

His line of work kept him primed for sharp diversions. "How do we know you didn't cause the accident?" I pointed to his son. "Ask your son."

At the same time, a sheriff's deputy car pulled down that incline to the altered accident scene. At last, I could feel vindication coming, explaining my innocent involvement in the accident, fully expecting to be exonerated and perhaps hugged, its being Christmas and my giving my life selflessly to the education of others and so on and so forth...

He was tall, dark, and fairly handsome, exiting that cruiser in slow motion, adjusting his aviator sunglasses, clipboard ready, hired talent straight out of a music video. A last ray of chilly December sun shone right on his badge hero bright, impeding my line of vision. Who was this hot Deputy Dawg in black leather? In fine deputy fashion, he put his hands on his narrow hips above his gun belt. Wow!

I thought. I want to kick *your* shins! Cuff me! Cuff *me*!

For once, I had one of those random musical cues for a song, and it came straight from Tornado Alley, via good old Rodgers & Hammerstein. I pulled from that ne'er-do-well high school musical I kept directing. Yes sir, here came a moment that was about to put an *"Oklahoma!"* song in my heart, and the law at my personal disposal. I hummed softly, saying the words with my lips shut, because I was pushing two of my few best features out, trying in vain to create a sensual pout. The cold had lowered the thermostat on my usual hot lips!

I sang:
> *Oh, what a beautiful morning*
> *Oh, what a beautiful day.*
> *I got a beautiful feeling,*
> *Everything's goin' my w-a-a-a-a-ay.*

"-----Hey! I know you!" Officer Hot exclaimed, ripping off the sunglasses. "You flunked my ass in high school!" It was (now **Deputy**) Steve Johnson, a former flop in my senior English class. A wiseacre, for sure, and yes, I'd flunked his ass in high school. He hated English and me, too, maybe. I felt embarrassed, with a shake of dirty on top. *Oh My God!!!!!!!*

Might as well call it a day! I was going to be cuffed, and not in the Biblical sense! House of Delegates plus paraplegic plus disgruntled failed former senior English student casualty with legal authority equals a not-pleasant call to my insurance company. I was about to tarnish the family education badge of honor some more. I prayed Dad was up there in Heaven's Half Acre growing winter squash with no time to watch his daily dose of daughter's lunatic career life below.

After he took statements and peered in my Lumina Deputy Steve said, "Guess that tree's going to Harry Green Chevy with the tow."

I was cold, and I was stranded, just Mom at home doing dinner, never a driver's license to her name. No cell phones in the eighties and, moreover, no hero dad any longer to hear say "I'll take care of it." The tow truck had come and already pulled away, towing my mashed silver accordion behind it, with the color-coded branches of my disassembled tree. I had a new song in my heart!

I sang:

> ***"Oh, Christmas tree, Oh, Christmas tree,***
> ***with Harry Green and not with me...."***

"Come on, Miss P.," Deputy Steve said, interrupting my cold stare into winter's dusk, lamenting that the peanut butter blossoms with Hershey Kisses would all be gone by the time I pulled in to the feed store. I wasn't going any place. Maybe if I thumbed there, one of the bake sale kids could help me chop a bush with Christmas lights out of Raymon's Restaurant parking area. Steve continued. "I'm going to take you home."

It sounded wonderful, like something Steve McGarrett would say to an old maid crime victim on *Hawaii Five-O*. No matter what he thought of me then, he felt a bit sorry for me now. We walked to his cruiser and he held the door open. Just like a Hallmark Christmas movie, the one titled *No Car for Christmas*. ---Wait! Had he just touched my head, *the way officers load prisoners?*

That trip took only minutes. He flew faster than Rudolph on special trail mix and my bottom literally flew under my wool dress coat across half that leather back seat. I wasn't even wearing a seat belt. I listened to his radio dispatcher, counting all the little law enforcement accoutrements I spied.

Quite the network! I softly hummed Andy Williams' classic, "Happy Holidays," and felt felon and festive all at once. I guess I'd made English a prison for kids like Steve, but now, here he was the jailer with the car keys and motive, and I was seated behind him in the seat of honor. Oh, big deal. He realized his dreams. He got to wear basic black every single day. And anyway, I was finally warm.

When she died, Lucille Ball stepped before God and said, "Someone's gotta carry on the screwball stuff, and *she's* the funny one! Just look at what she gets into--- no script needed. Give her the gift. Unreturnable."

As we flew, my eyes saw nothing but blur out the vapored glass. I was on one of Harrison County's Police Jumbo Jet Cruisers flying home. Would there be an in-flight movie? Unlike the usual passengers, my hands were free and I wanted to draw a little devil on the fogged back window. I was flying, but there were no complimentary Smokehouse Almonds.

Instead, a movie appeared before me. I recalled Dad's dinner story about a high school smarty he'd paddled. Going home that night after some whooshin' good swingin' and stingin', Dad's own brush with Karma hit. **BANG!** A blowout on old Tunnel Hill.

That old gray '48 tank decided to break out a few seconds pulling him back and forth on that two lane, then it surrendered and Dad got things under control. However, he was screwed, because changing a tire was not part of teacher college or apparently military training. And who should come along down that stretch and stop but the very boy on whom Father had made that lit-up, smart impression. He changed Dad's Chevy tire, zoom-*zoom*!

Then he turned to Dad and said something that hit Teacher Leo right in the proverbial kisser, except it hurt in the ego, not the face. He smiled and said: "You can't get it all in the books, now can you, Mr. Pilewski?"

That new epiphany sure brought it all home to me. Dad's spirit was with me again, there in a warm county sheriff deputy's car, with a holiday teachable moment. People can surprise. And show their humanity. Of all my students, Steve's career path surprised me the most. I hadn't been inside a police car since the Salem Police allowed J.D. Muldoon and me to sit in the city cruiser's back seat in 1972 for our "Most Likely to Succeed" yearbook pic. Here I was again sitting behind another officer, twice guiltless. Not a lot of felons can claim that distinction. There was only one question: Would I ever drop the "Most Likely" and cross over to full-on "*Succeed*"?

I felt like the secondary hound behind the lead dog in an Iditarod. Except the view was far better. Before we slid to a stop outside my door, I debated how to end this movie. What would make him always remember the day he prevented me from walking home at Christmas? (another good working title for a Hallmark holiday movie- --*Walking Home at Christmas*)! This deputy of the law had just given me a powerfully kind Christmas gift, and later, would go above and beyond to get all my accident bills and claims reimbursed.

"Merry Christmas, Steve....*thank you*," I said, getting out of the car and patting his elbow, all neighbors' eyes on police passenger me. He sped away so fast my coat whipped open.

I waved and said, shaking my head, sighing, "Hi, ho, Steverino!" because he would have put that pedal down the same damned way in high school. What a guy!

I vowed to myself as I crossed the highway to my door that if I ever wrote a book, my favorite deputy would be somewhere inside, at the halfway mark in our careers, where we met on his terms a second time.

Note to the reader: Of course, I rented a car the next morning at the airport for nearly a hundred dollars a day, retrieving my piecemeal tree from Harry Green Chevrolet for take-home and setup. Though I can no longer use it due to injuries sustained in that auto crash, I still have that old Christmas tree. It doesn't stand up quite as straight as it used to, but then, neither do I...

Lost Reports, Phallic Wind Sock Artists, Ron B. - Robbie, and Square-Headed Bathroom Humor

Back there in the pastures of teaching job number one, I was regularly called to the office, always to receive a bad luck prize. I got summonsed as often as the worst "bridge kids," who congregated day and night over a small bridge in a tiny pocket of civilization and plotted everything mean they would do next day starting on the school bus, ending with me. The good news was that I kept on treading and pedaling through troubles in tall Aigner pumps! The bad news was that a few of my more seasoned colleagues hoped I'd pedal right on out the door and become what they all thought I should be. A Hallmark card writer, specializing in bath-of-fire empathy cards for the misbegotten, misguided misfits of the world. They acted like I knew something about that particular class division!

"**MISS PILEWSKI!**" screamed the secretary through what seemed like a bull horn custom-fitted right over the intercom microphone on her desk. I hated that thing. My butt would jump from my armless teacher seat. The decibels were so high that dead flies buzzed again on my window sills, fully resuscitated. "**MISS PILEWSKI, WHERE IS YOUR MONTHLY REPORT? I ASKED YOU FOR IT YESTERDAY! SEND IT TO THE OFFICE-----ASAP!!**"

I was so frightened I couldn't decipher her acronym, much less find the paper. College had not bettered my organizational skills. When exactly had I decided that being in a school setting would colonize structure in my life? Did prison make Martha Stewart a porcelain termite? Certainly not.

"Okay, class, first senior to find my report for the county office gets---"

"Your red Nova?" a bridge boy asked.

"Extra credit......or a cake.......or money......I really don't care. We'll talk. Now get up and search!"

How 'bout snuff?' another voice asked before getting up to look. It sounded female, so I answered it without looking. "No, no, you'll have to rub it on your own time, sorry."

"You ever rubbed or done weed, Miss P?"

Invariably, one of the students found the always-late report before I had to answer that interview question, and then it was back to the normal stress of trying to teach without injury to anyone.

One of my students had suffered a head injury playing football during an intense Friday Night Lights match. He was a handsome young man, a senior football star, who sat in the back left (my left) corner of the afternoon class. After getting sacked, he did not move on that field. His serious injury halted any sound from the bleachers. He was taken to a waiting ambulance. He had a tough road ahead.

Much, much later, when he returned to school, he was different, unable to sit for long periods, nervous and forgetful. It was nothing for him to get up and chatter and walk out of class. It grieved me, but it also made teaching a daily surprise party, because I never knew when I would have to drop the chalk and gingerly run retrieve him.

Leaving my post was a no-no, but not keeping my student contained was a lawsuit in progress. I did not want him getting hurt, just the same.

It was important that, whenever possible, the bridge kids saw me at least as partially fearless as they were. I stepped up and took my office medicine, which came in liberal, refillable doses. Seniors placed bets while I was out of the room. They were always guessing who my replacement would be midyear, betting on how I would look on my return from a comprehensive ass chewing.

But this morning was different---no squawk box, no screaming, no jumping. I didn't have to come down the steps to the principal, this one my former high school counselor. He greeted me inside the cafeteria main door as I entered the building one sunny morning, already fumbling for my wayward keys.

"Miss Pilewski, come into my office."

Yikes! It was my favorite principal again! He had this long stride, like a gun slinger, and he always tilted his head sideways a little the way a horse does, in order to see better. I called it "the *Columbo* turn around," my own character analysis, based on the Peter Falk detective.

Once in the interior office with the door closed, the principal began his well-thought-out opening. "You're the yearbook advisor, correct?" he asked, rubbing his unusual nose. He talked with a raspy vocal, indicating he needed to clear that throat, and he always carried a big wad of cash in his front pants pocket. He would flash it once a week getting it close enough to grab, but damn, he was just too quick for me.

"Yes, I am. You know I am," I responded. "Did something happen?" (meaning: *Please! I am not your captured mouse. Don't paw me to death, just kill me now.*)

125

"Oh, yes. Y-e-e-e-s, something happened. First, I want to know how my picture made it all the way out of your cloakroom picture file, down to the cafeteria bulletin board."

"Maybe.......Some kids really like you?" I asked, biting the side of my lip.

"Well, I'm not sure about that, but I think maybe someone does. This person stole that photo of me, the one you had the photographer take, me seated on the front edge of my desk. I always think that's a dignified pose. Now, can you tell me how that picture got downstairs and who might have hung it on the main bulletin board? And---now here's the really amazing part-----how that picture got altered...?"

"Altered?"

"Altered."

"Mr.---, we handle a lot of pictures and layouts each day. It's a big class, a congressional district. It's a lot of kids all doing yearbook pages. It takes a lot out of me just keeping up with my bottle of rubber cement. I admit, there are a few huffers, Mr. ---. I try very hard, but apparently someone thought they'd be cute, and I will take full respons----"

"----No, you're way off," he interrupted me. "Someone took that picture, cut it in half, and they added their own artistic ability, sort of ...enhanced the picture, you might say. And..." He pulled the photo out of his middle desk drawer, flashing it at me a half-nano second, "as you can see, they added on some significant details."

And there it was. Two fairly hairy drawn-on legs and a big penis floating up like a car dealership wind sock man and my shocked face, beginning a feverish red-hot burn.

"Oh, **Oh, God!** I am so, so sorry." I felt dizzy and his face was prismatic, everywhere I looked in the room. "I will yell...until the offender confesses."

---Clearly, this was not exactly what I would do. I would pull my best snitch boy aside (just as he did), and offer to bake banana bread if he could just push the right instigator way, way under the bus, Number 100. Then, I'd-----

"No....no," Mr. Principal interrupted. "Let me finish. That student does have some art skills. You find him."

"I intend to," I said, planning to send him tripping down the staircase straight into the principal's lap for making me go through this visual hell. "Now, will he or she be suspended?"

"Suspended? Noooo...nooooo....I want to shake his hand! He was very, VERY generous." As I turned to leave his office, he was smiling. Generously.

I ran out of that jumbo art exhibit and through the double doors, charging upstairs to my room. and inside, let my back and my right raised foot slap against my cement block classroom wall, my hand clamped over my mouth to muffle my screams of hilarity and human anatomy.

When my eyes could focus completely, I was sullen. *Why* had something happened to me, *again*? If he knew, then the coaches would know. Locker room humor never changed, never matured. That meant eventually, everyone would know. I exhaled slowly, hanging my jacket in my coat room. I sat in my armless chair and spun, left to right in tempo, tabulating all the disgrace, all the trouble, all the many ways I knew I was an unfit bit of a flop.

And yet, out that pastoral window, I heard the birds and watched the cows swish their tails. They were free and nonjudgmental. Ten more minutes until first bell. I thought about the entire meeting and the anonymous little Picasso bastard who had ruined my day. But then, I saw the manual Photoshop job, sketched by hand, el grande, and decided I didn't give one flying flip.

My boss wasn't mad at me. Maybe the perpetrator actually wanted a buddy/bromance with the principal. But for putting me through that, I felt the perpetrator belonged in a penal institution for "hap-penis" artists.

I let that chair spin me into the realm of a better mood. I raised both hands toward Heaven, laughing like I just didn't care. Why? Because I had the mother of all teaching stories that evening for dinnertime with Dad.

I had more educational meetings with my favorite principal. They were equally jolly, the kind of stories that build connections and trust around campfires.

His name was Ron B., but he was not the principal. He was our high school yearbook sales rep and he was classy. When he came in my classroom, I always checked out his wardrobe: tweedy coats, shiny tassel oxblood loafers, silk rep ties, and the best socks going or coming through that Room 11 doorway. He reminded me of Robbie, the heart throb offspring, played by Don Grady on *My Three Sons*. I still recall that opening drawing of six shoes rocking out to the saxophone music, showing argyle socks. Ron was cool like that. Oh! I just loved Ron B.- Robbie!

On this particular day we were drawing chalk sticks to determine who was going to approach the principal about adding eight pages of color to the yearbook. After eight or nine turns of "You go," and "No! YOU GO!" declarations, we both decided to bite the biscuit and just go together.

"The principal's busy. Just stand there till you get his attention," the secretary said.

We waited. I had a five dollar bill in my pocket and felt like waving it through the glass in the principal's door.

But we could not get his attention; he was inert, splayed out on the kind of office chair that had been designed by NASA engineers. If the G-force measures the force against a body, one could only guess about the unseen tremendous force his frame was being subjected to in that office space to hold that body position. We glanced around, looking for suits and white jackets writing things on clipboards. They must have been watching the test proceedings from a remote location.

He saw us! "Come on in, boy!" he shouted to both of us. I allowed Ron B.-Robbie to take the lead. What strength this administrator exhibited, being able to speak in that supine, inert posture that way. His left arm was now visible, with a telephone in that hand.

"W-H-A-A-A-A-T?" he tease-screamed to the voice on the other end of the phone. I liked how my principal found the joy in living and joking. But, as the coaches reminded me, some of that joy I admired came from a little bit of betting. Fine by me. The phone call ended. "Now, what can I do for you, boy?"

He was looking right at me, so I spoke. "Well, Mr. Principal, Ron and I are thinking about eight pages of color. Kids want color these days in memory books. I guess they remember the blush of youth that way when they're old and gray. So, I know you're concerned about cost and the budget, so here I've drawn up---"

"---Stop right there. No can do this year. Color is expensive. No color. Budget won't allow it."

I was crushed. That was that. The yearbook would just have to be fifty shades grayer.

As we got up to leave, he pulled out the right-side bottom drawer on his NASA test desk and spat into something. In went a big "Phooooot!" It was a bullseye into some unseen vessel! Was it another G-force experiment? As Ron rose to leave, I noticed his eyebrows were up high and frozen; he threw a shoe, one of those soft Italian leather tassel loafers, in sheer disbelief. We left abruptly. I was clicking my pen nervously out in the hall, about to walk my shame stroll back upstairs. Ron was doing an impressive step-slide, trying to get that shoe back squarely on his foot, where it belonged.

I wondered what I should say to Ron B.-Robbie. I did not want to say what I was thinking, that I did not like education. Instead, I said, "I---I do not like education, Ron. I think I made a tragic mistake in college." I wanted him to touch my arm and reassure me and say, "Let's go out for a quick lunch, Lexsana. Say...Harper's Ferry?"

"I mean, I am always, always in trouble," I vomited out. "If trouble could be seen with the naked eye, it would be a picture of The Scream, wearing my home address on its T-shirt. I think high school necessities equal sports for most principals. Nothing else counts."

But I believe I wore that principal down. We finally persisted in getting spot-color approval, then full-on color.

Eventually, I ended up telling these stories a dozen times, because they were pretty funny. Other stories involving principals were not so phallic and jolly, like the day I was running off papers years later for my adult ed learners. In that sun-drenched, hot tiny teacher's lounge with an even tinier attached bathroom in a tinier school, prejudice was lurking. It was the late nineties.

As I straightened the copied paper to return to the annex building, the door knob turned. It reminded me of that groper assistant principal following me into the copier room. I uncapped my pen just in case he'd tracked me down again. But in walked a local retired teacher I really liked, carrying an old yearbook from a defunct high school right there in our area.

Patty said, "Look at this boy's senior picture, at the distinctive name underneath. The only other one we know with that unusual a name is a county administrator, right? And he's from Pennsylvania originally. Isn't that something? I mean, how many young people around here would share a different name like that? Wouldn't they have to be related?"

On cue, the principal came in, heading straight for the attached tiny bathroom. But now, I felt I couldn't leave because Patty was still talking. I didn't want to leave her alone there with the yearbook and the man blasts that were surely to come. Never trust that polite feeling to stay and be sociable. *Just get out!*

"You know," she continued, "they do sort of look alike." It was a compliment, because both were really handsome. As Mr. Principal passed, she thrust the book out towards him. "Look at this picture! Doesn't this fellow look like Mr. B at the county office?"

Oh God! Here it came. Mr. Principal, who had the voice of straight-up Goofy, went for the kill. And I can quote him to this day.

"Of course, he does!" he spouted off. "All Pollacks have square heads, isn't that right, Pilewski?" BIG smile on his face. "Uh...huh! Huh! Huh!" He felt so good with his tiny cut I knew it would make his bathroom going a real thunder bluster.

And in fine Lexsana fashion, I had nothing for a reply. Blank. It was out there and my verbal reflexes were still what they were in grade school. I smiled and continued onward. Sometimes it took years to think of what I should have said. Sometimes I thought I might have to write a book to let someone else fill in that blank for me.

My, but I felt attractive afterwards! It proved to me that, as every farmer knows, there is bad seed, and it's scattered about in all professions, including a few farmers maybe. I became self-conscious in a new way, pouring over family albums, analyzing head widths and arcs, looking for the right relative to blame. I bought every mousse and gel product that promised to create a rounder contour of my crown. There simply had to be a cure for ethnic squaring and I would find it. Pleasing even no-goodniks was my sealed birthright. Today, I would have locked him in that bathroom and barred it with my square head, plus the copy machine.

My dad had passed a decade earlier, giving that put-down more of a personal sting. Still, the principal shot hoops with the kids after school, watched out for the special needs kids, let teachers go attend to a smorgasbord of crazy emergencies, and best of all, he loved dogs. This fact alone made him the real deal, so I forgave him, making me into a better person.

In a few more years, our program for parents and children closed, and I was back to the high school setting. And because of this new (to me, I mean) principal's insistence, I became a county teacher of the year. After that gloss wore off there came a day in late fall we had a faculty meeting.

Mr. Principal announced yet another project and he needed staff to volunteer.

Two tables over a colleague said in an audible vocal: "Get the teacher of the year to do it. She can handle it." The driver's ed teacher's head turned and both he and I looked in separate directions to see who else had heard.

I couldn't wait for that meeting to be over. I visited the principal's office and let go of some of that held-back temper. "By God, I did **NOT** want to be teacher of the year. You wanted me to! I didn't even know what it was! What I don't want now is a person I work with making fun of that out in a meeting where others could hear it. Will you *please* tell my colleague that it was you who suggested this!"

The principal blinked. I was huffing in anger, causing a paper on his desk to jiggle. As always, I felt bad, unleashing on him like that. When I went to my room, I stayed there the rest of that continuing ed day with the door locked.

I received an apology. It didn't give me that Church Lady sense of superiority I had thought it would. I listened to the words, seated at my desk, but felt none of the power I'd planned to get from hearing it. *You drama queen!* I chided myself, even as that colleague told me he sometimes popped off about things he shouldn't. *Hadn't I done the same?*

Five years later, my mother died. It was New Year's 2013, a cold January. I was exhausted and semester tests were underway. My new husband took on the task of arranging for pallbearers. I planned Kitty Pilewski's funeral like a big play production, because she had said once, for pity, that she wanted no funeral.

"Who would come?" she asked me sorrowfully, the eyebrows drooping down to her ears. Whether she was serious or just seeking the big cheer ("Now you know that's not true!") from daughter truly, I took on a new project.

"Mom, you might be surprised," I said. But, of course, if she were gone, how could she be surprised? I thought that inappropriately, even though I was looking right at her. I condemned myself for it before realizing I was actually assuaging her again. Whatever I meant, I wasn't ready to lose another parent.

That chapel was filled with friends, flowers, singers, a touching video and eulogy, even "favors"--- a violet-washed card. One side had the lyrics to "The West Virginia Hills," a song we often harmonized at family gatherings or sang on shopping trips. The flip side had a poem Mom had written, "My West Virginia Home" about moving from Louisiana at eleven years old and loving the mountain state to her last breath.

Her eulogy read like a book chapter, because I wrote and delivered it:

"In 1964, a concerned mother sat down and wrote President Lyndon Johnson a heartfelt letter, enumerating her issues with the Vietnam War and with her son's potential drafting. Her impassioned plea got noticed. My brother never was drafted..."

Mom was not the weak, uneducated soul she'd sometimes painted herself to be, to make me feel worse during a fight. She was a master of debate, exceedingly observant, well spoken, well written, coy, beautiful, and brilliant. Even sadder than her passing was the fact that she had hidden all that ability under a Biblical bushel.

When the service concluded, one of my favorite colleagues came over. "I really enjoyed that eulogy,

Lexsana. It was like I was reading her life in a book. I didn't want it to end. I wanted it to go on."

Before me, delivering that compliment, was the person who had teased at the teachers' meeting, but on this day, he was one of my mother's pallbearers. This gentleman was fighting a tough battle himself.

I learned that even with a working filter, I still let my temper do the talking, instead of sitting apart quietly and sorting out why we *all* act out in different ways. That career "bath of fire" had screwed me over one more time. Did Dorothy Belle ever get anything wrong? No. She did not. Not where I was concerned.

Tears at the Midpoint

In my forties, being husbandless and childless was a fact of life that I pushed away, the way I used to push calcium and chondroitin away. The ignorants decided I must be gay. I guess their criteria for a life partner were moderate, lower than my own. I wanted "someone to watch over me," but the real person who would never break my heart was not yet on scene. The next best thing for me seemed to be school involvement and working with students of many ages. It gave me a convoluted sense of family, of having my own kids.

I was teaching adults at Family Connections, where parents could work on their GED while their preschool children prepared for kindergarten. "Miss Ana" (I) worked with parents on test prep while "Miss Ida" taught early education. "Miss Becky" directed.

Family learning had minuses. Right after lunch was P.A.C.T. (Parent and Child Together) time. (Yes, another official acronym, education's vaulted trademark). Our parents spent about an hour playing *with* their children. How familial it all sounds, but it wasn't. Some parents balked at having to do this as if they'd been asked to jump the Grand Canyon. "Do we have to do this?" a parent asked me. "It isn't half as painful as a root canal," I assured. "Or childbirth."

I knew nothing of that. But I said it any way, because it was true.

The smallest school members sensed their parents' level of involvement, because they were studying the other

136

families' interactions. It was hard for young learners to ignore other parents and children playing a game together, totally involved and having more fun. A small thing like shared playtime had a big effect on every single child. The less-sincere parents contributed to behavioral flags--- pitched fits thrown by their own indignant children.

Some kids (take me, for instance) purely required a heap of attention to mature.

A young parent named "Leeza" (now deceased) raised her hand during one of those happy family parenting lessons for which I knew nothing, because, as you may recall from your notes in the pre-lesson, *I was childless.* We were making collages from old magazine pictures to display three appropriate parenting practices. My parenting ineptitude must have been showing, apparently surpassing my poor picture ripping and cutting skills.

"Miss Lexzann," Leeza began, "is it hard for you to...well, teach parenting to us parents when you have no kids? Is that tough *at your age?* That must suck." And she said it with zero malice (or filter), instead with a look on her face that seared right inside my reproductive mash up.

She had decided that there was a tangled web *somewhere,* or I would have framed pictures of graduation gowns and great-grandchildren eating watermelon framing my desk. I believe it was her brand of "empathy awry," a state of mind characterized by sad, slanty eyebrows mixed with a head tilt and a pinhead of pity, kind of like the donor who throws a fifty in a Salvation Army kettle with a note attached: "*Sorry, but I just make **more** than you.*" She was clear and forthcoming as a draining cyst. I held my tongue after I asked myself, would I want my dog groomer giving me *stock tips*? That shut my face up fast. I grew even calmer with many other would-I-wants...

The point was made about my barren desk and body. Sideways glances shot out from the other adult learners. They were whispering: "Hey, why *doesn't* she have any kids?" and from a slightly older fellow who enjoyed all that ovarian real estate around him. "Doesn't she like kids?" Plus. this, from a mother of many: "So that's why all her outfits match her shoes. She's putting her money on her childless back." Maybe they thought: "Could she be a he? I'm moving to the back of the room!" "Can she have children?" And then the one I could swear I literally heard all those "inklers" say: "Wonder if her wife wants her to have kids---they could adopt."

The following Monday, Leeza's focus shifted to science, meaning number 104 on the Clairol Periodic Table of Color Elements.

"Miss Lexzann, do you dye your hair, because I'm pretty sure it looks blonder today." She approached my desk coon hound style, quick and sniffy, intent on my roots. "Yep, it's dye (because she was a natural blonde herself), I can smell the ammonia from here." From that moment, any time I attempted beginning algebra with those GED kids at the board, I made sure I stood beside them and was not seated, because now I was rooted in scalp-consciousness, holding my hand to my part often, hoping I did not reek with Mr. Clean-scented ammo hair.

One day during an intense A, B, and C equation problem at the board, Crystal, a sassy, funny blonde, was standing to my right, working out her problem, deep in thought. She appeared hypnotized by the sheer positioning of all those numbers, letters, parentheses. The following description should not infer that I was pushing her *to the point of collapse*. How could I? I didn't know an angle

138

obtuse from a train caboose.

"So, Miss Crystal, what you do on the left side, you do on the right," I tapped with my chalk.

In two words, <u>Crystal collapsed</u>. Her left forearm went up to her forehead. I remember a swoon and a toppling, and **BAM!** She hit me. Not in a way like "Bitch! You're crazy if you think I can do this! I've been out of school sixteen years!" It was more like "Ah.... AAAHHH!!!"

--- *AH???* I thought. Is A.H. my students' code for faux math teacher's Ammonia Head?

And then a real-life, dead weight faint fell on me, mid-thought. Picture two big blonde dominoes with square shoulders, a combined dress size of 24 together, falling sideways. Why was I doing this gig? I wasn't qualified. They needed Mother Hubbard with a good left brain set of skills.

My God! Bad teaching had killed Crystal! She was out cold, slain in the spirit of education. It nearly killed *me*. We laid there and the adult learner emergency division picked us up like reclaimable salvage. That bleached blonde implosion was an incidental engineering teachable moment. Crystal and I became human visual aids, illustrating how powerful dynamite charges imploded great buildings when enough force was applied, enough charges were set. If there was any dust in my classroom carpet, we brought a cloud out.

"I think you're trying to kill me!" Crystal said, drinking the glass of water one of the other ladies had brought her.

"Well, I was thinking the same thing, Miss Crystal *Math*." MATH, I emphasized, so she would not, in her resuscitated state, think I had just compared her to crystal meth.

Adults (meaning my teacher self), like preschoolers, say the darnedest things.

Preschool kids do say the darnedest things, too, about things they don't fully understand, yet they know that the meaning is borderline bad. One of them was Jamie, our blonde, feisty-ornery cutie who knew every cuss word from every bar in the eastern United States. He could croon that Hank Williams spiritual, "There's a Tear in my Beer," and cause a throat to go dry immediately. That kid warbled his language skills in song, with western nasality. Any Nashville lyricist worth the ink in his rhyming lines would have been deeply moved.

He and his little cousin, Kenny, had a thing for nylon hose. They loved to pet my calves when I wore dresses, the way kids stroke a puppy. Jamie was street smart summa cum laude, and absolutely nothing bothered him. He may well have been in his twenties instead of the age on his shot records, just vertically challenged. In summary, he simply knew too much.

Jamie moved on to the main campus two years later. He became an apathetic learner. There were issues, including a medical one.

"The kids are making fun of him, Lex," his mother cried on the phone. "One eye is crossed. We have an appointment in Pittsburgh. I don't think it's good."

In no time, doctors said, "squamous cell carcinoma," a malignant tumor growing in the center of Jamie's brain, inoperable. Mom and Dad still felt like part of us; they updated us. Ida and I went to Presbyterian Hospital in Pittsburgh to see Jamie, though we felt fairly helpless. After several stays, he had finally lapsed into a coma. Doctors said, "Get the family prepared."

"Those damn doctors said Jamie's gonna die," James cried on the phone to us at work one afternoon in spring. "Can you come? I---don't know what to do."

James stood tall and stout, a country boy used to hard work. He could birth a breech calf and make farm equipment hum. He applied a belt-tourniquet *to himself* after his forearm was taken off by a hay baler. But, potentially losing his only child was unparalleled pain, more hurt than he could bear.

When I walked in Jamie's room, James was there, pacing. Jamie had lost so much weight it was hard to spot his comma body in the rumpled hospital sheets. That signature blonde tow head hair was all gone. I looked above his wrinkled head, thinking he needed to hear country music. Total silence is the smell of death to me. Someone had put a figurine of an angel there on a shelf over him, keeping watch. I looked back down. Jamie's bed had a wash of an aura around it. "Jamie's not going to die," I said. "Can you see that...around the bed? I think God just gave him an extension, I do." I felt stupid yet compelled to say it. There was light there, as sure as I would be a second-go-round teacher till I retired. It was risky, making a layman's prognosis to a father dying for a miracle. "Thank Him. Pray, Dad," I said. James was learning to lean on a higher medical authority.

Days later, Jamie was out of that coma asking for a four-wheeler.

The family made their introductions to the *Make-a-Wish Foundation*. Jamie's parents asked the foundation for a trip to Oral Roberts University in Tulsa. They were believing for divine intervention. They asked me to go. I was all in.

We hosted a big yard sale in the middle of town to help with trip expenses. The temperature on the day of brisk sales exceeded ninety-six degrees. Jamie's mom and

I stayed cool by plunging our burning feet in a cooler of ice and jamming our hands down in the shaded money bag coinage, reminding us why we were baking there on the corner, two hot spuds. A local dealership lent us a van so Jamie could be more comfortable. Walmart donated trip snacks. There were 1,030 miles ahead of us that July.

The four of us appeared on a show called, *The Hour of Healing*. Richard Roberts laid hands on us and prayed. Unexpectedly, I went straight backwards in a spiritual swoon. This was my trust test moment, apparently caught by ushers, because there was no wham! kebam! body slam. I was motionless on the cold tile floor and happy as a human can be who isn't rich or yet retired. Catholics don't typically get that knock-down hit of the Holy Ghost.

Jamie's Crew on *The Hour of Healing*. Front row: Miss Sue, Prayer Partner Coordinator, with Jamie. Second row: Paige, an ORU singer, Donna (Jamie's mom), me, and Daddy James.

Jamie ate chili on the return trip. "I think I got my healing," he said, a little shy in saying it. But the endless trip home was much harder on him.

Though he enjoyed the rest of summer, there would be no further bold statements made by anyone about his future. Only a parent with a terminally-ill child understands the feeling that hope is suddenly hiding somewhere from you, teasing in the cruelest possible way.

In October, as a Pennsylvania college was celebrating Homecoming, its high-energy band of loud bass drum cadences came up through open windows, making them vibrate. Jamie now lay in a hospital ward, about to pass. Life and self-absorbed collegiate joy below in the street, passing and grief, just a few floors up.

His private room the past several weeks was already sterilized, made available for the next premature death. He lay there dying, in a large room of strangers hidden behind white privacy shrouds of passage. He had been placed in what I'd read in an essay once about doctors' secret codes----a CTD area (physicians' family-friendly term for "circling the drain"). There was nothing the hospital could or would do to prolong the suffering. His body was innocent and weightless as a newborn's. The fully-opened morphine drip was going to be removed. Ida, his father, a relative and I awkwardly surrounded his bed watching, unwilling witnesses to the death of a child who would never be a teenager, or an old man with family around his table at holidays. As his breaths grew more labored and seemed as if each one was the final, our standing there as premature mourners seemed ludicrous.

Suddenly Ida sat on the side of Jamie's bed, scooping him up into her open pure wings, rocking his lifeless body as if both were enjoying a secret lullaby, kissing his hairless head, helping him cross with inaudibly tender words. "It's alright, Jamie. You're safe. We're here. We all love you," she said, taking him back to his mother's arms as an infant, where nothing could ever hurt him. The drum cadences were gone. The rattling windows grew quiet.

Ida did what I could not. She took death's greedy grasp and loosed it off her student, protective as a mother bear. If it was to be his time, she would not have Jamie feel alone in his helpless, singular journey ahead. I realized then that emergencies don't make heroes, they make angels. The added proof of her transformation was my remembering right then her former life. Ida had previously been a nun for twenty years. Acts of love and mercy were involuntary for her. She could be crusty sometimes, but she well exceeded the requirements of goodness and kindness to others, as experienced in many lives, including her own wonderful family, and mine.

That one minute, the amount of time it takes a shooting star to note an earthly parting, reminded me I was in a kind of job post with no guarantees of ease or peace. Jamie's hand relaxed in mine; his pulse paused, then Eternity took over. Tears flowed naturally, quietly, because other stations of death readiness nearby needed silence to concentrate on what was coming for them.

All the things that made him so lovable and so bad as a four-year-old were again on his face, relieved, released from pain he could never describe or understand.

And all I could think about was that little face and a bow tie, standing onstage at dress rehearsal for *Cheaper By The Dozen*, playing Little Bob. A cast member said, "Miss P, that little dude is bad-ornery! He just told me a joke that was dirty. I had to think about it nearly a minute before I got it!"

Ida and I eulogized Jamie. But the moment I remember was earlier that morning, looking out my hall window. Unbelievable, but true, and I shared what I saw:

In the Heavens was the soft outline of a buck, colored white in cottony clouds. I ran to find my camera, remembering how Jamie's purpose in living was to get a deer the first day of hunting season.

There is another sad teaching unit from Family Connections' record books, sadly titled, *The Tragic Loss of Jesse*. That preschooler had a face our director, Becky, said smacked of Huck Finn with a southern twang that made you want to grab up a fishing line and drink apple pie moonshine. Jesse was just as cute as a Christmas puppy, with the ability to recite rhymes and sensational fairy tales in a brown-eyed P.T. Barnum kind of way. He was bright and bubbly, and he loved being outdoors. He loved his family, so, so much.

One weekend Jesse accidentally rode his bicycle past the end of a driveway and an oncoming truck could do nothing but brake and weirdly lock to the bicycle, dragging little Jesse. That's not an easy visual, but that is how the story was relayed. Our hearts were helplessly focused on the bottomless deep pain thrust upon his parents. Jesse's parents, both such nice folks, had to deal with the ultimate tragic loss and family devastation. The words didn't exist to alter their grief state, but everyone in that learning center said them anyway, to God and to them. Their lives were fully splintered; they could never be quite normal again.

Leeza was right. My childless existence gave me no concept of how it felt to lose the best part of yourself. I couldn't fully be the parenting instructor, much less a sympathy-doling fellow parent to my affected adults. I never even owned a Cabbage Patch Kid. But I did have two solid, good parents that always taught by example.

"T" was one of our most hopeful women with half a dozen small children and a troubled husband. The children were blonde and gorgeous. T. worked so hard on her certificate. She had several babies close together, and now there were health issues, including an apparent heart condition. Her children had the most cherubic faces. They were never school noisemakers.

But one day her husband set a vehicle on fire, then called to say he was coming to our center to do the same. We locked our building, pulled the shades, and took every child and parent into the restroom to shelter in place. After trying every door knob and knocking on every door, he left campus. Arrangements were made to get T. to a safe house. She called the center with updates and was getting her life back on track, though a new relationship had ended in more-than-hard feelings. That individual assaulted her on the street and she died there. Another passing, another cycle of loss.

Other parents passed, too. One of our adults, "C," was originally from the Centennial State, Colorado. She pronounced it "Colla-rahdo," which made her sound so Aspen-like. Her beautiful little fairy-like daughter was a sprite who skipped above the floor, lifted by her invisible fairy wings. "C" had mentioned problems with her heart. We heard about her passing, not long after that family exited the program. Another motherless child.

Another parent called Ida one evening. "Ida? I'm at UHC. They're going to transport Tim [name changed] to Ruby Memorial. Could you and Lexsana come?"

We met her at the hospital, where her husband was loaded into the waiting mouth of a Health Net helicopter. This was a scene right out of ER. We followed along the interstate, driving with an eye to the road, the other on the helicopter whirring on ahead of us, weaving through night's silver haze.

"S" had a beautiful heart and one big family, about to become fatherless. Again, our hearts were broken, for "S" was one of our most generous hearts, a Mother Mary with incredible baking skills, always gifting someone.

After his passing, we took the family out to eat and made sure there were funeral outfits. Weren't there other ways to help than always tossing money at misery and death? It seemed superficial, an alternative to what we should have been doing...However, who knew what that was?

Family Connections had done its part for learning and for the community: plays presented to our auxiliary school, poetry read at town hall meetings, Christmas craft shows, community read alouds, as well as our becoming a collection site for Franklin Graham's Shoebox Project.

We all survived days of anger, setbacks, tragedy, illness, miscarriages, leaves of absence, some shaky attendance at times, building equipment thefts, and an occasional fight, but above that were the outcomes for which we'd been trained-----GED degrees, so that adults could improve their families' lives and elevate their young learners by example. Crystal worked for the school system as a school cook; Linda became a nurse; Amy worked at a local hospital; others got a driver's license and subsequent jobs. We hoped those children would genuinely get an *Even Start* (our original program title), in school and life.

We received recognition. Department of Labor Secretary Margaret Chao was to visit our elementary school on September 11, 2001, but 9/11 arrived right before she ever stepped foot on that plane in Washington. She wasn't going anywhere.

Some tears at the midpoint were personal, cried at home. I'd become engaged to a younger man, a local news anchor, whom I met while performing in *Lilies of the Field*. Yep, East European nun and Irish priest, Father Murphy, hooked up one night after a particularly religious dialogue exchange and the rest was, as good Catholics would call it, "liturgical."

That didn't end well. A year later, I wrote the producers of *Oprah* to invite myself onto the show to talk about the Heart Bomb Law, involving the ethical question of giving back the (coincidentally heart-shaped) engagement ring after a breakup. They wanted to do the show!

But a few weeks later, a show producer telephoned me back. "Miss Pilewski? I'm an assistant producer with the *Oprah* show. Well, your ex-fiance declined appearing on the show, so we have to cancel. I'm sorry it didn't work out." Another potential fifteen minutes of fame dissolved. But, then I thought, *HOLD THE BUS!* What would *that* purge have been like? Fortunately, I wouldn't have to find out or humiliate myself further.

I lost oodles of Kluski Noodles on my Big, Fat Polish Wedding reception. That five hundred dollars reserving the banquet site turned out to be nonrefundable. "Food's already ordered," they said with all the sincere regret of homeowners who refuse Jehovah's Witnesses into their homes. The lady who sat and planned that big day event with me got one hell of a tip! I'm thinking my five hard-earned Ben Franklins went towards another diamond ring flasher, judging from the blinding ice on her helping hands. If the food was secured, *then who would be eating it?*

My brother, the idea generator of the family said, "You should have invited every homeless person in the area to your non-wedding reception and filled 'em up. No booze allowed, no baths required."

Naturally, I lacked the nerve. Today I might have done it because I'm older, retired, and have more time for confidence-building discovery weekends from those take-out-a-loan Tony Robbins seminars.

That decade-long flash on my timeline was a survival test. Tragedies times ten crushed me flatter than an old Chrysler in a junk yard. Hearing about students' trials and injustices made me hug that inner shred of innocence tighter. Even at the midpoint I still needed to grow and appreciate more. I had already learned what it meant to do without things, to have a wheel of misfortune hit you in the face between jobs. Standing in long lines to apply for Unemployment was like being fifth in line for the French Revolution's guillotine. It seemed completely disrespectful to my hard-working father, me, standing there with my hand out.

Even though he'd been gone a few years before my career track started derailing, I hated myself. I was doing nothing for the family name. "Your name is everything," he said to me. "Never do anything to tarnish it." And there I was, letting it rust away, staining its shine.

I still believe there was a reason the federal government established that family learning center, why the three of us ladies met and worked our degrees off providing for our unique student enrollees. Our GED students had been through more than *Jane Eyre*, and she was fictional. Their situations made mine into a thimble full of nothing.

I listened, but as they counted the ways, I was making a head list of my own. I thought of that one phone call that was both awful and transforming.

"Your family emergency time is up," an administrative secretary informed me in her steady, all-business voice, even though Dad was inches away from his final hospital stay. "You'll need to return to work." Her warmth burned me to a crisp.

This was not the time to unleash on a woman doing a work directive. Nor was it time to unleash on a young woman who was trying to steady herself for the death of her father.

"You know, I understand that. I do. I take work seriously. But... my father is *dying*. He never left my side during surgery or sorrow or trips halfway around the world. My place is with my dad, so you do whatever you feel you have to."

I hung up the receiver realizing I'd pretty much fired myself. Instead of obsessing, I kept that call and my inner joy quiet. Relating that call to Dad would have instantaneously alleviated his suffering. Nevertheless, the release made me feel my exit door had opened at the perfect time. *What had I just done?* I felt like I was gliding. I grew calm. My peace came by saying, for once, exactly what I meant. I'd just cured myself of decision paralysis.

Still, a lingering question: If I left education, would I stay gone, thus proving there were things teachers could do besides teach? ---Of course there were! Teachers had to be a dozen different professional people every day of work. Many teachers were actually working comedians. However, how many entertainers were (or would ever become) teachers? Well, other than Tony Danza, who decided to use his English degree and teach in a Philadelphia high school. He was a tear jerk almost daily, and he only did that gig for six big weeks. Students can be tougher than any director or audience, because critical thinking, critical commentary, and intense drama come so naturally to them.

Some of our adult learners seemed to learn to exist in a limited world of chaos and noise, generational lack and sorrow. Yet, finding their way, their voice, pushed them past neutral. If all teachers, administrators, and bureaucrats were required to make home visits as our center was, and see what our staff saw (things I would never share out to others), then education would find its heart fast.

Time double-stepped on, and those preschoolers grew up, married, and became parents themselves. I realized this two Christmases ago, when I picked out a theme-park-epic-light-show tree at a popular do-it-yourself-then-pay-a-contractor-to-fix-it-later store. That Christmas tree did everything but make corn dogs, which was a separate purchase. When I wheeled the tree to checkout, picturing the light works show it would perform in my living room...there was Paul, whose dad was air lifted to Ruby Memorial in Morgantown when Paul was barely chest high to me. He was incredibly hulky now, tall, handsome, with his own babies, sharing pictures, catching me up on the family.

The conversation diverted to our time back at Family Connections.

"Have you ever seen Miss Ida since school, Paul?"

"I haven't seen Miss Ida in years. She was a good person, good to my family," he said, loading that redwood into my Subaru. His brief tribute said it all. It impressed me he would even risk being old school and uncool. His mouth simply spoke from a pocket of gratitude. Sure, he was little when his mom brought him to our preschool. Absolutely he could get mean-mad and vent to near extremes. But something long ago maybe helped him. Nothing blocks out the fragrance of kindness. The heart never forgets it.

"Merry Christmas," he called as he returned to work, waving at me. I felt myself age more with his every step.

These days I can cry on a dime. When I see a commercial packed with clips of military family reunions I feel my lips start to dance. An opera audition on reality TV can knock me backwards in my Amish glider rocker, giving me goose flesh. I don't even like opera. I recall my parents doing the same thing, for which I frowned and turned my head, not understanding. Now I'm that dribbler.

Soon my phone calls to fellow retirees will revolve around my colon and my beautiful hands and hair I didn't appreciate enough in my twenties. I will talk madly about bygone things from this book, repeating myself, proud I stayed the course, tears and all. A former student (one I will mistake for a different former student), will see me in the grocery store and tolerate it about thirty seconds. "Well....good seeing you, Miss P., I gotta go pick up my granddaughter at soccer practice. But you take care now." Yep. I would be the frail old gal who kept all those school kids on a strict though improvised timeline, making them lie about where they needed to be. All that, just by appearing feeble or slightly askew, like my Jack-o-lantern lip line I was sure looked pouty and youthful. They would quick step it, exiting, leaving groceries behind if necessary, and I would toddle off, sighing, recalling many wonderful memories that may have never happened, Miss Daisy driving her big buggy right into the battery kiosk.

Refinement (meaning that familiar phrase, "bath of fire") prior to, at the midpoint, and later on brought deeper emotions than I have ever felt. And I am so thankful. Tears are validations, chapter markers, each one recycled from original episodes in our timelines, like moisture drawn back up into the clouds after soft rains, keeping earth tender.

Me and Mr. Lewinsky - Not a Love Story

May 22, 1997, and the majority of Clarksburg's Democrats needed EKGs. Some of the city folk were palpitating over the soon arrival of President Clinton, agitated to a medical condition called "the joy that possibly kills." Presidents visiting North Central West Virginia just didn't happen. My teacher friends with connections made well-placed calls to House of Delegates members, hoping for a hot seat in the airport bleachers. I did not care about having my hair restyled by Air Force One. I got a backstage pass, quite the accidental "visit participant/team member." Clarksburg and my tribe of OG (official greeter) homeys were about to be changed forever.*

William Jefferson Clinton was hosting a Town Hall Meeting at premiere Robert C. Byrd High in Clarksburg, West Virginia! It should be noted that the president had none of the usual hosting duties that exhaust, like appetizer prep, banner making, and deep cleaning the gym floor. Further, these intimate fireside "informal" chats were anything but informal. Staff people would take care of all the formal protocol. They could exceed even the creative prowess of Disney's Imagineers and Broadway's brilliant set builders.

I was unexpectedly involved in that gathering, about to get a big lesson plan in Washington politics as

*The word "forever," actually is a hyperbolic word choice here, meaning "for the rest of the afternoon."

153

well as the epiphany that locally, on that May day in 1997, nearly everyone was a Democrat when Air Force One touched down at our recently-expanded air strip and the thick exit door opened wide...But I was elsewhere, evaluating all the hoo-hah.

First came **Lesson One**: If a school in a district is awarded Blue Ribbon status, look out! Either a president will visit and complicate your small-town life for months, or your school will soon close. Awards tend to roll out the death knell in education. It's similar to the Lottery curse: win three times and die trying on the fourth attempt. And, as a lifelong loser in all award nominations, I can verify most of that theory.

Lesson Two: This awakening involved the village it took to bring the leader of the free world to a small arena. The village barely fit inside the perimeters of Clarksburg and Bridgeport. Big sections of suites were "roped off" at the local Holiday Inn. Washington's finest were the not-so-Secret Service, opening communications between themselves and D.C. The "Holidome" (Holiday Inn indoor pool, fitness sectors) was likely a network of invisible computer network cables and phone banks, cords -- a bonus amenity for the common guests fortunate enough to reserve the last broom closets available.

My involvement started when The White House phoned a tiny southern Harrison County elementary school. The principal spoke to a spokesman who spoke the news that the school's reading test scores were impressive, presidential, in fact. Our small elementary school in southern Harrison County had been given a state award earlier that spring, one of fifty state recipients, at a national ceremony in Atlanta, Georgia. The president's staff requested that a teacher from Lost Creek offer a

154

probing question during the town meeting. We on staff were impressed to varying degrees, our Pride Alert elevating mostly to pale peach. I was the appointee. Our little school's star was ascending.

That same evening, I picked up my phone at 8:00 p.m. sharp, as directed by the White House aide earlier via my spokesperson, the principal. The phone did not even have to ring.

"Lexsana?" This was the "WHA" call (my code for: White House aide). "My name is Reagan, I'm an aide to the president, and I will be coordinating the Town Hall event."

I laughed nervously. Was this a code name? A Democratic president and someone named Reagan was working for him? "Okay..." I answered Miss Ronald Wilson.

"Your Town Hall question will be pre-written.by a small cadre. I will call you tomorrow evening."

"Well... alright," I said, wondering how many people actually use that word "cadre" on a daily basis. Was that the same as a gaggle, a skulk, or a herd? I did not want to say anything further, guessing she or someone was listening, already knowing my weight from fourth grade. "I am very excited," I said, suddenly feeling indignant. That response may have been a lie. The subtext of them writing the question for me was: *What would a teacher or reading specialist know about delivering a proper reading comprehension question to a president?*

The next evening, Reagan called back. I was out and Donna (superb reading teacher-specialist) was in. She would ask POTUS a pre-written question longer than the opening paragraph of *Silas Marner*. The White House C.O.W. (more of my own clever code, this time meaning

Council of Writers) had already co-authored the prepped question. I, the suddenly displaced question-asker, would stand in as an official greeter, no questions required. Go, OGs!

"Now Reagan," I asked, "Will that assignment require anything special? How will I know exactly what to do?" Was this smart to ask? No, it was not.

"All directives will be given shortly before the president's arrival, okay?" she said. She was through with me, though I had wardrobe questions, refreshments questions, bathroom bladder-timed-out questions, important things!

Meanwhile, at the Holiday Inn a fleet of dark suits continued their massive spying production at their remote command center. Cables and phone banks were installed. My static-y phone line told me the gospel truth---my phone was likely being tapped. Oh well! No further hour-long phone calls to "Uncle" Boris Yeltsin for me!

Over at Bonnie Belle Pastries, expert bakers were preparing a "facial recognition cake" masterpiece with the president's portrait. He could literally eat his face off that evening, returning home to D.C., and no late night talk show host could see it as fodder for his monologue.

On that red-letter day in May, military guards lined every ditch and a few driveways of Pitcairn Hollow, the address of RCB High School. I felt like I was back there touring Poland with such a military presence before me and my Subaru. Those soldiers were spit-shined, standing at attention *facing* those driveways and homes, their backs to the road the president would travel. They would keep the house dwellers in check. Sharpshooters were in place in the plentiful woods for the president's visit. Step out of line and there might be one anonymous bullet. Lights out. A special tent had been erected beside a lesser school entryway selected for the president's secure arrival and limousine parking.

When I checked in to the secure check point, I was ushered to the school's library. Inside Byrd, near the 300 Section stood a far lesser head of state, the president and God-given minister of Salem College.

I felt my shellfish allergy-imitation face set in, where I get flustered and red and poppy-eyed, trying to hide from the coming confrontation. I had worked for that Little Dictator a few excruciating years between teaching jobs as SC Coordinator of Alumni Affairs and Publications. My whopping salary was $13,000. every fiscal year, rain or shine. If meanness is measured by height, it usually goes the shorter, the meaner. He was short and mean to the Salemites, his subjugates. He hated me, no matter what I did, wrote, coordinated, or alumni'd.

Once he had me called to his office when he smelled an "impeachment" plot afoot, a peasant-planned revolt. He called in his unwilling secretary, with whom I'd gone to high school. She was ordered to take notes as I made a confession of collusion for wanting him g-o-n-e.

"Now then, Miss Pilewski," he said touching his fingertips up and down his hair part, the way the SS might do before extracting confessions. Crickets from yours truly. He would never break me. "Since you seem to have no words today, I am calling you back to this meeting in exactly one week. At that time, you had better answer my questions directly, or else."

I never opened my mouth. I wasn't afraid of someone an entire head shorter than I. I stared him down. No, I stared DOWN on him. I would not buckle.

He did not call me back to his office to watch him finger pad his scalp line. I (and forty-five other kind hearts) lost our jobs that same spring. And to seal the deal, he sold the college, too.

Now here he stood like Browning's "Last Duchess," feeling superior, even to the library furniture where he stood. The sight of him and our past interfaces made me think deeply about the choices before me. My choice was that I would rather eat wet dog shed than hail him with zero-genuine greetings. He was the kind of man touted in Randy Newman's tune. I would have to pick his tweedy little body up just to say hello.

I could no longer hide behind magazines or books. They were being moved to make more space for the influx of invited guests.

"Hello, there Dr. -----," I said with politically correct faux joy. What a liar I was!

He returned faux friendliness. "It's so nice to see you, Lexsana," he said grinning like Wally Cox on *Hollywood Squares*. The resemblance was uncanny. What a liar *he* was! He didn't want to see me, except with tar or trapped in a gator hole. Adding this authentic, heartfelt question: "How have you been?"

If he was faux caring, then I was about to pour out my fancy pants bio. "Well, I'm wonderful. I am teaching in a high-achieving elementary setting, and today, I'm one of the appointed presidential greeters," I said. "Are you a greeter, too? No?...Oh...Well...Oh…Well….Our school had national recognition for its reading scores. So, I'll have a chance to chat with the president. Isn't that so nice?"

This pinched smile came over him. His eyes squinted the way Bogie's did lighting a cigarette, when you weren't sure he was a good guy or a gun runner. The Reverend wanted to kill me alright because he couldn't break me, not when I was his peon then, and certainly not now. He couldn't kill me. Too many witnesses.

Lesson Three: Karma did exist, though sometimes it took a few years to boomerang back to its source. I believe he always thought I had died in a county stampede for a teaching job. *But...here...I..was!*

In another hour I saw pudgy, bespectacled WHA, Reagan, and she was exactly WHA-t I'd imagined from our brief phone taps. She threw out her directives like candy from a firetruck in a Veteran's Day Parade. Except the candy was sweet. I was pretty sure she had been dipping into that candy stash for years!

"Official greeters! I need you to follow me and form a perfect line exactly six feet from the doorway where President Clinton will enter." She moved like a large animal, one arm up in the air to enhance her authority. "You must listen carefully. You will <u>not</u> veer from the formation. Do <u>not</u> turn your head when the limousine carrying the president arrives. Do <u>not</u> move at all as the president approaches or make any sudden moves towards him. If you do, you will be taken down. And, above all, do <u>not</u> speak to the president unless spoken to."

"Pardon, Ronald, but is this the *American* town hall meeting or did you use your powers and switch this show to Reykjavik? This stuff's harsh."

Lesson Four: There was little difference between a grand lecture before our family visited my aunt in Pennsylvania or a grand lecture before meeting the forty-second president.

"Your Aunt Jane doesn't eat like we do," Mom warned. "There are only two meals on Sunday and one snack. You'll just have to starve until we get back home. Do <u>not</u> ask for more food! I brought some snacks in one of the brown bags. And, do <u>not</u> ask for more than one slice of toast! Your aunt counts toast!" Mom could threaten all she wanted; Reagan was still scarier than parents or aunts.

I also realized that "to whom much was given, much was required." This chick with the Republican first name was tangled tighter than the one real gold chain in my jewelry box. The truth was, she was only as important as the *current* president. She would never be a Bush-man or a Trump-ster because she was too "unornamented." Someday, there would be no hall pass for her at The White House entrance gate.

I blocked out the rest of her blah-blah, refusing to look at her, suddenly knowing how the usual suspects feel in a police lineup. She was ruining the whole experience for me, talking down to board presidents, state senators, business owners, and the token teacher in the mix. We were her grunts, trickle-down inferiors. An approaching pristine motor finally silenced her.

Run, Reagan, run! She held her clipboard up to keep her breasts secured. There was POTUS butt to kiss.

The highly-polished First Car, a Cadillac called "The Beast" had pulled in, causing a power surge of running feet. The cattle run reminded me of watching old westerns with my dad, of a dusty Wells Fargo stagecoach arriving with important snail mail and money bags. I looked so far left out of the corner of my eyes to peek that I was afraid they would stay that way. If they froze, as Mom often warned, I would have to pivot forty-five degrees away in order to make eye contact.

The sight of that beastie fortress on wheels made me feel unsteady, like its missile-proof girth had caused a small fissure in the school's floor. Was the earth moving or were my locked knees slowly starting to sway in a coming topple? The appearance of the authoritarian glossy wingtip meeting the concrete and red carpet under it, a shoe custom designed for William J. Clinton, made me forget about fainting. I needed to use the bathroom. He stepped out, and *boy*! He was paler, thinner than David Letterman had claimed in his jabs about Clinton's big pasty thighs.

And there was the famous lip-biting smile and narrowed eyes. He talked to each greeter and I suddenly clammed up, trying to remember what <u>not</u> to do.

If only Dad were still around! I missed him so much at a moment I could never share. Once a minister on TV said, "When something really good happens down here, our relatives are allowed to peek over Heaven's banister and witness the achievement."

"Hello, Mr. President," I smiled, the fourth in line to receive the handshake Reagan would disinfect for him later with White House Rose Garden-scented anti-bacterial gel. "How is your leg doing since your nasty accident?" I asked him about a tumble downstairs playing golf or chasing someone, asking as sincerely as I could for Reagan's sake.

"I'm feeling fine, thank you," he said. "So glad to meet you. Tell me about what you do."

"I am a teacher, Mr. President. I work in a family learning center here in the southern part of the county. We had national recognition for high reading scores." *God! I sound like some kid bragging about his dad's old Camaro.* He probably thought I was a stand-in for the actual, accomplished educator.

Was he smiling at me or my answer, or neither? Here stood an intelligent man, smart enough to be a Rhodes Scholar, a world leader, a cheat. All that took talent, so without a doubt, he had the built-in smarts to look deep into a person in a sort of sneer-leer and smile and squeeze a hand and be thinking about how good it would be to squeeze something else right about now.

The biggest buildups in this life have the fastest letdowns: Christmas, weddings, souffles, and Town Hall Meetings. I went ahead and washed my hands when I got home.

Shaking a president's hand takes no more than ten seconds unless there is something else happening. Shaking a president's hand left me feeling ----flat, unfeeling. I swear, in that moment, I felt I was making contact with a body double.

Could it be? If it could, then there was a little bit of Stalin-ing going on, a leader famous for his body doubles. It seemed crazy, that is, until nineteen years later, when presidential hopeful Hillary Clinton was accused of using a stand-in after that now-famous New York flu faint.

That night, hanging up my presidential two-piece Maggie London dress, I wondered if I would keep it as a souvenir, for visual evidence of that meeting. I did. Unbeknownst to us official greeters and all the awestruck multitude that hot spring red-letter day, someone else, nearer to Washington, D.C., was doing the exact same dress thing that I was, for similar, though severely different reasons.

I Wanna Be a Producer-r-r-r

Spring 1990.

"How would you like to direct our school play?" he asked me over the telephone.

"Are you serious? You sound serious."

"Of course! I want to know if you want to do our show. We need a director."

I wondered if his fingers were crossed as he asked, or were they all just wrapped around a Snickers bar? I knew him; most assuredly, his hand was attached to an after-school candy grab. Wherever this conversation was going, I was going for a dinner-plate-sized Reese Cup just as soon as I could skip to goodbye.

His school was right down the road from my teaching job. He could have opened the office window and practically yelled it to me. Closeness in proximity meant minimal miles to trek after work from my job doing the adult education thing. I liked directing the way ghostwriters like writing for famous people with minimal writing chops. You watch your vision and investment grow and you just feel so...superior.

I was holding him up. Time isn't money to anyone in education. Time is car keys and sunglasses and adios to the day because there is not much overtime in teaching or administrating. I heard a clock ticking behind his head while I entertained mixed feelings for two reasons.

"You still there?" he wanted to know. "Yep, still here, still thinking," I said.

Hmmm...I'd been away from theater a while since my days with the eclectic troupe known as the Clarksburg Art Center. We were the motley masters of small-town comedy, drama, musicals. And some of that actually occurred on the stage. We considered it a big deal to act out our frustrations and talents. People paid to see us freestyle and work out our personal kinks. We were all guppies in a small pond. No, we were more like big guppies in the West Fork River.

"Sure. I think I can do that. That could be.......fun," I said to my *brother*. Yes sir, he was the asking principal, the one doing the inviting to direct. And there it was, Reason #2, the other cause for mixed feelings. Working with relatives always degenerates into a presidential debate, though the talking points get far less heated during those televised candidate exchanges.

"*Oklahoma!*" is a big musical, even for celebrities with big talents and PBS-backed productions starring Hugh Jackman as Curly. But since I loved the music and thought it was perfect for the spring season and the audience, this show was *on*!

When the dust settled from all the back-and-fourth with The Rodgers and Hammerstein Musical Organization, I had signed many confusing papers. I believe one of them had me married to either the ghost of Richard Rodgers or that of Oscar Hammerstein. Once New York got that commitment fax, you were slave to their terms. There was no going back on those estate boys, never mind both had been dead for a combined total of 41 years.

We signed, so we owed, regardless what disaster might prevent the actual production from making it to the stage (which happened to be part of the gymnasium). Creating a show, particularly a musical, in that acoustical all-purpose nightmare was not easy, because as any drama teacher knows, we must bow to the sports gods. A few rehearsals illustrated my point.

In February: "Yeah, we got the court tonight, so, uh, how much longer you gonna be here?" asked a coach, chewing on something disgusting. Coaches loved theater to a spine tingle. Musicals were the jock itch of their existence.

"Oh, okay, we'll just skip through to the last page," I said to no one, because coach had already sprinted off the gym floor to get the basketballs.

"Many a new day will please my eye—" sang Laurie and lady company up on the elevated stage of community action.

BAMP! BAMP! BAMP-BAMP! went the balls on the court.

"Many a new day will find me---" Laurie continued, louder.

If the entire team decided to make points with coach and turn their practice orbs into dodgeball, we onstage could be toothless or worse.

"Okies, let's blow!" I said, ending rehearsal, fuming, as if a funnel cloud had been spotted somewhere below us, in a hailstorm of burnt-orange basketballs. Things which could be batted, dribbled, punted, driven, kicked, spiked, or caught were the bane of *my* existence.

Spring is a difficult time for play production in a more rural area. For one thing, crops must be planted.

165

(You don't get that on old Broadway, no sir!) This big chore always created no-shows. It was hard for students present to simulate square dancing moves partner-less. Those half-dances put stress on the Martha Graham-like choreographer, a veteran dancer herself, all business. Non-teaching professionals find high school ambivalence and silliness their highest anger barometer. Professional educators find ambivalence the halfway point to getting a class's pulse.

After many attempts to pull together these constant joke-telling cow wranglers, she broke with her own patience, broke out into awful red welts. Tina smacked off her boom box. Everyone eventually shut up.

"I warned you that I wouldn't tolerate acting stupid in my rehearsal hall and not listening. **I am done!**" And with that, she took her swishing pony tail and pranced out of that room as only a dancer can.

As if I'd made a disgusting bodily function sound, most eyes and all heads turned to me. I drew on my old Art Center skills and smiled. It was one of those *I've-been-poisoned!---but-I-like-it* grins. Did they think I would whip out character shoes and set an entire show right there? All I knew in the way of steps were "The Virginia Reel," the polka, and a crazy little happy dance I did when Halloween candy got reduced on All Saint's Day.

It took me four hours to get the courage to phone Miss Tina. I did some big-girl groveling.

"Tina?" I swallowed, expecting a grand slam in my ear. "I am so sorry about what happened at rehearsal today----"

"No! I'm sorry. I shouldn't have done that." What a woman, sparing my reading of the shake-and-beg genuflect plea I'd jotted down on a Publisher's Clearinghouse envelope.

She returned and the students had learned a lesson. They did not waste her time again. Storm Number One had ended.

The play staff had its share of disagreements, too, and some were offended by the line from the song, "The Farmer and the Cowman" -- "Well, I'll be damned if I ain't jist as good." The jist of their upset stemmed from "the 'd' word." We honored Hammerstein's lyric, as I had no interest in entertaining his ghost-haunt. "Damned" would probably not rip the gingham fabric of society. There were bigger worries, like that surrey with the fringe on top. And there were props to build, like the whole farm house porch and "The Little Wonder," a type of "telescopic centerfold" cowboys used to leer at showgirl postcards through a twisty View Master. There were over-the-top props and costuming: chaps, pinafores, ballerina attire for the Dream Ballet, old wicker picnic baskets, a surrey, and moreover-----a calm surrey horse to steal from a nearby barn.

Fortunately, the shop teachers had game, real board game. They took lumber, students, nails, added water and stirred, and there stood a movie prop porch. My Uncle Mason produced that Little Wonder from the cavity of a large, painted flashlight, adding a turn crank that ended up looking authentic in a 1990 facsimile kind of way.

Then came The Great Trouser Robbery a couple days before dress rehearsal. I was checking the surrey, on loan from a local benefactor, when actor Curly walked up surreptitious-like.

"Um, Miss P., um, I know how stressed you already are, but I had five dollars in my wallet for gas money. Someone stole it and now I can't get home," Curly said, and I think his chaps were chattering. "My car is on 'E' and I can't call my dad. He'd flip."

"*WHAT*?" I yelled. That was it. I think I bellowed it out, channeling Dorothy Belle during *Harvey*. I whumped down that director's copy, went up the back "stage" steps and threw back that door like there were wedding cake samples waiting for me behind it. Hands flew over skivvies and some of those manly cowpokes squealed like girls.

"WHO TOOK FIVE DOLLARS OUT OF CURLY/ LARRY'S WALLET?" I screamed. That pee-soaked sports/ drama dressing room took on a brimstone aroma. It was an improvement.

Silence. No words. Sudden shock can bring on non-verbal tremors that resemble ice cream brain freeze.

"Let me revise that. Who **STOLE** five dollars out of Larry Z's wallet?" Years of cattle stampedes and gunfights had apparently deafened these cowpokes, still suspiciously in partial character, still not talking.

"Fine, get yourselves dressed and get out here on the gym floor. You have three minutes. We're going to collect a little gas fund for Curly. Now MOVE IT!"

Oh my God! I thought, clomping down the steps like Dorothy, down to the gym floor, pacing. Did I just go into a boys' room and see all that? If iPhones had existed, I'd probably have been cuffed in another ten minutes.

Curly got at least a half tank of gas that night. But the cowhands left pissed. That was the proof positive of my Dorothy Belle spot-on performance. I had raised my director-producer credentials to exploding bitch.

Finally, it was nearly dress rehearsal, when that pay check was almost in my hands. That ensemble reprise of the title song was roaring happily in my head, when suddenly, the winds actually came sweeping down the plain. A janitor came running in and started pulling out the bleachers, stored and collapsed in the gym wall, motioning me over. "Hurry!" he yelled.

"What's going on?" I asked.

"Tornado coming! Get these kids under the bleachers! You gotta get that sound system turned off NOW!"

I called for a cast meeting. It was one sentence. **"TORNADO! RUN! UNPLUG!"**

Boys took care of the speakers and mics. Girls searched for their purses in the gathering darkness. They wanted to die with their lips on. We regrouped behind the bleachers and waited. I thought about the day I had agreed to this madness. The question tonight was, *where would I be found the next morning*? Up in a pine tree? Under the surrey wheel? Or maybe in the boys' pissy dressing room, hanging on a hook with a sign, "Funeral Expenses Collection Envelope." I tried to remember if my underwear matched. My mother was a big proponent of matching lingerie and "all holes barred." I grew up hearing it every time I took keys in hand. "Where are you going? Put on your best bloomers if you're going out in that car! You could be in a bad accident and it would be embarrassing having holy panties on in the emergency room. We have more pride than that in the South!" Mom's disaster scenario was always a severe car wreck where my jeans would be ripped off by the flying stick shift, upon impact. A potential tornado seemed far less likely in the Mountain State.

Underwear was not that big of a deal right now. At least I wore some. I listened to the kids around me, some talking, a few whimpering. Could this be it? Lights out for all of us, only The Little Wonder prop surviving the weight of the gymnasium wreckage? Is this how kids should perish, just trying to be part of their school's musical? I was angry and afraid. Would I ever hear my

169

mother's sweet southern voice again saying those golden words: "Lexsana, would you like some more fried okra?" and the even more-endearing statement that moved me every time: "You need shoulder pads in that dress." "Will we be okay here?" a student asked.

"Sure we will. Stay close to the wall," I advised, which was a stupid directive, because nobody in that moment knew literally which way the wind would blow. "We'll be okay. I know it," I said in the same faux way you tell your peers that the show has been a sheer delight, start to end. The end was coming before the show. I pictured funeral hymns and overbooked undertakers, and the heavy scent of carnation bouquets. And again, I asked myself, *What Would Dorothy Belle Do?*... "PRAY! You idiot!" kept coming to mind. Boy! I was glad my Nova was paid for. Oddly, that was the only thought I had that brought me solace.

Someone said, "My mother's going to kill me for not being home on time." Oh! Wait...that was me.

In minutes we heard wind, then the freight train barreling over the gym roof, deafening like the laced-up hooves of a thousand River Dancers. We were a bowl of frightened meringue and that storm was the electric beaters. Surely that ceiling would come crashing down. If anyone was screaming, the dynamite charge above us drowned out all sound. And then, I heard my sainted mother's voice.

"Is there no phone in that school? I was worried sick! Worrying your mother like that! I could have a heart attack!" But in less than a minute there was pure peace and quiet. Except in my head. "You NEVER call. I thought someone had kidnapped you. I know how trusting you are. You drive along that deserted old country road every day and every night. Drifters watch for pretty blondes* in Novas on country roads. How have you already not been murdered?"

It was quiet, dead quiet, where you blink, finally close your mouth, and search for your rear with both hands while checking your inferior undergarments for wetness. I was relieved all of us were awake, meaning we all weren't obviously dead. We were in total darkness except for two small red and white exit signs at either end of the gym.

"I think it's over, guys. Is everybody okay?" I asked.

"Think so, Miss P." And, of course, from the tough-guy section: "You kiddin' me? That was lame!"

"Feel around for your friend. Are we all present because I can't see much!"

And just like that, as if covering for their former frightened mousiness, the lot of them began laughing and shaking off the semblance of fear, brushing their hair, making jokes about the storm. I wished there had been an ounce more of something scary, if only to make them cry "Mommy!"so I would not have been the only one doing so.

We went to the back gym exit doors for a peek. Trees down, no power, eerie quiet.

The prospect of an impromptu slumber party with that lively mob scared me worse than the storm. These forty kids, one janitor, and I were totally stranded. The custodian helped me corral the entire crew in the cafeteria with two flashlights. He opened up the cooler and got us chocolate milks and mustard packets, having no other keys to pinch some real food, like day-old rolls with a gallon of government peanut butter.

*"Pretty blonde" is a Kitty Pilewski euphemism for "homespun char girl." Those drifters were actually looking for pretty blondes with great shoulder pads and color in their faces and legs thin enough not to ignite like matches.

171

By 1:30 in the morning I had forgotten exactly where I was. The kids were still twirling and yapping from the "*Oklahoma!*" tornado and someone said, "Miss P., are we here for the night? I'm tired and hungry!"

"Help yourself to the ketchup packets at your tables, kids. Some presidents consider Heinz ketchup a vegetable," I said, sounding a little tiddly, like Queen Elizabeth on a toot. I was clearly out of my mind, dying for sleep and a couple Quarter Pounders with heavy pickles.

Why would I put myself through this? And then, I remembered...

I, like my father before me, like most educators, needed supplemental income: painting for the county board of ed; pie baking; crafting for Christmas Bazaars; directing; summer school teaching; Upward Bound teaching; house painting; cashiering; selling Avon; and the king of all kings, Amway----all second or third jobs that had a pay check attached. Five hundred dollars, the fee given a play sponsor, didn't go far when she sank most of that amount in play necessities, like chic prairie bonnet gingham. Obtaining a purchase order sometimes was as complicated as Mandarin Chinese. Even if the five hundred remained in tact, it wouldn't help much should a tornado funnel the play producer's car up to, say, Indiana, Pennsylvania, with barnyard animals as passengers.

Rescue workers had at last cut up and removed the large trees from the highway. The fire department and others checked on us. It had been quite a long day.

I locked the building and stumbled to my Nova. Still there! Hooray! I was feeling refreshed, alive, hardly able to wait for the big hug I would give my mom, Miss Kitty. How I would cry and cry and say, "Mom, just hold me! I nearly died tonight! I am still reeling from the shock of it all!" Mom would say, "Oh, Lexsana! I thought I'd never see you again! I just want to hug you and not let go!" Then we'd sit down and have a cruller and she'd make coffee and we would spend the rest of the night talking about tornadic activity and apple recipes and all the beautiful music in "*Oklahoma!*"

When I finally got home at three o'clock in the morning, I ran across the backyard, blocking out post-tornado/tomato ketchup hell. I didn't remember going to bed. But I can recall that moving reunion with my mother, seated at her living room vantage point, waiting for me in jammies, robe, and slippers.

"**Where have you been**? Is there no phone in that high school? You should have phoned."

There was no crying. No comforting. No Stroehmann crullers or coffee. I glanced around to make sure I was in the right kitchen. I felt my temper boiling like the water that was not boiling for Sanka.

"Mom! There was a tornado tonight! *(no response or facial surprise)* It nearly slammed into the damned gym! God, give me a break! I could have been killed! I had forty kids to babysit. Trees were down and no power and I had to---"

"Lexsana, *why* did you do this play? I told you not to. Directing a play is dangerous."

"It's three in the morning and I have to get up in two hours. I am *not* fighting with you!"

"Are you sure it was a bad storm? We didn't get much of a storm here. Why, I'd have heard a bad storm. I just put new batteries in my hearing aid."

Mom hated "that damned Bel-Tone," as she called it. She told the story of how that unreliable, inopportune whistling hearing aid came to be there, in her right ear. Told every boyfriend I ever dragged in the front door. More than one never entered it a second time.

"You may have to speak a little louder. I hate asking people to repeat themselves. You see, I've been going deaf since my thirties. I was out there on our lower front porch in the swing. Lexsana was a tiny baby in my arms.* Little brother was sitting on the arm at the other end, when those heavy chains broke. The swing gave way and all that heavy chain and screws fell on my skull. If my head hadn't been there, it would have killed Lexsana. And that's precisely why I can barely hear to this day. Deaf as a door nail!" she said. This original simile made her anguish and affliction almost edibly sweet, in what I call "marsh-melodramatics." Mom was just that Hollywood good.

She was angry. "Boy! Am I glad there was no tornado, because here I was by myself and I would have been petrified with you gone! What if something had happened to me? Would you have been in trouble!"

That was an often-recurring theme during the verbal jousting between us. As we got madder, the conversation got faster, like oil bubbles heated for fried chicken. I was getting fried. I was not just responsible for groceries, laundry, vacuuming, dishes, all our rescued pets, and keeping her supplied in Lancome and puzzles. I was also responsible for the outcome of any natural disasters that might befall our little home with the front porch swing of infamy.

"Night, Mom," I said, whipped, dragging up the steps, wondering if Dad's army rifle was still out in the yellow shed. I might need it. For protection.

* *"Tiny" was a purely intentional word here. Mom was careful to spare a pea-sized part of my feelings in her dramatic story. You can't look at my baby picture without wondering how my mother birthed a full-term anvil.*

174

In a few more seasons and leaps of faith, I'd been getting a pay check teaching adult ed for a dozen years. A rumor swirled that family learning was about to suffer a family breakup, namely the family learning center where I taught. There was talk our doors were closing forever, without even a going-out-of-business notice. We were the last to know.

Ida and I knew why. The one day every adult and preschooler stayed home, we only had Miss Kitty and Baby Apricot in attendance. They were the orange tabby family we rescued on the hilly grounds around our block building. Keeping those friendly cats clustered (hidden) was quite the chore some days. "Apie," as we called junior, was smart as any enrollee, able to navigate a tricycle if there were a booster hand to push. "Miss Kitty" helped with daily discipline. Our families loved them. Some children responded to fluffy kittens when they could not communicate well with adults. They were our school therapy pets, and yes, their shot records were up to date.

On the morning of the no-show, we were petting the cats and talking about how not good it was to have a school day and no attendees.

The front door opened. In walked our favorite principal with the svelte superintendent.

"Hello," Mr. F smiled to us, taking roll around my room. "I see we've got two eager learners here." What a cover! A fitting fairy tale came to mind. *Fee fie foe, fear! I smell the blood of The Closer near!*

Apricot jumped atop one of the round tables and the super petted him. That silver-haired wonder was already closing our center in his head. This man did not strike me as an animal lover, especially since his undefiled, spotless suit literally shone with antiseptic hygiene. Hosting a wildlife feline habitat within the confines of a learning center wasn't working for him.

He had it hidden, but clearly, Jack had an ax, and he was there as a bean counter, about to cut down the dried beanstock.

Two staff and four big rooms of materials to clean out by the last day of work. My friend, Karen, also learned her position was being eliminated. A Christian and one fabulous teacher, I knew that she would prayerfully help me decide my next job. That big decision was cobbler with ice cream compared to the grumpy principal who said in a snarky bark to Ida and me: "You'd better get this damned stuff outta hear. My vacation starts next week and I'm not waiting. I want those keys turned in!" And he turned his ass to both of us and it was the last time I had to look at his happy face. I grabbed up my belongings like a teacher in a blowing money chamber. My car looked like Jed Clampet's pickup, packed to overflowing, the way we hill people like it. I backed down from our white block building and started to cry.

Halfway home I realized this was not my first departure/rodeo. I'd left a school before. I'd quit teaching in 1984 after Dad died. Maybe my mistake was returning to teaching. Ida chose the path more logically traveled. She retired and took Apie and Miss Kitty with her. I rode home thinking about Ida, about Hilda, the awesome sub who filled in when Ida fell ill, and Becky, our director. It was all good. We had all contributed so much.

Explaining this job closure is proof positive that destiny always rewards, for God opened another door immediately, taking me right back into the theater.

That same June I learned I had gotten the open English position where I had student taught over twenty-five years earlier. The full-circle career was manifesting itself. It all started with my phone ringing.

"Miss Pilewski, I am about to make you an offer you can't refuse," my new principal said. "I know you have theater skills. I want you to produce our school productions, and I won't take no as an answer." I felt Deja-vu in that drama invitation call. Here was I, at forty-eight, experiencing Old Newbie Syndrome in a different position, and I thought fast. To refuse a new boss's proposal was questionable if I wanted to start off on a positive note.

"Principals are problem solvers," Dad told me many times. "*Don't* be the problem the principal has to solve." I had gotten better at not being a principal's raspberry seed under his partial plate. But if I said no to play producing, I would be creating my first problem.

"Can I think about it?" I asked, but I already knew what I'd be doing come early spring of 2003. Director Gregg Brown and I would be casting a show. And to make things extra easy and a little familiar, we would produce a musical that would be right for the season and the area. We would find the right talent, the right cowboy dancers, and I knew where we could get a surrey with fringe and that iconic Little Wonder, the one that had survived the earlier tornado. And so, *Oklahoma!* enjoyed a revival in a different school theater, but troubled winds blew once more.

That Sunday night in April 1990 was a cast dinner between final dress rehearsals. Everyone ate like the ranch hands we all were. During the cleanup parts of the second run-through, several adults appeared in the double doors. They approached and asked to speak to Josh, who was playing Jud Fry. In a few moments Josh burst into wails

177

and tears, a young man in shock by awful news.

"My father just died!" Josh said to Gregg and me, in frantic breaths, looking around the room, ready to bolt.

Dear Heavenly Father! What does one say to a young man when that deepest tragedy hits without warning? Rehearsal stopped. Nobody said a word, but as if on cue, the cast began moving into a circle, surrounding Josh, everyone hugging, crying. We stayed that way a long time. Finally, after Jud left with relatives, we again spoke, this time about consequences and solutions. Without Jud Fry, there would be no show.

"What do we do now?" someone in the cast asked. I answered, "We honor his dad by going on. Josh wouldn't want the show canceled, right?"

"But what about his part? Who will be Jud?" another asked.

"I will," said Liam, a teacher's dream of a student, portraying the territory sheriff. "I know the lines. I'll stay up all night and learn it by Tuesday morning show time." And he would. He was a brilliant student, a nice young man. I had graduated college with his parents. They were so wonderful, I sometimes wished they were my parents.

That night required an extra staff meeting. I got home late. I couldn't wait to convey everything to my mother, who would offer support and a few helpful suggestions. She knew things! Because she reminded me of this all...the...time.

Instead, I got a wallop of a welcome. And there they were! Those four words that were my reality check. "WHERE HAVE YOU BEEN?" Then, she added,"What time was play practice over? Doesn't that school have a phone? Why don't you ever call me? That school is on a lonely road. Hoodlums travel those kind of roads. I know.

178

(*See? She knew things!*) They're just waiting for blondes alone in fancy Outback Subarus to come along so they can follow behind and take advantage of them. And you know what *that* means!"

No, Mom, what does that mean? Maybe you need to make me some flash cards!

"Did you just say something?" she asked, pricking up her ears.

"Good night, Mom. I'll scoop the litter pan. And I'll walk the dogs."

"You should have called!"

These encounters always led to my thinking creatively about common household items. Surely one of them could aid in my self-inflicted demise: curtain tiebacks, an old pack of matches from my town's First National Bank, defunct for decades, Dad's turpentine. Or, maybe I would just run down the steps full throttle and crash my head into the low stair landing. But, if I were conscious, Mom's face would be hovering over mine. She would say: "I told you to duck your head, Lexsana. You never listen. I know these things. Steps can be dangerous. I knew you'd hurt yourself one day. You're bleeding on the new carpet, right on the landing where all the relatives will step when they visit. How am I going to explain *that*?"

How did I function normally in society?

Fear was one of the dark clouds Mom projected over my head, with the daily rain. God! How my southern belle momma loved me!

The next Tuesday, we would perform "*Oklahoma!*" for the student body. Jud came through those theater doors bright and early, ready for showtime. We were stunned, the entire cast applauding, again forming a circle of support around him.

"I want to dedicate my performance to my father," Josh told us.

We'd already planned that announcement/ voiceover. This young man had had some rough rehearsals but by curtain, he was as good as Broadway bound. He got thunderous applause and I saw his tears. A young man was about to graduate and go into military life. He'd already had the worst of boot camp hell the previous few days.

Every musical that followed (and there were several) involved a crisis (and there were many). From lockdowns and fire alarms set off by stage smoke during *Little Shop of Horrors*, to acts-of-God weather events. During the musical, "Seussical," cast members were scheduled to appear on the noon news community spot.

An impressive snow had canceled school. When I arrived, brilliant Tanner, the Cat in the Hat, had some sorrowful rhyming news: "We can't go....It's shocking.... I know....I know... The principal says since there's no school today… we can't appear on Channel 12 anyway....."

The theater had turned me into a full-on DBUD stormer. I stormed into the principal's office. "Why can't these kids go on TV? They got here, even though there's no school, and they're out there in full costume. That damned cat face isn't easy to apply, either."

Principal was the calmer to my stormer. "Whoa.... deep breaths," he said. "The county policy is that if there's no school due to a weather event, then there's no extra-curricular activities." One thing about that principal I had learned over time. He did hold back with control, especially when crazed women were yelling at him until their earrings flew off.

"I know that!" I continued with my vein-popping rant. "Listen, this isn't a stupid ball game. This is television! This spot was planned months ago. You just don't *not* show up after a station puts you on the damned news. You know what that means to them? Dead air time, that's what. If you ever want them to cover anything out here again, you'd better let us go. We're supposed to be there five minutes ago."

We waited for the official decree from her royal superintendent-ness. She was merciful. Key cast members were already in seat belts, and when the principal said go, Dale Earnhardt, Jr. had nothing on me. Mayzie La Bird lost some yellow tail feathers. Horton the Elephant got flapped in the face with his own ears. The cat's hat toppled. We were late, but anchor Don Graye was exceptionally professional and we pitched our show to the viewers. Every obstacle was as worth it as the pangs of childbirth.* As any play producer will tell you, the show does go on and the awesomely-talented kids who find their perfect fit in theater, help make it go on.

During *Oliver*, the brooding young man playing Bill Sykes revealed he could not perform because he could not remember lines and had other emotional issues. From his angry posture, I believed him. Why was it always the actor playing the villain who had the life issues?

A colleague---and my future husband---had already earned my respect in building an amazing stage bridge over the Thames. We called it our "Bridge Over Troubled [Theatrical] Water." And if that weren't sufficient to hook me, he quickly drafted one of his vo-ag (vocational agriculture) boys as the new, improved Bill Sykes. Nick was a tall building made fully of concrete and untapped

---

I never gave birth, but my mom had and she reminded me often what she went through, even though in that age of obstetrics, Dr. Rose knocked out all mothers-about-to-be before the blessed event. VERY harrowing!

abilities. That wonderful colleague allowed his protégé class time to run lines with another student. Out popped an amazing Cockney accent and a realistic darkness that made even the orchestra pit shutter.

"Who are you, and where were you the past four years of auditions?" I asked him.

Nick and a talented cast saved our floundering behinds. The dramedy continued. To show my colleague the full measure of my gratitude, I eventually agreed to marry him. After all, I sang to him with Oliver's accent, "I'd do anything for you, dear, anything......" That translated to him as our eventual "getting hitched."

During *Annie Get Your Gun* rehearsals, flooding occurred, and for the show to go on, a couple students had to row across Ten Mile Creek (not the creek's width, thankfully) to reach the road and get to school by curtain time.

One no-good bad day before an opening, a colleague at school remarked, "Lexsana enjoys being the martyr." Word traveled straight back the hall to my room. I want to tell that colleague something I could not say then, because I was gravely offended, as was my performance ability. I am pretty sure I would insult martyrs everywhere by being lumped in with the conquering spirits of that singular genre. But, in hindsight, I may be one hell of an actress. If I weren't such a method actor with extra control, *would I have taken that crack from you without a fight, toots*?

Mel Brooks, lyricist/book author and demigod of *The Producers*, was thinking a lot about the producer's lot when he wrote the funniest musical in the world. I wrote this little song parody straight from that show, as an homage to the high school teacher-sap who produces show after show and threatens every semester to quit the madness but stays. I've sung it in my head many times:

I wanna be a producer-r-r-r
And pitch a fit the old broad's way
I wanna be a producer
Dine at Burger King every day

I wanna be a producer
And sleep in till half-past six
I wanna be a producer
And burn the candle at both wicks

I wanna be a producer
Wear some faux mink, gems, et al
I wanna be a producer
And see my name-----
on the bathroom wall?
On opening night!!!
What??----"Pilewski SUCKS"???!!!

Little Women, the eighth production I produced at that school, shrank my health until I really was a little woman, whisked to the hospital with a serious infection. I missed weeks of school. The wound required packing every day. Mornings were not orange juice and bud vases. What joy it was to have my colleague/future husband see me that way. He didn't care in the least. His gentle hands took that eight-inch pointy wooden swab and stuffed clean packing deep into my left shin and under my right arm every day. The pain seemed close to what a gunshot must feel like.

But opening night of *LW*, I was in the hospital, dreaming of the entire cast coming through the door, in tableau, singing "Off to Massachusetts" for me—Jo, Meg, Marmie, the whole lot of the Marsh family. It didn't happen. That is when I admitted the show does go on, but this time, not the way I wanted it to. Either my expectations were too great, or people just don't have time for hospital visiting any more.

I'd been balancing too many weights between school and home, with my mother in failing health. In your fifties, it's time to increase your vocabulary usage to include this foreign-sounding phrase: "No! Enough!" Right there I learned something. Sometimes we are forced to make some really serious decisions lying flat out in an uncomfortable hospital bed. Sometimes, we know in our hearts those decisions already.

I noticed when I turned my head to the large picture window in my hospital room, I was framed in its reflection, a minor character without words. Hell yes, I felt sorry for myself. I had no one else to blame. *Are you telling me something, God?* The light streaming in from sunset's blazing orange burned so brightly I closed my eyes. I looked out again but couldn't focus.

Everything I looked at had a halo around it.

"Oh Dear God! This better be angels and not cataracts," I prayed. "NO ONE touches my eyes!" *Sure...*

I laid there in bed thinking deeply, a convalescing prospector sifting the bad out until only the good thoughts and actions remained. All was not bad, because with every show came a rush when the show hit high on the applause meter.

Even so, it would take this hospital stay to realize I had always been too busy talking big and fast and hurrying like a triage doctor to listen to Someone who could either kill or heal me. Where was that old lusting fire to be the burning martyr? Extinguished.

184

Emergency surgery yet again. I felt the ER doctor draw a large circle around my red left breast before I was put in a private room. Later that night I was facing surgery alone. My legs jumped around the operating table in outright fear. I wondered if I would wake up. The entire team of surgical nurses surrounded me, stroking my arms, smiling, promising that I would be fine and in good hands. "God sends us angels," I heard my Dad saying. Tonight, they were nurses.

It was difficult not to embarrass myself, but I started to cry anyway. I called forth some funny movie scenes in the bright overhead light and started praying. My God! I had regressed to the age of eight, remembering a scared somewhat-little girl, mask over my frightened face, prepped for that emergency tonsillectomy.

As I drifted off to sleep 'n slice land this time, I hated that my less-than-Kardashian breast was about to be the focal point for discussion the next hour and a half. Appropriately, that fact made *me* a little woman. I wanted to wake up with the same paltry mammary material with which I fell asleep. Gales of applause would be nice, honoring my brave acting talents, smiling through tears.

But first, I just wanted my daddy.

I finally closed up my little suitcase of producer things and, with minor reluctance, handed it off to a younger teacher, Ashley, for good.

And then, the voices started, both real and imagined:

Real:

"You're getting 'of a certain age,' Lexsana. Things start falling apart. You can't do everything. You just need a hobby. Stay home and write. You enjoy doing that," Mom said.

And maybe, imagined voice:

"Finally! A half a century later, she *hears* me! Sto-o-p-p wearing the shoulder pads! I'm tapping, tapping you on the shoulder and you can't even feel it. Your shoulders are fine. I mean, I made them for you, right? Who do you trust more, your mother, or me?" I believed I heard the voice of God again, celebrating my little breakthrough, my suitcase handoff. And he sounded suspiciously like Mel Brooks.

My time in the theater went dark.

Note: My choices got me in heaps of trouble, yet I stubbornly wouldn't quit. I want to blame my parents for always telling me not to give up. "Giving up shows weakness." But, I found out, so did staying the course. My inner voice was screaming at me, like Mick growel-yelling to Rocky in the ring, "You've taken one to the leg! It's cellulitis! Stay down, Lexy! Stay down!" But getting up was what I continued to do, staggering a bit. On crutches or in a wheel chair, in school or dying at home, I wasn't impressing anyone. At least I learned that from teaching, me, the pugilist pedagogue, fighting through like the champ I didn't have to be. Eventually, I heard footsteps. It wasn't a group of girls wanting a pass to my room to work on projects. It was Time. I paid him no mind.

How I Got Rooked -- A "Humane Tail"

Family Connections, our little school of parents and preschoolers and a staff of three, had found a good home on the campus of my favorite elementary school. Partnering with the elementary school grafted us into a few of their awards and honors. Unfortunately, one award eventually turned into my brush with pseudo-celebrity purgatory. The main elementary campus was quite the pseudo-celebrity itself, churning out high test scores of readers as leaders. Adult students one building up were getting their GEDs somehow, even with me as their teacher. It created the perfect storm for recognition. Washington D.C. took notice. So much so that our elementary school got a national reading recognition. Our little department was invited to travel with the main campus reading teachers elite and receive the award in Atlanta, home of the Braves, CNN, and grits on everything. I loved grits!

Georgia braced for fifty nationwide winning teams of party animal educators. The award dinner turned out to be a high key big deal. Walter Anderson, author and then editor of *Parade* magazine, distributed the state awards, which meant West Virginia had much obligatory hand clapping before our low-on-the-alphabet state would be called forth to smile, wave, and receive. What a nice man he was, autographing copies of his book and posing with us for pictures. After pictures, we invaded the City of Peaches.

We were all still in the mall age/phases of our lives: Lisa, Libby, Donna, and I, ripe for shopping. Lisa was looking for wedding gowns, something foreign to me as dirty martinis. I couldn't concentrate on our hunting expedition once inside, for CNN was there, about to broadcast live my mother's favorite talk news show. Here was an impressive theater in the round, with lights, cables, cameras, and important lackeys with thick headsets.

"Have you guys ever watched *Talk Back Live* on CNN?" I asked, giving them that "Johnny just called me a dike" sad face that instantly stirs both commiseration and support in colleagues. It's part of the sisterhood of educators that when out on furlough, where everyone deserves indulgence, lady teachers will go along with just about everything. With amiable "why not's?" all around, we lined up for free passes, picking out seats.

"Do you know who Susan Rook is?" I asked them with great glee. "She's the host of this news show. My mom just loves her." I was all up in my own joy, but looking at them, I saw their one question through fake interest smiles, "Who's Susan Rook?"

Each audience member had the opportunity to write a brilliant question for real-life asking on camera. I've forgotten the topic that day, but I just wanted to meet Susan Rook. My mother fully loved watching her. I was there for an autograph and I would get it, because 1) I loved a challenge and 2) if someone ever let it slip I rubbed elbows with THE Susan Rook and didn't tackle her for her signature, I would be dead to my mom, canceled like a too-wholesome sit com on cable.

"Ms. Rook?" I approached her afterwards, ready with my pity story card, which I was a little ashamed of pulling out, though it was true. "My mother is a big fan of yours. She watches your show every day and, truth be told, wishes you were her daughter. Anyway, she's having a breast procedure next week. It would mean a lot if I could take her home your autograph."

"Come with me," she said. "I understand about health scares. We'll go up the escalator to my office and I'll sign a picture for you." I turned and gave the girls my "Holy crap! This is happening!" face and they smiled back. "We'll wait right here," Donna said.

It was a big office with more empty desks than people. Nobody looked at us. They only looked up if someone staggered in with an ax in his arm. Those noses-for-news reporters had no time for star-struck Rook-ies because they were CNN and they were the most trusted news team in the galaxy.

I thought about my old trip to Atlanta where my cousins had just moved. Traffic in Atlanta was menacing, but I just *had* to get to CNN for a job. We could see those major-news tall red CNN letters from the Interstate, but they eventually faded away as we found our way back to Norcross, defeated.

Now, here I was, standing on their major news network carpet, picturing myself with a dumpster-sized bin, delivering their mail. What might have been! How I'd wanted to work there after I quit teaching *the first time*. Like waiting in eighth grade for Dorothy Belle, here was another slice of Heaven for me one floor up from our ground-floor shopping expedition. Why was Blue Heaven always just one flight above my head?

She signed the photo "To: Kitty, Love and Best Wishes, Susan Rook." She was a big-boned beauty and it seemed like she had the world by its proverbial tail. Ms. Rook even wrote down her office number. "Let me know how your mom's procedure goes." On her crowded desk in that large hospital ward for journalists were many little wind-up critters. She handed me a tiny plastic rabbit who drove himself crazy driving around in circles, just

189

like me on my earlier, directionless CNN trek. He clacked when you wound him up. Big ears. Big teeth. Interesting choice. Was that rabbit the hare of friendship between two professionals? "Give this to your mom, from me. Guaranteed for a smile."

I had the picture and the big-toothed directionless hare, so now I just got ballsy. "Susan, would you ever consider a travel stop to Clarksburg, West Virginia, to speak at a Humane Society banquet?"

I blurted it out without thinking it through. I had to produce a fundraiser on that board or I would soon be strapped to the "Eject" button seat of honor. At this point she was discreetly moving me to the escalator. She knew now for sure I was a stan (stalker + fan).

"What would you want me to talk about?" she asked, confused. This from the host of *Talk Back Live* who earned a living talking on talking points.

"It's a fundraiser for our local humane society. Are you even mildly an animal lover?" I asked.

"Sure, just call with the details and we'll try and arrange something, okay?"

This was extremely foreign-sounding for the entrenched educator. Our lives were planned down to the millisecond, including bodily functions. Our plans had to reflect embedded everything, from getting a fountain drink (no, not BK Coke Zero with flavor fixin's, *hall fountain* slurps with lukewarm water and spat snuff) to multi-cultural inclusions (not even mandated at the state ed level). Multi-cultural activities might include, but not be limited to: Hindu Sanskrit word searches with definitions; recipes with harissa, siracha, or curry; or Native American ritual dances taught via video link by hottie wolf dancer, Kevin Costner. But "we'll try and arrange something" was not in my plan house.

For sure, this was the celebrity brush-off. That banquet would never happen. When I said goodbye I couldn't wait to hop back to my ed friends and relay every word. Was it remotely possible I could score BIG with the Humane Society board? I had just asked a celebrity journalist to deliver a God-knows-what-topic speech to a vast audience of Susan Rook worshippers at a banquet I would have to arrange, including her travel. A cinch! What could be easier?

"Wow, nice," they all said, nodding approvingly, the way over-fifty friends lie to each other when trying on skinny jeans in another state, far away from their students.

The entire next month was another hit on the DBUD bath-of-fire prophecy scale from so many years earlier. The soon-to-be-speaker-less fundraiser was not going smoothly. There was no connecting flight for Ms. Rook from Pittsburgh to Bridgeport on the scheduled Saturday of the banquet. Barb, a fellow board member, had to ask Dr. Church, a heart doctor and a happy pilot with appropriate transportation, to fly to Pitt Airport and scoop up Rooks I and II (Susan and her personal assistant).

It took days to finalize. Everyone I called (A through Z of the C & P Telephone Directory) to invite to Via Veneto for the banquet personally expressed what the masses (minus my mother) were chorusing, "Who's Susan Rook?"

Susan Rook was practically on her way, though things still looked grim.

"So, I was hoping, senator, that you and your lovely wife might be able to----"

"----Um, now who is speaking? Would I be speaking?" the senator asked.

"No. No, Susan Rook is the keynote speaker."

"Yeah, I don't know who that is. We have another fundraiser that day. Two would be pushing it," he said.

I was begging people to come to this dinner. This needed to go well, because I had a mother who expected to be Queen [Elizabeth] for a Day, and because I was one mother of an approval seeker, an apple head apple polisher. I did what I've seen female teachers do right before Thanksgiving. When there is no time to visit the stylist and the holidays have rendered women fuzz heads before the five-day labor of feast prep, women grab shears. I grabbed a pair of pinking shears and went for my neck. In fifteen minutes, I was wearing an old, old Carol Burnett do from 1970-ish. It's so true that you can always tell a woman in crisis based on the deckled-edge crew cut she self-styles to save herself from harming someone else. I stood there looking at my squirrel reflection in the mirror, except I was a *square*-head squirrel about to be totally nut free, meaning flat broke.

I was in muddy water up to my deranged eyes, like Captain Willard (Martin Sheen) in *Apocalypse Now*. Further, I found out that planning a fundraiser in the middle of vacation season will not yield immediate Disney World cancellations for one dinner with one unknown female journalist. But at least those rich folks were polite enough to lengthen their invitation-declining phone call. After thanking me for thinking of them, the same question got asked, "Who's Susan Rook?"

"Ron?" I said, calling House of Delegates member Ron Fragale, who I'd taught with in my original bath-of-fire days of impersonating a teacher. He was a good guy. He wouldn't tell me no. "I'm planning this great fundraiser for the Humane Society and Susan Rook of *Talk Back Live* will be the keynote speaker. Would love it if you and your wife could come."

"Wow, thanks so much for the personal invitation, Lexsana," he said the way cool delegates thank the crowds at spaghetti dinners before elections. He was pretty sure he knew who Susan Rook was! And, he and his wife would attend! This was huge for me, he and his wife doubling the attendance that way!

Feeling validated by the yeppers, I mustered my best invitation plea, straight from my revised phone script, yielding a smattering of obliging acceptances. I did vocal warm-ups ("Lexsana is not a lousy loser") five times in rapid succession to keep my throat moist and non-desperate sounding. I was sure I was slaying it on the phone now with my rebranded pitch.

"How do we purchase tickets?" someone asked me on the phone. I about died.

"Tickets! I'll call you back with that information," I promised vaguely, because I'd forgotten the necessity of tickets. I hadn't had the tickets printed. *Ka-ching!*

Rook at us at the airfield! Her Girl Friday, me and that damned pink pantsuit I wore to meet important people, Aunt Patty, CNN's Susan Rook, and my star-struck Mom meeting her adoptive daughter for the first time!

My eager mother, my Aunt Patty, and Percy Ashcraft, member of the House of Delegates, joined me at the Bridgeport Airport to greet Susan and Her Girl Friday. I had a bouquet of flowers ready. The bouquet and Percy both smelled pretty good.

"Who's Susan Rook?" he asked as we stood a short distance from the air strip, his arms crossed in fine Percy fashion. No security was necessary, because nothing wicked happened at airports in the years leading up to 2000, except for a handful of bigger-city old Moonies selling very old flowers.

"You're not the first inquiring mind to ask me that," I answered him.

Incoming! Dr. Church to the rescue, my hero delivering Rooks I and II. We waited for her to descend the short steps to vast scores of adoring fans (the four of us). I introduced all the women, then Percy. I think he spoke for all of us when he finally got a chance to speak for all of us. He drove our guest entourage to the banquet. I don't know how he, Susan, and Friday all fit in that big Mercury Cougar of his.

The banquet was small. I ate little of the lovely spread of selections: pastas, chicken, salad, vegetables, dessert choices, the best not-gourmet fare that Lexsana's big-bucks teacher check could charge on her Visa. I spoke, tossing in a literary quote of flattery while introducing Susan. Everyone smiled vaguely, as though I'd tried to teach them future perfect tense, as in "Don't worry, in a year you *will have forgotten* me and this dinner lemon, at least, I hope so." Their pity clap, something I just seemed to draw out of people repeatedly, and their unnatural half-smiles barely masked their clueless question: "Who is this Susan Rook you speak of?" followed closely by, "Is there cheesecake?"

194

When I finished my introduction, I returned to the head table. I, the head table's English and speech teacher, had a silent question: *Where were her note cards?* I realized Susan had pulled an Abe-Lincoln-on-the-train-to-Gettysburg speech, jotting five words on a grocer's coupon. I scanned the banquet prisoners' weak applause because it sounded a little like they were wearing gloves.

"Um, I don't have a watch with me. I need to know what time I begin and end," Susan said to me. No doubt, this was second nature, needing a visual clock, hosting an hour-long TV show with CNN sponsors and timed-out interviews. I got that.

"Oh! Well...here, have mine," I said, unclasping my favorite watch, a unique little brass parade of doggies linked noses-to-tails, marching around my wrist. I'd had that timepiece a very long time, two whole months; I wanted to tighten my grip as she took it and put it on her own wrist, walking away to the podium. I sat there and imagined it's the way most mother dogs feel when their babies are ripped away from them abruptly. Goodbye, appropriate animal-themed banquet watch that I wanted to wear some day in my casket. Me, the crazy dog lady (which is another book).

I didn't pay enough attention to Susan's speech. I kept thinking: 1) Hope I get my watch back and 2) Is she charging by the word, because remarkably, she made discourse from a fifty cents off coupon. A celebrity can stand before a mic and just say, "My actual roots are greener than McDonald's pickles!" to screams and applause. But I stand before a seated tribe of teenagers and deliver a haunting, memorized wintertime rendition of *Stopping by Woods on a Snowy Evening* by Robert Frost, and I get one hand up. Not the church praise hand up. The "I gotta pee, like right now!" hand. But maybe my poetry reading talent from my intense college oral interpretation class came from Professor Venita Zinn. I lovingly say Venita was a starita ---in *Our Gang/Little Rascals* comedy shorts in Hollywood in her younger days. She tweaked a syllable, intoned it to a fine aria. Why wouldn't I think I was slaying Frost, reciting those poetry lines until the temperature dropped in my class and icicles formed on my face. My most captivated student felt those fervent words on his insides, as if sitting in that chilly sleigh, frosting his renal region. He had to *go!!!*

He r-r-r-eally wanted to go. That handy-up kid had gotten a silent text: **Drug Sale! Bathroom! Five Minutes!!!!** He didn't go.

But I digress. Because I am retired and lesson plan withdrawal has left me ... more patternless, easily distracted, and overly-spontaneous. A teacher's mind is a terrible thing to take "off schedule." Thus, I digress again.

In a show I had directed for the Art Center, *The Front Page*, Hildy Johnson, a star newspaper reporter for the *Examiner*, has been trying to escape editor Walter Burns' attempts to keep him from marrying and leaving the paper. After many failed attempts to rein Hildy back in, Walter has a thug take Walter's own watch and gently plant it in Hildy's pocket. Hildy and his fiancé go to the train station to head for their new life. As the play ends, Walter smiles, dialing law enforcement. He yells as he tells the police to detain Hildy at the train station. "Arrest him," he orders. "The son-of-a-bitch stole my watch!"

Susan wasn't rooking around. She flew out that door, on schedule, escorted back to the airport, where Dr. Church would be waiting meanwhile, perhaps doing mobile surgeries right on the tarmac.

The banquet was over. Toast. I smiled like a wild-eyed ventriloquist's dummy because that's what I do before I fall over dead from crazed exhaustion. My eyes bug and I can't fully close my own smiling mouth. That end line from *The Front Page*, came back to me, post-disaster. When I got back in my car to go home, I made a mental list of all the places I might find spare change on which to live the next two weeks. I looked down to note the time my whole Hindenburg had crashed. *No watch*. I thought about Walter and that well-placed phone call in the play. Too bad I hadn't thought about it sooner before the guest of honor beat a retreat with my litter of brass puppies crying, clinging to her abducting arm.

Rook II remained behind to attend the Miss West Virginia Pageant that night. "I've never been to a state pageant," she gushed, her pony tail scrunchie still on her wrist. That meant a hotel tab for wherever she stayed. I would have to pick up that bill at some point, too.

Now *I* needed a fundraiser. I had as much chance of paying off this debt as a deer in the Wild and Wonderful West Virginia hillsides in mid-November.

What was I thinking when I set up Barnum & Bailey's Colossal-Fail Banquet? Being on a board of anything requires mutual funds, lucrative book deals, and a rich old spouse who may have been Clark Gable's movie physician in the fifties.

Teachers know our rewards are _not_ our paychecks. Still, we can only drive by the new housing developments in dark glasses and drool, "One thing I can tell you about that house with four garage stalls. No teacher lives there!" Our gems are either simulants or beach finds hot glued onto shower curtain rings. We can take an old bed sheet and make it double as everything from table linens to handkerchiefs. Our dinner tables cluck with chicken, and worst of all, we re-gift. And, for the really random "local color" portion of teacher frugality, there's this: any teacher with DNA roots to alcohol stills who's worth his weight in corn, knows how to get from mash to moonshine minus the essential long-handled spoon and a reduced amount of corn. We mountaineers call that "liquid conservation," livin' large off the land.

Rook II's staying over meant a gas fill-up then a trip to Pittsburgh Airport following breakfast Sunday morning. I picked her up and when Eat 'n Park burned my Belgian waffle, I knew it was a sign. I always got lost like a toad in a hailstorm in Pittsburgh. Signs of doom were easy to read. State route signs…no.

I saw Rook II off, waving at the boarding gate. Oh my God! What a scourge from another brilliant plan gone to perdition. Did I ever learn? No. Did I remember exactly where I'd parked? No. There it was, the curse of the apple head. Teacher to hundreds, learner of nothing. I'd wrapped another predictable episode of *I Love Lexy*.

I *did* get lost headed out of the city, after finding my Lumina. Headed *out of the city. Who does that?* When I finally got past Waynesburg, I was going home for yet another private breakdown with tears, an hour of red nose blowing, and two hours of kicking the Serta, asking with Nancy Kerrigan-style weeping, *"Why? Why-y-y-y?"*

So, in the spirit of reteach-reinforce, I asked myself later over pie what I had learned from one more bath of fire. My mother joined in.

"Wasn't today fun?" she asked. "Bushels," I answered. "Yes, everyone just loved Susan. What a great gal!" "She's a---peach," I said, and sliced more pie with angry ease.

Not only did I admit I was my own worst enemy, always taking on too much, but I also realized I was my own worst student. I never listened to the still small voice of low-key choices. Here was a crash, a cheek-burner for its organizer. I felt hypocritical. I was always lecturing to teens to change, then mad and hurt when they got called yet again to the principal's office. But, as reading specialist Bev Eisele reminded me during a school visit, "Hey, to a child needing approval or love, negative attention is still attention." Would this finally be the moment I kicked the habit of seeking out attention, universal approval? No, no it would not.

I _might have_ learned that sometimes, instead of aging the body five years planning a bomb of a dinner, it's easier to pick up the phone and speed dial the bank. I _could have_ saved time and a smooth several hundred by transferring savings to checking and writing that donation straight to one of my favorite charities, The Humane Society of Harrison County.

But that near lesson faded fast. I would eventually need more projects to complete me, validate me, punish me. It's what I thought I needed to do. This woe without end was a slavish, servile circle of life I'd drawn around myself.

A Much Lesser-Known T.O.Y. Story

Picture it...We were about to begin Beowulf, dragon master/hero champ of the Geats, who, I assured my seniors, was a hero to many. "Alright, class...with a partner" (------- "Miss Pilewski, did you just say 'teats'?")---- ----make a list of ten of your ultimate heroes. Justify your choices, explaining in complete sentences what makes them so heroic. Let's say ten minutes. Go!"

I liked this new bell ringer business! Ten minutes would give me time to take roll, which I always forgot to do, and put my Stouffer's frozen entree in my mini fridge/freezer, so I would avoid a ptomaine event.

Glitch! ---Nobody in that class went go. Just dead air and blank faces, like Anglican royals getting a dose of preached soul at an American actress/princess's royal wedding. Then, the barrage: *"Ten?"* "Can we just make it none?" "Do we have to use a pen?" "Do you have a pen I can use the rest of the semester, even though I'll lose it?" "Is this a class participation grade?" and the clincher: "I don't have any heroes. Honest to God. I don't. There's nobody to look up to."

Yessir, I LOVED TEACHING!!!--- "Yes, you have at least one hero, and they don't have to be famous people, because heroes can be well, almost anybody, right?"

Too bad I hadn't auditioned for Disney World. But, since they didn't allow facial hair....

Fortunately, for this particular bell ringer of pre-lesson Beowulf heroes, I had anticipated glitches. I had prepped a backup package for the bell ringer, in case of dead air and blank faces. I told the story from 1982 of Lenny Skutnik, a federal worker who jumped off the 14th Street Bridge into the January ice of the Potomac River. I described how he saved a drowning flight attendant from an Air Florida flight when it skidded off the runway. Her frozen hands could not hold onto the lifesaver dangling from the rescue operator. Skutnik's tall leap from the bridge shocked his entire system, but he was able to drag the woman to safety. "I'm not a hero," Lenny said later. "I just did what anyone else would have." ----*Silence all around*...

"And class, shouldn't a hero be that amazingly humble?" My seniors did not care about flawed, old heroes or ancient Teat Geats in canoes.

"No one would do what that guy had done and risk drowning," and then: "The world is Lenny-less!" They tore into a popcorn commentary around the room, telling me they were over being disappointed and let down by celebrities and athletes and the cast of *Atlanta Housewives*. They were sick of hollow stars, as they called them, repulsed by these "drunks, whores, cheaters" wearing the mantle of celebrity while secretly screwing mankind's vulnerable belief systems.

"Well then, you're going to love Beowulf!" I smiled, raising my eyebrows, nodding.

Now *I* had no heroes! They had turned my ship of hope around, written off the entire subject, and called it a day at 9:45 a.m.

But, of course, I promised ten free minutes at the end of class to get them to put stubby or borrowed pencils

201

to paper. Only one answer popped up on multiple lists: grandparents. Why had I assumed that teenagers found oldsters too early twentieth century? Grandparents were some kids' primary parents, for whatever reason. I had never considered all this. While I assumed they were insulted by graysters getting in their pathway to the food court at the mall, elders meant nobility, wisdom, and most importantly, *home.*

Though my assignment was shot, I briefly considered what I'd have felt had I two parents *some place* but was being raised by two grandparents, or an aunt, or worse, no one. But, there was hope for the ages, in one generation revering another. For once in my life, I wished I were older, not to retire, but to gain more of their respect.

"Who's your hero, Miss P.?" a senior asked. They took to heart when I told them I would never make them do anything I would not also do.

"Besides Lenny Skutnik?　　Well.....Jesus..... um, Thoreau, (----"Justin Theroux, really?")----Emily Dickinson, my dad, Lincoln, and.............Sheriff Woody."

"Nooooo! *Toy Story* Woody? Wait! Really?" they asked. "You're funny!" someone laughed and someone else added, "No! She means it!" Then this: "You *do know* he's a Disney toy, right, Miss P.?" Further laughter.

"I realize he's not real. But.....oohhhhh, how I l-o-o-ove those surprised eyes, those natural gas pipe arms flailing, teeth white as hot grits, tight jeans, tiny caboose, silver spurs.....Yep, if he were real, I'd be married."

That classroom got quiet fast, more like frozen, except for the plop of some gum wads dropping out of mouths onto blank hero short lists. I would never call on my acting skills again, or finish any thought my conscience advised me against. There was no point now in sharing that

I had Sheriff Woody sheets with "Toys Forever" written across the pillow cases. I did not want to experience a medical Code Blue in my room.

"Who wants to wear my Viking helmet and be big ol' King Bey?" I asked, to deflect their attention and mental images elsewhere.

...Somehow, I never quite verbally got my true smarts across, because, as my mother loved to point out, "Lexsana, you say too much. With you, there is never any mystery, and *surprise*! ---people [meaning tall, dark, and full-head-of-handsome-haired men], like a good mystery." Mom used her own kind of bell ringers on me.

My stupid admission about Woody stayed with me. Would my fourth-grade teacher, Georgie Washington, have said something like that to a class of fourth graders? I could see her towering over me still, shaking her yellow-white head, withered lips tight with disgust. "You'll *never* be the teacher I am, tubby, because you can't be tough. You're afraid you'll offend somebody and then they won't like you. You can't stand up for yourself. And you tell too much, like your mother just said."

A couple school days after The Woody Reveal, I crawled to my desk at 1:25, spent. It was fourth block, my ninety-minute planning time till the end of the day.

My mother, who wouldn't go to bed the previous night until she had 39 Across locked down ("a bread crumb") in the evening puzzle, kept me up till 1:00 in the morning, talking about that book of southern wisdom she'd never finished.

Sure as I was her second-favorite child, the next morning she'd have an update on my puffy eyes. "Lexsana, your eyes are puffy, just like your dad's. You surely didn't get that from me. And put on some lipstick." Never mind I'd just come down the stairs still asleep and just stepped barefooted into a cold, squishy, long hairball.

My lack of sleep and baggy bulges had nothing to do with 39 Across. I put an ice cube in a wash cloth and tapped those flubber-puffs hanging under my eyes, my consolation being that I had a new vocab word and, if desperate enough, could use it for a bell ringer---"ort". An ort was a bread crumb, for 39 Across. It would be a cinch to remember, having so many orts in my own life and hot rolls and butter being God's most perfect food duo.

It had been a trying third block of enough freshmen to fill *The Voice's* audience seats, twice as loud. The fourth block tardy bell rang and the rumbling floors fell silent. I locked my door, counted the days till Spring Break, took the pillow out of my wooden rocker from Goodwill, and put my head down. It was 1:35, and on this one day (because sleep washes the human brain), it was about to be nappy time at the automated brain wash.

I opened a couple windows. I tried to hose out all thoughts of fart smells, dried manure mud pies fallen off work boots just for me, old-school "huh-huh-huh ...huh-huh" *Beavis and Butthead* laughing at whatever about my outfit entertained them, the stench of sweat glands that exceeded my dogs' anal gland expressions. The list had no end.

Knock! Knock! went my door in fifteen minutes. I shot up, papers scattering. My Joan Rivers yellow watch had made an imprint on my left cheek. I flipped on the lights and opened the door. It was the towering bald principal, big enough to be Brad Garrett's hairless brother.

"Can I come in?" Brad's-bro asked. "I need to ask you a personal question," he said, flashing me a manila envelope. He came in my room and closed the door. Sliding out the envelope contents and narrowing his eyes, he announced, "I want you to consider doing this for me."

What exactly was on those papers he wanted done to him? I had to sit down for this.

"And what might that be?" I asked, scratching my head with an uncapped pen, rubbing my watch imprint.

"It's for a T.O.Y. award."

H-o-l-y PIXAR! Word had traveled fast down that hall about my crush on a kid's toy! Those ingrate seniors! No more punch for *them*! "Toy?" I repeated with darting eyes, wondering if he was playing me here.

"T.O.Y.---West Virginia Teacher of the Year award," principal clarified. "Who better than you? It's your time. Read this over the weekend. Think about it," he said, handing me the information. "You're a wonderful teacher. You've earned it. You love your job."

"Love" was a little too big of a word choice here.

I pictured him taking his empty Diet Coke can from lunch and spinning it, game-like, on top of the faculty directory list, where it landed and dripped its last on my name.

Crap! I had my Spring Break all planned. I would not even read a fortune cookie. No school work, just walk my dogs, eat, sleep, and hang upside down over the edge of my bed licking marshmallow creme off a spoon the entire hippity hoppin' Easter holiday.

I was not loving my job. Further, I was consuming Vitamin D3 for more energy and bone mass, half dead from being the family butler. Here was a prize offer regarding my ardor for teaching. Ordering cardboard sunglasses for three quarters from Kellogg's Tony the Tiger would have brought more joy. Something was very wrong here.

Here, yet another epiphany! The profession boat I missed was clearly----acting. The faux spring in my hallway steps down to the cafeteria, and my pearly smile and my fake lithium battery energy in class were all playing my work world but good. Suddenly, none of that acting was to my advantage.

"I really hope you'll do this," he said, leaving my classroom.

I paced through the chairs, listening to my shoes squeak, thinking how little teachers got recognized, making it even harder for a singled-out one being elevated by her principal. I smelled complexity, excommunication, and a tough Spring Break week with my mother. She'd read me the evening paper while I tried to enhance my past life experiences on that manuscript of an application. No way. But, would I be angry if someone else at my school took that manila envelope and ran with it?

No! I would <u>not</u> bend. Schoolwork was exhausting. I did not need more of it taking away my precious minutes of Spring Break. There was not enough marshmallow creme on earth for that much effort and all the comments I'd hear from my mother. I deserved one duty-free spring vacation…

"This frigging application is driving me c-r-a-a-a-z-y!" I yelled, sitting side saddle at the sofa table, hunched over my old Acer. "I'm so tired I can't remember graduating college. I'm telling these people more about me than *you* know, Mom!---Mom?"

Mom took her critical time, put down the newspaper, the glasses came off, then she answered me with a leathery tongue lash. "You should have said no,

Lexsana. Why can't you say no? I always tried to teach you that, plus, to never tell your entire love history on the first date. You make yourself a slave one way and single the other. Besides, you're never home. The dogs are all depressed. You're always too tired to talk to me very much in the evening, and---"

"---MOM! *I talk for a living.* I bet my vocal cords have a dozen lumps for all the ways I have to use my voice. I'm tired!"

"Well, I'm tired, too, and I'm thirty-two years older. I can hardly walk and I have pain all the time. You don't know what tired is. I worked for almost two years in a dusty old glass factory. And just because I didn't get to wear fancy clothes like you, doesn't make you better than me!"

"Oh, my God! Are we going there again, Mom?"

"So, explain to me! Why are you doing this award thing for a toy? What kind of toy, Lexsana? Because that's odd."

"MOM! It's not for a toy; it's a T.O.Y. AWARD, for Teacher of the Year, Mom! If I win, I get the use of a brand-new car for a year to travel and talk to schools about my teaching methods. I'd get to travel and get a break from teaching. It's a big darned deal. The principal asked ME, mom, not the other way around."

"And you couldn't say no, could you, Lexsana?" Mom never used my middle name "Kay," when angry because she didn't need to. She called me "Lex" half the time, but the madder she was she used my first name only, making those three syllables into ten, depending on her level of ire (rage, 24 Down).

How ironic! I suddenly had another epiphany. I *couldn't* say no because I'd heard it nonstop all my life from hers truly mouth. "No" was her favorite word. Why would I make someone else that miserable by saying no to anything?

Eighth Grade: "Mom, the Four Tops are coming to Morgantown! Richard's mom will drive us----"

"-----No! You're not going there. You just say no, you can't go. That's not safe!"

Eleventh Grade: "Mom, I want to go to the state fair in July with----"

"-----No! You're not going that far in a car with anyone! Tell them you can't go. I'd drive you before letting you go off in someone else's car."

"You don't even drive!"

"Exactly my point!"

Twelfth Grade: "Mom, I can go to Virginia Beach this summer! You know I want to see the ocean----"

"-----No! You can't swim. Why, the very idea! You'd jump right in that ocean with the swimmers, then who wouldn't be around to eat shrimp that night? Lexsana, there are *sharks* in the ocean. If you read more, you'd know these things. Boy, your brother is the reader..."

College: "Mom, I'm in *The Miracle Worker*. I got the role of Mrs. Kel----"

"-----No! You.....oh, a play? Well, do you have to go anywhere?"

"No!"

"Then.....yes! I'll come see you. I hope whoever is playing Helen won't be testing her mother the way you test me."

"But I <u>AM</u> the mother. I'm Mrs. Keller!"

"Exactly! You'll find out how hard it is to say "NO!' to a special needs child!"

Fourth Year College: "Mom, I'm going to be a school teacher, like Dad, and Dorothy Belle, and not like that fourth grade nightmare of a teacher I lived through."

"No, no, no, no, NO!!!! Your dad was always gone, and he always brought his school germs home to us, and he took everything bad out on me. I was always baking for some bake sale and then he'd drop the cake on black ice and put my hard work right back on that cake carrier with ice balls, gravel and all!! I will **NOT** live through that with Leo Jr.! N-O-O-O!" (Who do you think Leo Jr. might be?)

My careerless Mom and her mom, my equally-critical grandma, hailed from the deep south (Shreveport, Louisiana), where they were deftly educated in the four C's: cooking, cotton, criticizing, and catering---to menfolk. They were Steel Chinkapins----tough (local color *and* locally harvested) nuts to crack. My sibling got the good catering and I got the criticism. He was clearly the cotton blossom of their eye. I knew two names hands down he'd put on *his* heroes list.

Maybe Leo Jr. just needed to rise up and defeat some of that southern sensibility. Sure I would teach. Dad expected it and my mom forbade it. Weren't those fair and balanced reasons for picking a career to appease one and taunt the other?

"Get that thing finished so you can talk to me. I never see anyone and you always have your back, well side, to me at that old computer. Will you please get me a Cherry Pepsi?"

"Would you say I am highly motivated or more subjectively idealistic?" I asked her without turning, fingers and eyeballs hovering over the keys, ready to type.

Waiting....waiting....holding....waiting...tired   of waiting...kidneys floating...

"Cherry Pepsi," she repeated, and I typed it right on the application.

209

"Miss Pilewski?" the school secretary called on the intercom, "state department of ed on the phone for you." I shook for a minute, not because this would be the T.O.Y people, but because of those younger intercom summonses that sent me flying right off my chair, always, always in trouble with missing paperwork to prove it.

"Miss Pilewski?" the voice said. "This is the West Virginia State Department of Education. Well, congratulations! You are one of six finalists for West Virginia Teacher of the Year. Interviews will be conducted this summer and the awards banquet will be in September. You'll be receiving a packet in the mail at the end of June. Do you have any questions?"

"Yes!" I said. "Is this a crank call? I mean, I don't want to jump up and down right here in the office with no good reason."

"It's official, Miss Pilewski. You have no worries there. Good luck!"

The news I'd waited for---T.O.Y. winner for Harrison County, and one of six state finalists. Me, Miss Begotten! Hot diggity! A loser no longer!

Would my mother say no to the banquet in September? Would she salt my wound if I came home a loser? *No*--- she would do neither.

There went summer: writing for weeks, editing, trying to sound like teacher perfection, spending summer as a whiter shade of pale, angry at myself for yet again taking on a big project.

But I had committed to it, and winners never quit. So...Create! Type! Revise! Print! Repeat! Oh...my...God!

For the interview, I bought a hundred-dollar briefcase and put a stencil number, "24," on the outside, representing the total number of years I'd survived a checkered career. Inside were a dozen or so pictures, exemplary of my students' accomplishments. The numbered briefcase was a prop like the models carried on *Deal or No Deal*, except there would be no hot model carrying it, and no dollar amount surprise inside unless I went for a bribe.

As I studied the photos, they did not tell my full story. The mental pictures of too many years of: scary threats ("I know where you live"); snuff spat on my raincoat and shoes; stolen jewelry, clothing, and perfume; seasoned teacher smackdowns over plucked plants; illnesses of every nasty kind; student deaths; my father's death; leaving teaching, then returning; play crises; ethnic slurs; slug fests; subpoenas; car wreck-----and none of it appropriate or admissible as "evidentiary support." I deserved to be Teacher of the Many Years of Hell (T.O.T.M.Y.O.H. for those who enjoy yet another good-to-the-last-letter education acronym).

At that winner-take-car awards banquet in Charleston, odds for my winning were nil, as my mother probably figured. I really didn't deserve it. Maybe a new refrigerator on a game show, but not T.O.Y., not with my story history.

"Two and a Half Celebrities" at board of education T.O.Y. recognition: Miss Kitty, the "half" with pink corsage from colleagues (the only reason her face had any color at all), and brother, past West Virginia Principal of the Year. I look oh so elegant wearing my grandmother's hair, and, oh, so -----slouchy.

A Different Kind of Dinner for Schmucks

The Marriott banquet room was dimly lit, filled with low-keyed county Teacher of the Year winners. I could smell the menu: pasta and chicken. Chatter was as abundant as the drizzling rain outside. My fifty-four competitors looked completely happy. They had the career bull by the horns. Their teaching stories were positive, with nobody getting maimed or arrested. My career colleagues were decked out in sport jackets (and a few of those, loud and ill-fitted), Alfred Dunner, and glass pearls.

One of the more flamboyant judges from the summer interview panel flitted by, recognizing me and my stupid briefcase shtick from late June.

"Well, Lexsana! Look at you! You're as nervous as can be!" he said, that diminutive little character touching my arm, not missing a beat in his pretend haste. This was a banquet bit of literary foreshadowing. Since his touch did not result in goosebumps or feeling I was soaring. I got a sinking suspicion that he was my harpy of ill report.

We were seated at the right hand of the dais, with the godhead, the state superintendent presiding, his key followers at his side. He broke bread with us all, everyone anticipating his keynote address. But before all that pontification, came the end of supper and dessert --- cheesecake, and the one hundred fifty forks scraping across those plates sounded like sinners repenting. Or just sinners operating road graders.

Someone from the head table began blabbing into the mic about the earnest importance of educators' sacrifices. It didn't even register. Sacrifices was too mild of a word.

My peripheral glances told me I was the brown shoes in a sea of black clothes. What pulled the shame out of me was the feeling in the room, simple joy as far as the eye could see, teachers happy to have a school night out, not grading projects or tests. I noted lots of head nodding, so typical at awards of great and powerful magnitude. My competitors weren't there for the competition; this supper meant something honorable to them, just being county winners. They were in-the-moment relaxed, not full of themselves, not anticipating a win, fully enjoying the proceedings. If they were foaming at the mouth to take home the prize, they must have had another drainage tube I could not see. They were flat out happy to be there.

Oh!--- **Happy to be there?** OH MY GOD!

I suddenly knew why my mother hadn't come. She would never make the effort to see me win a chance to travel West Virginia and speak about my teaching philosophies (which would have been pretty rich, in hindsight). If I were away, then she would be alone, something she despised. I was making her unhappy.

"...so richly deserving, our fifty-five county teachers of the year, dedicating themselves..." Sup. P. said.

I quit listening, because of my startling epiphany, though I clapped along on cue to the blah-blah.

So...I'd dragged my family out in bad, foggy weather, which upset me. My mother was upset that I might be spending more time away from her. Maybe I'd upset a few of my fellow faculty by that T.O.Y. business. What about them? *Weren't they equally deserving? Of course they were!* I needed a Tums. The whole bottle.

Two questions spoke to me: *Would picking up the grand prize make me like my job any better? Did I need a fake gold-plated symbol to prove I had worth or ability?*

That acceptance speech burning a hole in my pocket, with references to my family tree of many teachers, was not so red hot now. I had come to the state capital for all the wrong reasons, devoting misguided months to the entire process. This was my last career chance to shine, and suddenly I didn't care to glitz. Looking at the genuine faces of education, I felt like a traitor within the ranks. I knew this was not going to end well, no matter what. I felt I never quite did enough to earn accolades, and yet I craved them like candy.

Miss Demeanor wanted to bolt with Judas haste. Except, Judas had to stay and pose with the state board of ed president for a picture. *Smile, you small little teacher-imposter!*

It was a night of poor pasta, poor weather, and yes, a poor loser. The winner (certainly not I) was a petite, pale youngster with very short flapper bangs. She had accompanied the state board members and state super on an educational mission to Japan. This put my kimono in a bunch. And I thought my application piece about being Senator Jennings Randolph's *personal assistant* while working at Salem College might give me an edge! *HA!* Senator Randolph was responsible for the 26th Amendment, giving eighteen-year-olds the right to vote. Maybe if eighteen-year-olds had gotten to judge the T.O.Y. candidates, they might have felt a connection to my application catalog and the namedrop of Jennings, their constitutional standard bearer. Here is a note I think I may have included in my bragging rights. Maybe the judges thought I had somehow photoshopped the good senator's

counterfeit handwriting onto a stolen copy of Jennings'
private letterhead? But it is an authentic example of much
long-distance snail correspondence between the senator
and the assistant.

JENNINGS RANDOLPH
1730 M STREET, N.W.
SUITE 515
WASHINGTON, D.C. 20036

(202) 429-0041

June 26
1987

My dear Lexsana —
Your cherished
June 16 letter is
appreciated. Thanks
for the clipping. We
had a Top Time at The
University of Hard Knocks.
The Pisces folks must
keep together in joy
and service. Our
best wishes to Shirley
and Sandy. You are
The Sparkplug! always near is
Jennings

*Jennings and I shared March birthdays that were close together. We had
pet names, too! I called him "Teen Angel Hero" and as you can see, he called me
"spark plug."*

*Wherever we stopped for fast food, he insisted on sandwiches with
"liberal onions," apparently the recognized topping of fast-food congressional
D.C. Democrats. He occasionally had a hand seizure, affecting his right thumb and
pointer finger, resulting in an unexpected, drawn "pinch." We gals who assisted with
his Salem College visits decided the "JR grab" was likely a potassium deficiency,
causing his afflicted fingers to contract and affix themselves onto unsuspecting
buttocks. Regardless, we loved Jennings, disabilites and all.*

215

A hometown winner of the coveted state T.O.Y. award later said to me, "Oh! I wish I'd known you were trying for the state title. I could have helped you with your interview questions, and given you some pointers."

Pointers? Ohhhhh...like, schmoozing? Or using an important connection? Speaking in jargon-bursting sentences? Y-e-a-h...wasn't doing that. The interview portion of *this* pageant was a formality, like interviews where teacher panels ask educational job post candidates useless questions, make a hiring recommendation, which is typically and totally disregarded (as evidenced by whom the county hires, post-interview).

When we were able to bolt from our table and hurry to the parking garage to beat the teacher traffic, there was already a phalanx of tottering educators walking before our stopped car. We inched toward the exit gate. It was quite a parade passing by, many plainer ladies moving to the identical pace of sleepy students during morning fire drills.

Staring at the teachers, I remembered how someone always seemed to be asking me, "Are you a teacher?" as if their son were down a well and I were the only person who could save him. I guess the frantic questioner could take me to the site, to the well's windlass and hand me the well escape route manual so I could read and teach the at-risk child, quiz him on the bulleted material, then wait for the trapped boy to scale his way to success. If this is so, the next person who asks me "Are you a teacher?" will be answered with: "Do you happen to have a son who's trapped down a well?" End of discussion. I did not like specific inquiries that branded me, reminded me constantly of my delicious, juicy head.

Tapping the steering wheel, my brother was watching that flow of sandalfoots in front of us, too. I

216

was staring out my window, sitting behind him, already worrying about tomorrow. I would be tired, sad, and even more sad having to be interviewed by the Clarksburg *Exponent-Telegram*. That was going to hur-r-r-t.

Suddenly he turned round to me to deliver the best line of the night. "Well, Sis, I know exactly why you lost..." (Brother knew about perfect comedy timing.) "It's simple! (Wait for it...) He gestured over to the good folks schlepping to their own vehicles, prepping to drive home, indicating the women passing in front of our car. "You're too good looking!" he said smiling, to make me feel better about being the loser I felt I was.

That compliment, while uplifting, was the second time I got trumped that night, because it happened to come out of the mouth of a past *West Virginia State Principal of the Year*.

Something unexpected had happened that dismal September evening and nobody had caught the mistake. It involved a plaque, both on my teeth from eating pasta and cheesecake, and also in the form of a half-pound wood plank. And the denouement, the award end of all that hoopla and "grandeurian" preparation, would make me laugh when I looked at the engraving. Six months later.

After the T.O.Y. event, the mother of all stupid time wastes, I had forgotten about the dinner, the big "runner-up award of a lifetime." It was a Saturday, time for some semi-annual dusting. On a desk shelf that sits above my computer was the award that meant nothing. So very nothing that I'd never examined it out of the envelope. Until today. Now I had proof that I was one of the predetermined also-rans, because that goofy slab read as follows:

217

**The West Virginia
Board of Education
Recognizes**

**Lexsana Pile<u>sw</u>ki
(misspelled my last name!--How would you even
pronounce that??)**

**as a
2007**

**TEACHER OF THE YEAR
FINALIST**

**For Her Dedication and Contribution (no "s"?)
To The Education Profession (capital "T" for "the"?)**

September 12, 2006

Wow! All that work for a crappy plaque of errors. I showed it to my future husband.

"The state board of ed was not that concerned about loser engravings," I said. "The state board of ed needed *Strunk and White* at the very least," he responded.

Dad had given me a good tip once about any student who faced disciplinary action after being caught doing heinous acts of stupidity. Leo always looked at the guilty party and asked this question, "So, what did you learn from all this?"

I know what I learned from that award election that may have included a few hanging chads in the voting.

I would write what I learned down, to post at work and home, in case someone, someday, unexpectantly knocked at my door, stepped inside and squarely asked me once more the following: *Would you consider doing something for me?*

Read my response to what I learned about awards, It is also suitable for framing!

What the Teacher Learned about the Value of Awards:

There is no value in an award.
Students are a teacher's awards.
The challenging ones award patience.
The attainers award industry.
The teacher has all she needs
by doing the job,
serving her students,
receiving their accolades
--which are not political
-- or forced

A Prom Rom-Com 🐑

How many women teachers in their fifties can boast that they found love at a high school prom? I did, and it did not result in my being arrested for a "minor" infraction. I went to the prom that year, 2007, because faculty and staff told me encouragingly that a certain widowed vo-ag teacher would be there. Naturally, he got a similar memo with the same lively encouragement about a certain "un-tethered" senior English teacher. I always hated arranged dates because both parties had to seem wholly accepting to the kindly machinations of their match coaches. Apparently staff found us a perfect fit in a complementary, lonely kind of way. Just like that, I landed in the pomp, pageantry, and floral infestation of the junior-senior prom, the spring runway for eighteen-year-olds in dresses that cost what I earned in a month. Most teenagers spend an entire pre-prom day in the same way Oscar nominees prep for the awards ceremony. Some teens may have personal stylists or hairdressers flown in, with wardrobe and wind machines at the ready. It's really that ostentatious. High schoolers plan for a celebrity kind of fun night ----the kind of fun night that only occurs after the prom, or Oscars. For two teachers there would be awkward pleasantries, but no swag bags, stylists, or after-ceremonies fun night. No fun for a long, long time.

"Nice, evening tonight, don't you think?" Mr. Carr asked me. It was downright balmy for April in north central West Virginia. He was innocently posed on the event veranda, and there we were, two single oldsters in their own scene from a Hallmark Spring Spectacular

220

movie. I hadn't had a Hallmark movie moment (or a date) since Deputy Steve stuffed me into his cruiser after my holiday car crunch. Tonight's movie would be titled *Surviving Senior Prom Twice*, starring us, the two authentic seniors--- (*citizens*).

This whole being at the prom for a possible hookup was daunting and foreign. I wondered how the "OF" (Over -fifty) crowd did electronically-paired first dates. Were cheat sheets involved with the other person's interests and life hacks? For example: "Now tell me more about this... this...uh, I have to sneeze. Excuse me for a moment," (turning backwards to force out a faux sneeze, push up a sleeve, and review the date's on-the-arm bulleted bio highlights, flipping back around confidently)--- "Sorry about that...so, tell me more about this hobby you have of collecting miniature pitchforks. Is it all agricultural or more culinary for you?"

I finally answered his opening weather question, but had no idea what I was saying. I felt just like a news anchor! Words were coming out of my own mouth for which I had neither reason or excuse. *Who had written them?* Further, I had no cheat sheet inked anywhere on my person about this teacher/male/peer. My matchers hadn't thought enough about secondary information I needed to know.

Eventually, I realized I was giving him---the weather report, plus a medical bulletin about my asthmatic reaction to rain. NOT GOOD. Then, my mother appeared, floating over the railings of the vined veranda, reiterating her cautionary words about the reason I deserved my own ash bin. If I angrily threw my evening bag over the railing at her now, she would win and I would be going home. I didn't throw that little black bag, but I wanted to. I glanced around at happy couples one-third my age and wanted to scream at all of them, "Graduate a year early if you can! And for God's sake, LEAVE HOME! If you stay, it's a hellish tr-a-a-a-p! You'll die th-e-r-r-r-e!"

"You're not going to yell anything! You're always alone because you always reveal too much. Why can't you leave a question mark? Men love a mystery."

I knew what men loved, but deferentially I smiled, then made an immature face and considered my veranda flight plan.

As soon as Mr. C. turned to say hello to a couple eager to show off the effects of their teeth whitening pens, I bolted back inside to look for all the committee members responsible for making me that match. I wasn't sure this was going to work. I needed food and a posse to make sense of things. Prom is the place for many things, just not date comfort food. I opened my clutch to look for any leftovers from my last function requiring an evening clutch, but there was no clutchable food. It would have been petrified anyway.

There they were, all the Yentas from *Fiddler on the Roof!* I ran to the table with a smeared cracker and a celery stick, desperate as the refreshments.

"Did you see him?" "Where is he?" "Are you remotely interested?" "Could this thing develop?" "What did he say?" "Do you like him?" "I saw him looking around, and I can tell you, he wasn't looking for the men's room, either!" "He doesn't even look like himself! Make sure you talk to the right guy!"

"Well, yeah, he's out there on the veranda. We just said hello and that was about it. For an 'out-of-school environment' meeting, it was kind of wobbly. Who knows? But, it's okay either way, really."

I sat down for girl support and a nice vantage point. Our secretary, Deb, had a really cool do.

"I really love your hair tonight," I told her.

"Thanks," she said. "My beautician gave me this up do and I liked it, but now I look just like Opie's Aunt Bee."

Himself, the gentleman prince, strode towards us with a Gatsby mystique, minus the linen suit and shady wealth. After all, he was a teacher, like the rest of us, not a member of The Three Comma Club.

What happened next was that scene straight out of *Uncle Buck*. Macaulay Culkin sits down in the school cafeteria with the lunch Buck has packed, pulls out a Hellman's jar of milk and a black banana and maybe a pickle in waxed paper and asks his lunch buddies, "Would you be interested in talking about a possible lunch trade?" The camera shoots down on the table as every chair flies backward and the table dwellers do a screaming exit. Only, for my mature girl table mates, the exit was apparently soundless.

"Is this seat occupied?" Mr. C. asked, regarding the only empty seat to the left of me.

I looked back at my table mates to confirm that the chair was not reserved for any other would-be movie musical matchmakers. "Where did everybody go?" I asked, turning my head to sweep the room for my Yiddish Gone Girls. I looked back at him. "I swear, there were people here just a minute ago." *Such a preaching they'd get on Monday! Oy!*

"What people?" he smiled. "You look nice," Mr. Carr said sitting down, and, of course, I reciprocated by assuring him he could gain admission into most any country club on a non-prom night. I glanced at the tie. It was rather youthful and I wondered if he'd sneaked it right out of his son's closet.

"Nice dress. I like it," he said, so I believed him. His face was just that honest. Earlier that day when I looked through my closet I had zero dating clothes. Just a closet

223

of Christopher and Banks, one piece embroidered (ye gods!) with an apple. Desperate times called for desperate quick-stop-near-home discount stores. A weekend warrior has little time for couture fittings.

Maybe I said it because I hadn't had table talk with a date in over a decade. Maybe there was a brief pause that became too long in our conversation and I knew it was my turn to speak. Deprivation of the opposite sex can cloud good judgment. I popped out a whopper: "Thanks! You know where I got my dress? (pause that I still wish had been an eternal pause)--- at the Dollar Store! It cost me twelve bucks!"

Immediately, I heard Mom admonishing me, with gusto. "Again, you mistake a date for a priest! Men like dresses from a catalog, like Macy's or Appleseed's. Never, never tell a man what anythings costs, especially after marriage, which may never be a big concern with you."

The one damned time I lacked a filter, it boomeranged! On me! I dissed and pissed myself off at the same time. He would think I was tight, and obsessive, fixated on frugality! And I really wasn't! I was just low on cash from buying the weekly truckload of pet needs!

I knew I would stick that glad rag in the cross-cutter paper shredder at home, right after I heard that DJ play "YMCA." That would have made things better. But then there was kind of a big pause, and I got nervous and weak and needed a plate of french fries and a big Reuben with Diet Coke.

And I said: "I got my jewelry at Gabe's. And my shoes came from somewhere. I may have worn them for my college graduation." *...Oh my God! Now I'd made my outfit into a big discount headline, like a January White Sale flier. And worse, this "arrangement" would not be an*

224

OTO (one time only) face-to-face. I had another month and a half with this colleague who might tell other colleagues: "She's pretty, but she's also pretty blonde. I don't think she can handle things, things that cost full price. It frightens her, I assure you. There's a rich story there, I bet. Such a pity!"

"Did you say something to offend our colleagues? They aren't coming back."

He glanced about the long table, every chair pushed out and vacant. "Apparently, yes," he laughed. We evaluated some of the bolder prom ensembles where there were visible cracks and cleavage. Just like at The Oscars! Things were getting odd now. And then, I asked him something.

"What happened to the old proms without hotel rooms and instant families? It's all so...advanced now. Is that what fun is now?" *Oh no! Antiquated! Dull! Too straight-laced-sounding!*

Whatever he answered, I didn't care. All I cared about were his quiet, kind eyes. I felt physically pulled by them, by the type of maturity and living they revealed, life not even my father had known.

My friends had filled in that blank for me, about his loving a wonderful wife completely, beside her every day of a twelve-year illness, securing himself for whatever was to be. He was steady, committed, a comforter. Looking at him, I saw a minister, a doctor, a veterinarian, and yes, Sheriff Woody. He had a different strength, the kind that the soul sees before eyes do.

What might it be like dating him? He was not needy, greedy, or seedy. I saw someone with a full depth of caring. Here was someone with whom I could eat sloppy spaghetti and not be judged. Here was a man who, after an

225

argument, might dress up in a suit and stand outside my door softly, at full attention, until I decided to come out and let him speak, apologize. (He later did just that, which was better than the all-too-common tropical paradise proposal.)

He would never be appalled at seeing me without mascara or witnessing a childish outburst. He would never criticize or ask about my past. He wouldn't whine to his aging buddies about a specific run of "bad judgment." If he were ever to fall in love with me, I would feel it without words. He was that kind of man who cannot be dissuaded from a one-woman full-on declaration of commitment. All that from just one exchanged glance at a kids' prom. It was all so possible it frightened my spinster heart to warmth and then, faint hope and I thought, What T.O.Y. Award? Who cares? My *re*-ward is sitting right here and it isn't going to tarnish.

I ran my list of permanent mate prerequisites to "The Electric Slide." This DJ was old school! I'd been sitting on that sheet of bullets a half century, which fully explains my singular status. Said list was as unrealistic and stupid as *The Bachelorette*, because any self-respecting list of potential spouses needed to address wealth. My list did not include doctors. Doctors and teachers are fully different species. Doctors found me attractive only in my sickliness and a full-PEIA-coverage kind of way. Maybe men aren't really from a red planet; maybe some women's great expectations are.

The list was surprisingly familiar after forty years:

- Must have his own teeth and know his dentist's hobbies, as proof of oral health maintenance
- Must be at least half-a-head taller than I (no more ballet flats for OTO shorty dates)
- Must have plentiful hair; it doesn't have to be thick as Berber, but it needs to have a little heft
- Must speak in full sentences, especially at dinnertime, and understand "future tense" completely
- Must love animals enough to rescue them without reservation
- Must never put a cigarette to his soft lips or whiskey, either
- Must know the Bible is the greatest book on earth, followed closely by *The Great Gatsby*
- Must have broad shoulders for supporting me always, plus a tight, skinny butt
- Must have a sharp sense of humor and the ability to spin a good yarn
- Must appreciate the arts with unusual artsy talents, like flying Peter Pan or building a London Bridge
- Must have a separate identity and manly hobbies (saving me on car repairs)
- Must not be coarse or embarrassing or lack compassion, a respecter of women

The entire prom assembly did The Village People proud, young and old arms alike (including mine), flying into alphabet formations, bouncing flesh about. It felt more like a big wedding reception with lots of happy drunks full of extra cake, but it was not.

I ran to the exit, checking for all my belongings.

"Leaving us, Miss P?" a senior boy asked.

"Yes! I've------- got to go."

"There's a ladies room right over there," he comforted.

Then dollar store Cinderella did the mystery date dash, running across the curvy highway oblivious to oncoming traffic, to the far edge of the parking lot.

He never saw me leave. I put the hammer down and spun that SUV pumpkin out of the parking lot on two wheels, careening home, home to a list of nighttime chores and a houseful of cacophonous barking. The dogs might be barking a bit, too.

"I thought you might be home a little bit earlier because there were probably plenty other chaperones there," Mom woofed out. "Did you have a nice time? I bet nobody had on a dress like...yours. "

"Nope. Sure didn't," I said.

While walking the dogs I decided not to shred the dress. I liked my dress. So I would either save it or make it Cinderella's future thrift shop donation. I replayed the night a few times. If my mind had cable, it would live on a network called "I-REP" for the choosy few, neurotic viewers who lived life by exhausting instant replays.

But the question that night, standing out there in heels in the dog fence of escapism, under a bit of old moonlight, seemed to be: *What can ever come of this? How could I allow him inside my life and spoil his allusions and risk being embarrassed by my unreasonable, jealous mother? If the dogs didn't eat him alive, she surely would.*

I would soon be allowed to see behind the veil, before it was nearly torn in two.

...Unfortunately, this is as far as this chapter can go. Husband's request!

"Please! I prefer to be a man of mysteries!" He surprised me with that at supper one evening when I had been working on the book so much it seemed more natural to keyboard my food rather than use a fork.

"What an odd thing to say," I said. "Sounds just like my mother. She preferred mystery. Did she raise you, too?"

I had thought for eleven years just what to write about Mr. James Carr and now my fingers were seemingly tied by my new editor. I wiped them off with my napkin several times in protest, the way the newly-arrested wipe off their indignance at having been fingerprinted.

"But I want to give hope to older people waiting on love!" I pleaded. "It's a very fragile time for the 'olders' among us. Like bone loss. Besides, there's the Mom angle, trying to run you away, maybe with paid assistance. Don't you want people to know how you accepted her anyway? The way you proposed, and then saved that litter of six puppies one night, running through a creek and brier bushes refusing to give up, and how we sneaked to Maryland to get married? There's all the medical drama when you sawed off part of your hand cutting play scenery, then went to Ruby Memorial by ambulance, nearly bleeding out your pointer finger, and..."

But the M.O.M. (Man of Mystery) remained unmovable, adamant. "Book number two," he said. "Pace yourself."

Another epiphany! Though he'd never met Dorothy Belle of Sagacity, JC was saying what she always said. Just in his own words. "Pace yourself" sounded a lot like her "make haste slowly." I'd forgotten that advice. Was this why, in my rush to overdo and excel, I always condemned myself, repeating the past?

JC's words made sense. We feel differently about things as we age. We should! I made my declaration right then to slow down, because the world should not be so rushed. Not real love, time, a good meal, success. Nothing.

* <u>Thought for Your Day</u> (where applicable):

If you're running so fast you can't keep up, it's time to "make haste slowly." You're missing *living*.

Allow your brain to run a diagnostic. If cars have warning lights, how much more, then, do people? We have a "check engine" light, too. The still, small voice dings when we overwhelm ourselves. Some of us are just anti-dingers.

Check your stomach. Are those muscles tangled like Christmas lights?

Hold out your hands. Do those productive fingers tremble a little?

Roll your neck. Is this noisy and painful?

Can you feel knots in your shoulders like blocks of cheese?

Is your heart speed beating to "The William Tell Overture?" (Lone Ranger TV theme*)*

Breathe! ---Ohhh! You *do that already*, <u>and</u> you're *insulted* by the oversimplification?--- NOT sorry. Yoga teaches us to breathe in *slowly* to the count of four, then exhale to the same count. Maybe we all need a refrigerator list. Not for groceries but speed limits, pacing reminders.

Let that list have a scripture, like Matthew 11:28 ("...*and I will give you rest*"). Now, when I get overwrought, I ask: *What am I rushing (hurling) towards?* If the sped-up dead could speak, many would chant back, "An open grave." (There is nothing attractive about an open grave. I have seen my share.)

Thoreau said, "Time is but the stream I go a-fishin' in." He knew what the original definition of streaming meant. No pole and no hurry-up access.

If you put your BP in fourth gear to meet a lifetime-overload agenda, make certain your will is updated and notarized. Life just isn't good enough for you.

From the brilliant Lily Tomlin: "For fast-acting relief try slowing down."

Pace yourself. --- It's really a thing. It's how JC and I fell in love. For keeps.

West Side [Salem] Story and Revived Plants - A Teachable Moment

Teachers know about bad days. Little Mary Sunshine got bad days almost daily. My hope of having one fantastic school day from homeroom to dismissal bell was as likely as my being a famous writer, though I kept hoping. On one particular spring morning all things were moving in perfect symmetry. And then came second block. Anger is a problem, and its elite importance was pointed out to me on the first day of every new semester. Eager to share their distinctive and debilitating student health condition, those elitist pouters flopped down and let their mouths resemble a grumpy horseshoe. Their crossed arms made them look so...laced up and Nike-like. The odds are good that nearly every teacher in America knows about this protruding lower lip condition in youth. And frankly, a few of the less-receptive educators want to rip those lower lips off.

Typical event on the first day of a new semester:
"Hi, I'm Miss P., and I'm glad you're in my class! And you are...?"

She spun around and smacked me in the boobs with her big brown Samson hair. Her eyes looked extra mean with a little help from Maybelline New York. Her teeth were angry, filed down from excessive grinding. Her lovely diamond-studded nostrils flared out, bullish. Fernando sized me up and gave me her educational mission statement in one snorty compound sentence. "Don't ever touch me or call on me because I have really bad anger issues."

Plural! She had issue<u>s</u>, which she hoped conveyed that I should always cower in fear. I counted silently how many times I had heard that excuse for laziness. Apparently this order of a secret society had degrees, like the Masons. I encountered these kinds of "issue<u>s</u>" weekly, frequently as eyebrow and chin stubble. What I wish I could have said to all that unwanted drudgery and bristly ugliness was, "pluck you."

Anger among the pouters always began when there was any assignment that required group share-outs. I never learned. I called on Ferdinand-Samson anyway. She could easily have lifted me, my chair, and my desk and drop kicked me outside towards the school's fragrant septic system. Girl had nothing but pout and dirty looks, giving me a prelude to exactly what might happen if I attempted to make her talk. When I asked her to do a grammar workbook sentence I saw kids silently counting backwards from ten for the boom. After awkward dead air space, I decided on a little quick class improv, making a big dramatic gesture out of searching for a writing instrument, then dashing something odious into the grade book, with all the joy an educator feels in her heart at that special grade-cutting moment.

Son of a gun, if I didn't have an epiphany that, like my elitist pouter, *I* had "red pen issue<u>s</u>" and a daring desire to record minus signs! My actions spoke louder than her lack of words. I glanced at her and said my own inner complex sentence response: Don't piss *me* off, because I have the power of the red pen! Additionally, *Can you find the conjunction, direct object, and prepositional phrase in <u>that</u> sentence, you cheeky little teacher hater?"* I put down the red pen of ire and brushed my hands together like I'd just polished off a hunk of crumbly chocolate cake and felt that same kind of sweet, satiated rush.

One indifferent snort from Ferdinand told me maybe I had something to dread. I hated when students used their snort to decry my grand acting skills.

Nearly typical event on the day of West Side Story Girl Brawl that rumbled my second block:

As stated in this chapter's opening bell ringer to the reader, I had a great first block that happy spring day. Maybe due to an absence of pouters. First block's attentive kindness and energy that early in the morning brought out more of the calm professor in me. It is true that students who want to learn make teachers into smarter people. We educators will take extra pains to add vocabulary words and analogies into our teaching to make ourselves exhibit all the I.Q. those interested students think we possess.

"Have a great day and be good to your other teachers!" I said. "We'll reconvene this loveliness tomorrow."

"But Miss P., we won't see you till Thursday. Split block schedule, remember?"

I was never down with split block scheduling. One week students had my class Monday, Wednesday, and Friday The following week, Tuesday and Thursday. Not only did this make planning sometimes a challenge, but matching all the names and faces every other day was a bigger challenge. Students were stumped and forgetful every time we reconnected. But we made it work. I think.

"Whatever," I said, letting my smile evaporate.

As second block filed through my portal of peace, the tardy bell rang. I noticed two potential angry pouters were absent. Then my phone rang. When I heard the voice on the other end of the line I knew my cheery tree was about to be chopped down. Why did I always pin my hopes on the unlikely, always on an imagined sense of false security, like a car full of Driver's Ed students eating Happy Meals, oblivious to the unmarked sink hole on an alternate route back to school. That silent moment of professional pride, "Hey, I'm going to make it to fourth block without a Xanax," changes in a heartbeat to "Where is my riot gear? Lost somewhere, probably with all my vital state department English curriculum ----things."

A sinking feeling pervaded as I listened on the phone dutifully. All my euphoric little state department English head adjectives I'd just used to describe my first block experience (halcyon, euphoric, and my favorite, unperturbed), followed the unsuspecting Driver's Ed car straight into that sink hole. A dark mood swing was a-comin' straight through what I termed "the educational fourth wall," the one I erected to hold back education's bad angry.

It all started with a phone call. "MissPThisisMr.G." It was our soft-spoken but very fast-speaking vice-principal.

When Mr. G. called, you listened, because he spoke even faster than that *Wheel of Fortune* flapper sound. He was a beneficent administrator, the kind who saves his dialing digit for emergencies. Immediately, I knew this could be bad.

"SomegirlshadagangfightinWestSalemover theweekend. Twoofthemareinyoursecondblock. They weren'tonthesameside."

Wow! I was having trouble keeping up here, like when Mom critiqued my overall appearance on any given school morning in one long, debasing sentence. She could find and speak my flaws faster than hot water freezes midair in a Minnesota winter. With Gibby and with Mom, it was a lot of rapid-fire dialogue requiring rapid-fire

235

processing. I was slow to take that splash all in.

"Twoof them're inner cell block?" I asked. He repeated, but I would not further show my age or sudden hearing loss by asking him to repeat himself another round. I kept trying to decode this news. *Tooth'em in your sec-blah?* I was getting nervous now. I did catch the phrase, "girl gang fight."

Ah, yes! I had heard about a couple of Caucasian Gangnam group members being mortal enemies, one a recent transfer student about to join the military, the other, a Salemite with a peppered temperament. Both could be pouters and both were missing from second block senior English. The weekend's West Side Story After-Party had conflicting issues, probably over guys, their favorite gang fight theme. I pictured them that Saturday night full on in their ripping, scratching-good Clash of the Titians where bras got ripped off, nails were broken, eyes were blued, and thick heads of hair got some pull-style layering. Such pre-Easter rumbles indicated it was tough girl makeover season.

Mr. G. continued. "Theyjustleftmyofficeandshould bearrivingthereanysecond," he spewed in my ear with haste, though softly, without taking a breath. I bet his were the fastest wedding vows repeated to a minister in nuptial history. Did he just say, *They justlet moffus and should berry thrinny second?* Berry Thrinny...wasn't he a foreign exchange student from England?

Oh, goodie! I thought, putting my hand on the pill bottle I didn't own but wished could magically appear in my blazer pocket. I needed a Reese Cup!

As was the daily necessity, I put on my big-girl referee panties.

Cue the door! *Wham!* It flew open Cosmo Kramer style. I almost dropped the receiver as the two stomped in with renewed anger, one lagging behind, ready to trip the other at the first opportunity. Here stomped the pair of them, one Jet and one Shark. That made me Officer Pilewski-Krupke, as in that gang lyric line from West Side Story, "Gee, Officer Krupke, KRUP YOU!"

"Well, thanks for sharing that report. Unfortunately, it's a little late. I appreciate it so much," I said on the phone.

"Ifyouneedmecallme, he said. My eyes were on the godless. *Did he just say, "F'knee'd, meek-ally?" What?*

No, I wasn't going to call for backup, if that's what he had maybe said. I had street cred in the classroom brawl division.

"Where are we supposed to sit?" one barked, as I directed them to opposite ends of the class. The seats were arranged in clusters of four in what the trendy new education gurus called "cooperative learning" seating in groups of four. This made it harder to place those very angry girls apart. One of them was muttering and one said under her breath, "Bitch!" For a split moment I almost answered, "Here!"

They continued sparring verbally and I had had all the crap sandwich I could take for one day. I was growing impatient.

Inspiration! Growing impatient-----Yes! *Growing IMPATIENS.* I had a banger of a story sermon about withered roots and rough-looking flowers and the greenhouse patrons who leave them behind. Imagine the gratitude I felt, dating the school's agriculture teacher who ran the greenhouse where I picked up all the unloved, withered pots of impatiens, pansies, petunias, and perennials and nursed them back to health. (I promise not to use that much alliteration elsewhere.)

I treated those flowers like all my past boyfriends, investing every ounce of care in their crumpled sorry behinds because I was convinced I could save them.

But, it turns out, I could only save flowers because they had better sense. Mr. C. and I always left school and the greenhouse after the paying clients skimmed off the bright, even-tempered-looking plants. The scrubs seemed to look to me. Though I did not understand The Greenhouse Effect, my greenhouse effect was to grab the watering can and tell every single withered plant it was beautiful. They drank it all in. I leave it to the reader to determine if the more-responsive-to-flattery flowers were male or female.

"Shut your books...*NOW!*" I directed, suddenly a barker myself. I paused for a good half minute to let them wonder what was coming next. That way, maybe *I* would know what was coming next. I paced angrily. I read their minds with my discreet but sharp peripheral vision.

Me: "Those little twerps are nervous. They know they're gonna get it! I LOVE IT!"

Them: "She's pacing! Oh my God! She's gonna cage fight those bitches! Alright, al-r-i-i-i-ght! Can ol' Miss P. handle girl on girl hits with her flappy bird arms?"

HA! They didn't know teach had prior skills in *that* department. I had seen *West Side Story* on stage, on screen, and even more impressively, in classroom. I knew the rumble drill, beginning to end. I could stop a gang fight fast, because our fast-flapping vice-principal could run like he talked and was younger than the principal who broke up the last turf war years before. It also didn't hurt that he was six feet four and college-football-shaped. Gibby didn't fibby. If he said he'd be there, then he'd be there.

Nine out of ten English teachers cannot diagram *The Pledge of Allegiance*. But, nine out of ten English teachers probably have seen either *West Side Story* or

Dead Poets Society. English educators can quote Mr. John Keating to their students, though most of us are too old to climb upon our desks and recite, "O Captain, My Captain" by gregarious misfit himself, Walt Whitman. Professor Keating makes a point about life by taking his class of lads out to the mighty athletes' trophy case. He asks those boys to lean in and listen until they can hear the long-ago team faces whispering to them "carpe diem."

CAR-pe DI-em! Did I ever seize *that* day, channeling Robin Williams: "Lean in, class, go ahead, that's right. Can you hear it? Perhaps out there? Did someone just call you a loser outside my door? Why would they speak that of you? Because you waste your time being rough and tough. It's sooooo noble! So attractive! What an act!"

I yammered on. "I want you to know I loiter in the school greenhouse, that's right, I scan the plants that no one loves. And you thought I was picking through that gravel for change. *You* are those plants, the leftovers. You get looked over because you *choose* not to be good. You look tough, because you want to be tough. So now, nobody wants you in her garden stinking it up with your dead brownness. Teachers talk. You are the ugliness plant, cursed at the root. Soon, everyone sees only that in you.

I try to put you in a safe place, nurture you here, keep you pleasant as much as I can. (No one so much as farts here. Silence.) I believe you start to blossom. It *is* tough trying to figure out who we are and who we should be. You come off crazy to other people. I do, too. Don't fall into the dirty earth and die a dry sprout. You know what? At my age, I want to say that I hate ugly. I detest discord of any kind. It makes me mad and sad for you to ruin my day being immature. I want peace, people. I'm a caregiver 24/7, and let me report without the details, it's rough. Maybe when I die---and I hope that's not till after I make my point---even though I've screwed up a LOT in my own life, you know what I wish would be carved on my tombstone? (No farts *or* burps). 'She was kind.' Because for the most part, I have been. I put everyone's cares above my own and I still feel like the goat! Just know that kindness counts in the end. But we have to earn that. Don't waste time being mad. Time is too precious for that. Let it finish growing you up."

It wouldn't sell a screenplay, and it was rather disjointed and rambling, but maybe it stopped a few future lunch punches.

Thank God the bell finally rang. I felt lighter, having had that opportunity to vent. I was pumped for lunch a little more than usual. Too bad nobody else at our feeding trough in the back of the library appreciated my teachable moments borrowed from 1989 movie releases. I ate in partial silence, smiling. I knew someone who would have appreciated that tale at dinner. I ate lunch all gone. Calories didn't count today for Reverend Pilewski and her golden sermonette!

I hope the "good kids" (yes, that term does exist in the secret society of teacherdom vernacular) tuned out my acting rant that morning. Surely they knew which perennials they were. Maybe the tough kids tuned me out, too. Maybe they wanted their lives to be dried up and short. But the future doctor in the house, Brett, must have told his mother a little about my plant-based epistle during class, because at the next board of ed meeting, when rumors swirled that our high school might eventually close, Mrs. F, Brett's mom, stood and to God and the board announced, "There are good people in that place, and Mrs. Marino and Miss Pilewski are the best teachers you have."

I'm not worthy of that compliment, because after two decades, I was feeling a little bent and browned and rough myself, collecting a bit of an uneven temperament because nothing in my life made any sense. My mother and I were no longer close, putting it mildly. Two sentences in, and an escalating fight would ensue between us.

One day my future husband brought me home from work. He was so exhausted he went upstairs to lie down. I picked up the evening paper. My mother, in the kitchen, was talking to herself, apparently thinking that I was not downstairs. "I know that bitch went upstairs to be with him. What a bitch she is!" I looked up from the paper, sitting there in our living room, my mouth open as a broken back door. I was in my late fifties and my own mother had just suggested something coarse and topped it off with a double helping of the word "bitch." She had never said anything like that before. But she would many times afterwards, and the word would be screamed many times back and forth between us.

"I'm going to report you to the sheriff if you ever think about leaving me," she said with the repetition of the boy who cried wolf. "You'll be nothing. You'll lose your teaching job." My mother was no longer well. At times I heard my own heart tearing.

I felt something go out of me at my mother's new definition of her daughter. *What was I doing there?*

It was a milestone I did not want to remember. I cannot forget it. That day started our fast track to full alienation. I wanted to leave. I could not tell my seniors that portion of my sermon, though I wanted to in order to shame them over their classroom high drama. They were making life harder for me. Maybe I should have just held out my hands in surrender to them, making sure they saw the gross palms of my skin-eaten hands, two ground turkey hand patties, the result of unrealized gluten and sugar allergies, exhaustion, and stress. I was coming apart inside and out. My principal carefully wrapped my hands in gauze bandage and sent me to the emergency room. The pain and severe burning were my tipping point. I really wanted to give up. I was back in fourth grade.

But my dad was in my spirit in that exam room whispering, "You can do this baby daughter. You're stronger than all of this." Like always, Dad was with me at the hospital. What example would I set if I allowed myself to fade to brown?

I may have fudged a little in that oratory to the class with rumbling seniors. We bloom, but all of us go through brown patches. Sometimes it does take a good tussle to clear away the Weekend Fight After-Party trash of dollar store nails, hair weaves, and broken bras strewn in the streets. That should only happen on New Year's Eve anyway. It certainly shouldn't happen at my own home address. With my mother. One enabling younger Jet and one older Shark, ready always for a rumble.

In the case of girl ganging up on girl, I'm fairly certain that happened again somewhere. Christian-tinged words and plant-based teachable moments melt away faster than church social ice cream under a July shade tree. Watering a soul takes much more than just one sprinkling.

I can honestly say I got passed over for hosting any more classroom fights the rest of my career, something for which I was grateful every Thanksgiving. But better still, that spring, a few more of the wilty greenhouse plants got homes.

MRSA, MRSA Me!
The Infectious Joys of Teaching!

The year was 1976, a big birthday for America and a big goodbye to the former US of C--- The United States of Cleanliness. I was starting my teaching career as the US of C was fading away. I stayed, and it never came back.

I was hot off the education assembly line. For a brief time, I had that crisp new-teacher smell, health on wheels. I was *stupid*: I touched a dozen doorknobs daily; swept my hands across thirty-five desktops (not the computer variety, *real* desktops); shooed the flies off the last teacher's lounge doughnut and licked the glaze off my fingers; and rubbed both eyes till the cows in the pasture across from the high school came home. I was rather *lucky*: no pink eye, tummy rot, or infections with oozing not-so-awesome sauce. Nobody used latex gloves as a career accessory, not even my doctor. In my older world, antibacterial protection strictly meant a shot of whiskey, a prophylactic, or an alcohol swipe before a shot. People didn't smell like rotting vegetable drawers, either. Most of us washed up well and often in society.

Leave it to society to get lazier, dirtier, necessitating The CDC (Center for Dirt/Dumbness Control), a societal necessity, the same way big-and-heavy couch cushions became necessity when TV remotes hit stores. There was I, a young, careless teacher still eating potato chips right after collecting contaminated lunch money, still oblivious to pinworms, hookworms, ringworms, earthworms, and assistant principal worms. Most of those species are found in the earth or the digestive tract. Only one is found in education, with a much dirtier, gropier life cycle.

He followed me into the copier room and turned off the lights and grabbed me, kissing me. NOT acceptable and likely a very unclean tongue. I forgot about copies, leaving that room fast. I said nothing, being a first-year teacher. I said nothing because my father would have made that little germ apologize, before getting his ass both kicked and reported to the board of ed.

That little episode was proof enough that The Age of Grunge (and character filth) was solidly underway. I stood at my class door witnessing something uncanny. Dirty-looking, stand-alone jeans had no inseam hems. They simply slid down under students' feet like denim shoe extensions, walking through the sepsis of humanity. Germs had a ticket to ride. The New World Order of Bad Smells, NWOOBS, was real.

One morning I noticed my classroom was more tolerable in an olfactory sort of way. While taking roll in that senior English class I asked, "Where's Dan?"

"You mean stinky Cooper? Follow your nose," someone said a little maliciously. I pretended not to hear him, but that answer made me realize that body scents define us. BO, then, was the first glandular GPS. No batteries required.

"Lexsana, you have bronchitis again," the doctor at MedBrook said. "I'm going to put you on Levaquin. Start it tomorrow. Lots of water." If a doctor stayed in a room more than two minutes, he got gonged by Big Brother Medical Policy, code name: IHOP! MF! (Instantaneous

Handling of Patients---Make it Fast!). Infections came fast. Treatments, even faster. I didn't fly often, but I had frequent infirmity miles aplenty.

After my one-minute timed diagnosis, a nurse always walked into my exam room carrying a syringe as big as a celery stalk from a Bloody Mary. I missed my dear old Dr. Ritter coming to the house, sitting a spell, part of the family.

"You! You're back again?" she said, the shot held straight up between her fingers like a Virginia Slim. I instinctively pulled my arm out from under my sweater. "No, not there," she shook her head. "Depo-Medrol. You've got quite a bug. You have to drop 'em. Sorry."

Bare-assed, broken-in teacher me was already depreciating in value. Blimey! There *were* parts that could rot, ooze, and drop off. These bacterial bugs were depleting my good bacteria and slimming down my number of sick days. I sensed that something wicked in a medical way was coming.

"Okay. This is going to sting pretty hard. You'll feel it going in."

Ouch! I got stung yet again. I felt every drip of that awful shot. Immediately my left leg filled with cold concrete and I had no further feeling. It was a sensation I was getting to know. I would leave that place with a step-THUD, step-THUD, dragging my porch column behind me suddenly remembering I had not once taught *Moby Dick* to my seniors.

"Aw....I know it hurts," the nurse said with a feigned pity, finishing her shot business, tossing her contaminated stinger into the Hazardous Waste bin. But what she really meant was "Get yourself some big girl panties, chick. These have holes."

"Don't get so close to those kids," my mom, the non-teacher in our family warned. "You don't have to tell them to get away, just be nice and keep your arms straight out so you won't inhale their exhale. They'll get the message. You're breathing in all their germs."

Mom's solution for world health was for mankind to walk like germaphobe zombies, establishing safe-distance health shields with their outstretched arms. I wasn't yet dry behind the ears to know this, my mother pointed out, moving aside the hair behind my ears, drying that ear area like I was a Lexus. She dug in with a Bounty towel. "Germs multiply in moist places," she said. I was twenty-four at the time.

Some of my health issues were off-campus. One was even compliments of my mom. There was no infection with this particular pain picnic. God looked down on Job's descendant (that would be I) and said, "Ooooo, that had to hurt. So! We'll see what she learned from heavy lifting." It wouldn't be the first of many, *many* times I thought I heard the voice of God. He sounded a lot like Mel Brooks.

My mother had said: "Wait! Before you leave for your yearbook trip, I need you to go to the garage and bring me over that bucket of plaster patch."

Plaster patch? It was early summer. I was on my way to Gettysburg with my yearbook staff for a Herff-Jones publishing tour. I wished even then it could be the other kind of publishing tour, the one celebrating me, me, *me* as an author. But apparently, I had not yet suffered sufficiently to fill my own book's sorry pages.

But first, the all-important plaster bucket---over in the garage, all five heavy gallons of it. I was already sweating out the nape of my neck, but that did not bother my mother at all. "I got this," I said. I bent over, jerked up on that skinny handle and snap! thought my torso had popped off my hips. Fiery pain cut across my lower spine. I stayed bent in half for ten minutes, and went back to the house, knuckles grazing our lawn. Wow! It needed cutting.

"Why are you bent over like that? You're wrinkling your outfit. Straighten up, Lexsana," Mom said in clueless mother-ness, "before you stay that way! Where's my patch?"

"That damned bucket weighed a ton, Mom! *Why*--- did you think--- I could--- lift it?" I panted, twisting my head upwards.

"---But Lexsana, all I needed was enough to fill a nail hole where that picture of Mary was."

"Would Dad be okay with you removing the Blessed Mother from the house?" I asked, rubbing the small of my back. "Haven't you heard of The Curse of Mary for those who remove the symbol of Catholicism's faith?" I lied.

"Did you think there was a crater under the couch that needed filled?" She never directly answered anything I asked, including that question I posed much later in both our lives, *do you love me, Mom?*

So, I didn't win that one. However, most always (meaning never), I usually won. In place of Jesus's sainted mother's face in our drafty hallway went a non-denominational framed nature print, "October Morn," a points-earned print in a gold-brushed frame that had pie crimping around it. She'd gotten it with those perks-earned S & H Green Stamps. She bent over and put the orangey picture close to the floor, under my nose, where I could see its autumnal beauty. It actually was pretty.

"Don't hold it so close, Mom. It reminds me of school starting back in August."

I drove over to the high school to pick up my students with my nose on the steering wheel like a napping nanny. "Here're the kids, keys. Draw straws to be my chauffeur. I'm getting in the trunk." Pain had made me delerious.

"You okay, Miss P?" they asked, glancing at each other, grabbing for my keys, me at their mercy. I saw they were thinking about a much different drive, perhaps cross country.

Those crazy kids meant well.

I stayed in that fetal position for the four-hour-plus drive, pure homage to the Polish endurance in me. I made myself straighten up for the whole guided tour, a letter "C" painfully postured into a letter "I." It was the worst pain of my life. I know we shrink as we age like hot-cycle machine-washed wool, but by thirty, my spine was a string of matchsticks glued onto a leather barber strap after that big bucket grab attempt. While I sat through a few years of liquid spinal fire, I also shrank two and a half inches following in my Dad's footsteps, burdened and shortened by the weight of mother's heavy directives and walking on concrete floors and a concrete leg filled with Qwik-Set Depo-Medrol.

I should have used the bucket of patch stuff to build one of those inversion spine stretchers. Anything left could have plugged up any chinks in my classroom wall where a few critters entered as illegal aliens. But by the time I thought of doing this, I was junior humane society advisor and any classroom bugs had pet names.

The inferior crawling bugs of childhood were nothing compared to the invisible ones migrating into The United States of Unclean. This was the deal: We Americans traveled abroad far less forty years earlier; there were less imported illnesses to declare at customs. The only risk I ever took was in Poland in 1979 eating unpasteurized ice cream, peach melba. Best stuff I ever ate; worst diarrhea I ever sat through.

I got my germ denial from Dad. He always thought his WW II service tour of duty made him impervious to germs. But Dad watched the world change hygienically right on the *NBC Nightly News* when Legionnaire's Disease hit in 1976. It made both of us realize that other things made us sick besides bad cheese.

"Put the (fill in the blank) in the sink and I'll wash it," Dad said. "They put watermelons in a pyramid on the floor. You know how dirty store floors are."

Dad became a "hoser," not the Canadian (or anatomical) kind. He hosed down every gallon of milk, every glass pop bottle, orange juice jug, melons, nuts in the shell, and my brother and I, if we needed hosing. Once he polished an apple from our backyard tree on his work shirt and crackle-bit into it. I felt like writing him a citation. He spat on his first two fingers, not in the Jewish way to ward off evil, but to spit-open produce bags. Sealing an envelope required middle management---spit he spat onto his index finger that then went onto the glue portion of the envelope. "Never, *never* lick a postage stamp," he told the entire family during a demo family meeting, "or eat the flat bottom of an ice cream cone bought at an ice cream joint. Eat one of those germ balls and you'll never live to see if the Pirates win the World Series again."

He sat me down for "the talk" at twenty-five. This was big. He was going to give away his career confidential---and it killed 99.9% of bacteria on surface contact. Dad, then a junior high (yes, yes, old school term) principal, shared with me the secret to his ten-strike. "Janitors cannot be everywhere. One word, baby daughter----*LYSOL*." He ordered it by the case, commanding his remarkable custodians and secretary, Becky, to fumigate everything within ten feet of them: office phones, phone books, the hallway, doorknobs, pens, glass counters, desktops, thresholds. "And if anyone bitches," he whispered to Becky, "spray that fungus, too."

Ninety-five percent of my medical mayhem occurred at work. Except for my southern discomfort, which I blame on the late Eva Peron.

One freezing night in November while rehearsing *Evita* upstairs in the old Elks Lodge in Clarksburg, West Virginia, I got a painfully vile condition that was *not* germ-related. There was no heat in the room and naturally, the only seats were old metal folding chairs. Who cared? It was the Art Center, after all, and we were unaffected by the cold and bad reviews. The seat temperature was about thirteen  degrees. "Don't sit on the cold sidewalk October through May," Mom said to me every fall. "You'll get piles. They are the worst."

But I would get to wear *pearls, a beehive, and a sparkly chiffon gown* as Eva Peron's ghost, stand on a catwalk, and wave like a queen. After trying to sit on the palm of my right hand for hours in that ice block, I removed it, flat as cardboard, vainly attempting to revive life to it. "Que sera sera," I said to my abandoned behind while doing hand compressions.

What a painful, BIG mistake. In twenty-four hours I got an instant full-blown butt balloon like the swell in a knotted garden hose. It was the dimensions of a goiter, a man ball. After that frigid night and the plaster bucket lift, I knew I would never sit to teach again, except on my face. Holy backstage! How that hemmy throbbed! Was my mother ever wrong?

"Lexsana, you act like it hurts to sit. Do you have something wrong down there?" she asked, pointing to my southern extremity. "Oh! You've got a hemorrhoid, don't you? Now you'll suffer. Why didn't you roll up your coat and sit on that instead of that cold metal?" Mom said to me. "So what if you were a head taller than the biggest man there? You've been like that since first grade! You never listen!"

That disregard for my sainted mother's warning led to major surgery for which I desperately wanted to put my anal apparatus up on a very high shelf for a long rest. I postponed surgery to do the Eva Wave-a in the ghost gown, powdered and pearled. Theater-goers said I made the most beautiful ghost they'd ever not seen. But now, post-*Evita*, I was a soothing aloe wipe veteran, a sitz bath diva, enduring the worst-ever surgery ever written in the anus of mankind. After two prelims to Pittsburgh, I had more reconstructive surgery at <u>Shady</u>side, in Pittsburgh, on my <u>shady</u> <u>side</u>... Did everything I said, did, or wore always have to match? Ask any of my former students.

The morning of surgery brought a funny little tete-a-tete with the surgeon and anesthesiologist, that era's

"Rowan and Martin of the proctology set."

The IV had commenced. "Morning, Lexsana," said one of the two face-floating cuties. "I guess this is it. I promise, you will feel better, just not today. You have an unusually small back street exit. We're going to widen it."

"Ohhh..." I half-groaned. "Is the Department of Highways assisting?"

"Well, yes. And, after these two surgeries, you know what?"

"What?" I asked.

"Well, today's procedure qualifies you for the Perfect Asshole award!" --- *Gauche*, but funny, I thought, before snoring.

What a stitch! (Well, not technically. They said there would be none of that sewing business. Maybe I needed to see these guys' medical degrees).

Part II   *The Health Twist List*

Some hygienic safeguards I could not rally behind, like hermetically sealing my lunch tray with Saran Wrap for transport out of the kitchen and back to my classroom thus keeping my formed meat patty spore-free. One older teacher did that, but we all suspected Ethyl had a little methyl in her thermos and we dismissed her bacteria hysteria as pish posh. Little did we know pish posh could live in a petrie dish for forever, and surprisingly enough, even to her critics' surprise, gin had antiseptic properties. The old girl was never sick much, so, who's sorry now?

Some manish county health coordinator should have warned young teachers about germ-to-teacher combat. I wish some tough Clorox Coach had said: "Look, okay, teachers and aides have some of the dirtiest jobs on the planet. It's a fact you will be sick. Septic system work will begin to look good and sanitary to you. Stay strong! Never go near your filthy desk. Never sit on your filthy chair. Treat your own hands like they were stubs. We can help make that part happen if you take too many sick days! QUIT CRYING!! Fingers are your enemies. Optionally, of course, will be a spray hosing once a day by the janitor, for which you may need extra work clothes and shoes. Got that?----I CAN'T HEAR YOU!!!"

If I hadn't been made to move like a maverick to a new room each period, (known in educationville as "the floating teacher"), and if students in those crowded halls hadn't pushed me flat against lockers, I would have been fine. Trying to apply lipstick using the shiny silver of a Diet Coke can as a mirror during class changes made it hard to hit my target. With magazines advising me a pale mouth made one look weak, I applied lipstick liberally and often, but only occasionally on the actual lip line. With every slam into a locker came finger-to-teeth erasures. Just as "there's no crying in baseball," there's no irresponsible teeth touching in teaching. Mittens were a must during planning period, when the desire to dig or rub behind a closed door was greatest.

Here are the wheeziest, itchiest, pus-iest, painful-est, swollen-est, vomity benefits a thankless, un-disinfected job can offer:

Top Twelve Teaching-Related Medical Conditions That Are Trying to Tell You Something

12) Nonstop Conjunctivitis – goopy red-eye mucilage discharge sticky enough to seal documents and outgoing bills

11) Ringworm - long sleeves year round, and positively NO leaning on anything---except Jesus

10) Bronchitis - follow doctor's orders or become president of the Old Wheezer's Cough Club

9) Constant Sinus Infections - building mold, plus breathing all the high school girls' Cotton Candy Eau de Toilette

8) Graveled Knees from Falls - "Watch out for that ice patch, Miss P.!--Aw, never mind. That's gonna need stitches."--- Hi ho, hi ho to Medbrook, back I go...

7) Influenza – all jungle types A through Z, and Types AA through ZZ Top

6) Gastroenteritis - became a five-day hospital stay after school's "vegetable soup revenge"

5) Strep - you'll be fine, just don't swallow until you're over it, just like after your grade school tonsillectomy

4) Pneumonia - see number 10, plus extra sick days for this, your pulmonary staycation in bed

3) Bruxism - TMJ! and nighttime mouth guard, costing $500, never used for fear of swallowing it, creating nightly insomnia, leading to Ambien.

2) C.O.P.D.- PSSSSSST!!!!! Pepper Spray Aftermath. A temporary turnoff to tolerating job and/or certain teens --- getting kicks at my lungs' expense.

1) MRSA Infections/Surgeries - horrid lancings, irrigations, and packings, set to the tune of Marvin Gaye's "Mercy Me"--- "Oh, MRSA, MRSA me...Things [meaning I] ain't what they used to b-e-e-e..."

Too bad I didn't use my letter writing skills to write Hasbro and propose an *Operation II* game, "Infected Teacher Edition." I could have inspired young players to become doctors, specializing in Teacher Detox and Microbe Management. How in this cootie-filled world did I ever bypass lice? That's a head scratcher.

I got pepper sprayed indirectly right in the safety of my own classroom, stepping in from hall duty before class. Though I choose to believe I was not the target, I got it anyway. By the time all students were coughing, tumbling out of the room, I couldn't inhale for the burning. I left the office that November after telling the incident to my administrators and sat out the rest of the year at home. I was physically altered. Those little alveoli and bronchioles had been killed like --- well, Raid-sprayed bugs. Those two breathing buddies were never going to function naturally again, and I was in full-blown "pulmon-opause." Every physical action was work. I was an autoimmune disease whiz.

Back to Medbrook! "Did you miss me?" I asked.

"Short visit tonight, Lexsana, because you're going straight to the hospital," Doc said. It was a bad sign when an actual doctor saw a patient at a Quik-Stop and gave a directive in one fell swoop. "Your blood oxygen is eighty percent. You're going to UHC by ambulance."

"No, no I can't. I have to go home and take care of my mom and pets first. Then I'll go."

"Promise!" Dr. Bowers said.

While I knew this was crazy-serious, I stopped listening to some of what he was telling me. I needed to stop at Family Dollar, (the only direct-route store on my way home), and buy some youth size XL Ninja Turtle jammies or "Coffee Grinds My Beans" One-Circus-Tent-

Fits-Most nightshirt. My slippers at home looked like two drowned rodents. I dressed like a classy professional on the job, but sometimes at home I was Little Ratty Rundown. But I wasn't telling Doc that.

"Here's what's happening," Dr. B. said. "If an elderly man falls and breaks his leg crossing the street on Friday, he might develop shingles Monday morning. Stress on his system creates a secondary medical condition, something that's been dormant in the body for some time. Well, that's what happened with you and the pepper spray. It triggered stress on your lungs. Now you've got bronchitis and the beginning of COPD. There is no cure for COPD."

"Or stupid," I said. I really wanted to hurt those two boys. Maybe hire a boxer to bite off some ears or body parts.

"I'll be calling the hospital in a couple hours to check on you," he warned, like a father committed to checking on an untrustworthy child.

"We thought about taking those guys for a ride to 'rehabilitate' 'em, but we're seniors, Miss P, and we all need to graduate," Mike said later. What a great feeling it was just to picture it in my mind like a Quinton Tarantino flick, where most restitution takes place promptly with little reaction time.*

That next fall, I was back at work. The PRO (public relations officer) assigned to our building swaggered into my class, mid-lesson, and in his best lowered cool voice pondered the reason it took me a school year to recuperate from pepper spray. "You know, maybe one in a million has that bad a reaction to pepper spray," he said, fishing.

Don't judge! I always ask forgiveness at bedtime for thinking such thoughts, if I stay awake long enough. I hope the reader and Mr. Q.T. do likewise!

Was he being cute about this? "Yes, and I guess I am the one percent," I said. Dorothy Davis would have sent him flying out backwards with a single belch of fire. "Take that gun out of this room before I bite the hammer off and spit it down your gullet!" I couldn't say it. Dorothy would have done it.

In some states, a similar pepper spray incident requires that a Haz Mat team arrive on school grounds and investigate, even treat the contaminated places. Other states have in-place laws regarding that type of incident directly affecting a *teacher's* health and well-being. In our state, teachers are treated fairly, right behind students, then parents, then the adoring public.

Then teachers.

In a few years, it was a different and equally serious issue---MRSA. However that infectious distemper got in, my left leg swelled like a junior blimp. Fever came. The pain was intolerable. An extensive yellow core was excised at the emergency room, and I had a book-of-plagues title in mind: *I Know Why the Scalpeled Teacher Screams.* OW! My husband watched the fat string of infection pulled out by the PA. No numbing. Unfortunately, MRSA continues its vileness debut in public places and worse, in schools. Every school district needs a MRSA prevention and control policy in place. It could be a little better world if everyone simply washed his/her hands often.

"Sorry, I know it hurts, but I need to remove tissue around the infection and irrigate, so we can get all of the bad out, okay?" Why did things that hurt always end in an 'okay?' It wasn't okay. Having live tissue scraped and removed like porcupine quills hurt like hell.

"It looked like a squeeze of rotten yellow toothpaste," "JC," my husband, said. He patted my arm in the car. "They took out a lot of skin tissue. It was a deep infection. You were a brave girl!"

And I got a Whopper for being a brave girl. If girls do marry men just like their fathers, I was in trouble. I could weigh two hundred pounds in no time just on doctor visit rewards.

Infections returned. I was put on the "fast track" at the ER and never had to wait long. I sported crutches first. Later, after a second and third issue, I had to get around school in a wheelchair for a while. My understanding of disabilities was immediate. One teacher friend of mine even suggested I was "milking it." Was I? While I debated that crack, I thought about all the kindness and mercies I'd been shown with my big leg boo boo: doors held, principal driving me down the hallways, students getting my lunch. No, I wasn't milking anything. I hated all that fussing and personal attention. *Bleah!* ...But, of course (and once more), I might be lying.

Years of fighting odd infections followed. I never felt comfortable discussing the root cause with the school community. How many times can you be referred to a disease control doctor and still not get a disease under control?

And here's what I learned from this little bacterial bomb:

If you have this scary condition, know that you can overcome it. But not completely through mainstream professionals. Doctors were <u>essential</u> for treating my immediate serious condition with the appropriate antibiotics. People die from MRSA. However, the natural doctor treats *the systemic root. Additionally, no one can or will tell you the directions for getting through the deep, dark pathway to returned health: sugar ("the white devil," as a colleague called it one day while I was carrying a cupcake past his classroom door, lost in vanillaville), colonizes disease, and that is a statement straight from my healing doctors. Stop eating sugar. Period. Eating right heals. Olive Leaf Extract helped me heal, also. Do the research.*

I cannot prove my job led to a twisted top ten medical malaise list. It really is a germy world, no matter what your career requires, wherever it puts you. Jobs can hurt you. Unfortunately for educators, students may choose to use their germy little school fingers to pull triggers, accuse, push, flip off, dispense toxic chemicals, or finger stir your coffee for you while you are monitoring the bathroom. Fingers (and in the average class size, that equals three hundred little digits), can spell trouble, if they choose to do so. The unexpected outcome is an equal opportunity surprise that even the veteran teacher cannot always anticipate or prevent.

Do the Right Thing --
Students to the Rescue

After the midpoint, I figured more out about my teaching. And it was not all bad. As life moved on and damning surprises passed, I had better work days. My mother grew more frail and suspicious of my future plans, because of my affection for a certain vo-ag teacher. Our once-predictable, mildly amusing "Kitty and mouse" relationship faded. A doctor thought Mom had suffered a few mini-strokes. Her personality changed. She could not always keep her food down, though she downplayed this condition, not wanting to go to a doctor. She went just the same. Ironically, I found solace in my work hours, in the company of a different generation. The reality was that at my waning age, I was suffering from parental woes, something my teen students understood personally. On my uneven odyssey (when a few not-so-thoughtful students seemed like The Book of Revelation come to life), there came grand surprises during my final teaching years, support from unexpected sources.

The pepper spray incident in my classroom yielded great news. There were still honest people in the world, unafraid to speak the truth, and some were not of AARP age. 'Post-PS' (pepper spray), one student spoke up and directly related to the principal the five w's and one h (who, what, when, where, why, and how) regarding the guilty party that nearly blew up my lungs. I later learned her witness account of the boys getting the pepper spray from a girl's purse and setting it off over the trashcan told me she had a place in a Spike Lee film, doing the right thing. Chelsie was both honest and fierce. This told me her parents had likewise done the right thing in how they had raised her.

"They let off the pepper spray and threw the canister out the window before Miss P. came back in the room," she said, when no one else would speak up or answer the principal's questions.

Today, Chelsie is a nurse. Her high school classmate, now spouse, Mike, is a business owner. They may well have the most adorable little baby boy I have ever held. In an interesting sub-plot, my former students bought my old family home. My husband and I could no longer maintain all the house needed. We were at the same life phase where our parents began downsizing, where we admitted we had age-enforced limits, which is not an easy truth.

This was the second most difficult decision of my life. This would be the last time I could sit in that empty house screaming at me with its memories. My dad was bursting through the front door cursing, a five-gallon dirt bucket and an unwilling thick blue spruce being dragged like a resistance fighter to the hall corner. The old ceiling tiles where he made that behemoth fit had tree pox scars. I heard my Oil City aunties storming up the steps with their luggage every August, singing their joy at being with Leo's family, ready to start their vacation and add five pounds from gourmand eats in Kitty's Kitchen. Warm hugs touched my arms as company came and left at holidays. I tasted Mom's magical three-layer Neapolitan birthday cakes and matching ice cream, enjoyed with grade school classmates wearing cheesy party hats, singing me "Happy Birthday" off-key. My brother was sitting on the living room floor reading, asking our grandma, "Nan, would you scratch my back...just for a minute?" I had stood outside the big bathroom door while Davis Funeral Home, led by Paul Carvelli and visiting Hospice nurses, prepared my grandma's body for transport, loading her remains into the hearse, knowing that Phase II of Mom's grieving was starting all over again. Upstairs was the beautiful built-in wardrobe with end-cap bookshelves designed by my dear Uncle Mason, where Dorothy Belle's books were displayed proudly. I opened one of the louvered closet doors. A few empty hangers where Dad's expensive striped shirts with white collars and cuffs had once properly hung, clanged at me like chimes do before a storm. This was my house, but my home, no longer.

In the old laundromat basement, the building where Dad operated a not-for-much-profit side business, Mike showed my husband a few things he had recovered. "I think Miss P. will want this," he said, coming out to where I was standing, purveying the property I was passing on to a younger, responsible owner. "Miss P., did this belong to your dad maybe?" he asked. "I didn't want to load it up for takeaway until I showed it to you. I think you'll want it." A son I never had had just picked me the equivalent of little-boy blue violets from the backyard.

I was floored. "How did that hard hat get in Dad's garage?" Why did he think I would want that hat? "No, that's not his, honey," I said. "I've never seen that before." A minute later, I remembered. "Wait, I know what that is," I said.

Dad had gone to work in the steel mills of Pennsylvania at the very mature age of twelve, walking to work beside his father, one hard hat to another. I had never seen the hat, nor a sword that surfaced. Leo had apparently brought that menacing slicer back from WW II while stationed in the Philippines. I knew why Dad had hidden that long, weighty saber. He knew his two offspring had some mighty lively word exchanges and that sword might make a close haircut for one of them. Samurai Kitty would have used it in the kitchen, holding it high over a big Georgia Rattler watermelon, ready to half it for one of our picnic treks to an old state park site near Salem. But the hat had a less obvious reason to hide from our family all those years.

Driving home with my husband, I tilted the seat back a little and touched that gritty hat resting in my lap. Though it hadn't rusted, I sensed it had witnessed and felt a lot. Did Dad hide it from us because it reminded him of the dangerous hellish-hot job of molding steel day after day instead of playing sports or riding a salvaged set of skates around his neighborhood? Or was it part of his '48 Fleetline man cave shelves where it sat on a high place of honor, the steel symbol that pushed him to enroll in Salem College and graduate more fiscally sound than his own father?

Dorothy Belle was right about our students becoming our later family. Mike had done many tasks for me while my student. But that moment of thoughtfulness graduated him to a distant layer of family. He was smiling, so proud of finding that hat! Those students we love we meet again. This was one of those times I would quietly tap my big yellow watch and recall teaching the concept of full-circle story action, of time completing the plot.

Eric, a Student Council member and peer remediation mentor, happened to walk by my classroom one day as a tall teen jumped straight out of his seat, challenging me face to face, refusing to do the assignment the rest of the class was doing. Yep, I felt I was staring down the bat of a mailbox smasher and maybe worse. I feared my tongue would end up standing at attention like a mailbox red flag.

Eric crooked his pointer finger the way any seasoned principal might, and said to that young man, "Let's take a walk, you and me." Eric was a football star, with game cred, on and off the field. About twenty minutes later, my student reentered the room like a human shell returned from a UFO abduction. He sat down and started on the assignment. Class was a little different moving forward. That's all I ever wanted.

Jill was a Boho chic free soul, a dancer, singer, guitarist, poetess. I have known her since forever, when my career began. She saved me from making a terrible mistake once, because she cared enough to risk my being angry or alienating her. It is never a sign of weakness to allow a student to advise you later on when both parties have lived through like experiences. Jilly has had a rich life! A Christian, she is a breast cancer survivor, plus an elementary principal who knows every trick in the book. Students cannot fool her. If I were young again, I think I'd want Jill to be my principal. She saved me from making a mistake. It bears repeating.

Deanne was a cheerleader, a senior English student from the same original haunt as Jill. I held her baby while she completed my senior English final exam. Joel grew into a handsome man! Deanne graduated college with a business degree and we remained friends; but moreover, she led me to the Lord again and again. Had she not been such a fervent prayer partner, I might have degenerated even lower than I did at times. My soul illuminated because of her bright light.

Brenda, beautiful heel-kickin' half-Native-American Brenda. She had sass, especially in high school, exactly at the time and place I started teaching. Brenda would be the first to say that she was a wild child, making no bones about her stormy past. She told me something she felt important. It had come from AA: "Always remember that when you point your finger in ridicule at somebody else, there's three fingers pointing right back at you." I had never heard that gem of humility, but like the rest of humanity, I needed to hear it.

She married a good man, Perry, had two children, and shored up her shortcomings. Brenda brought her two children to Family Connections for early-learning before kindergarten. A local stylist, she gave a new look to one of our mothers getting ready to interview for jobs.

Close to Easter, my southern grandma passed. My mom was having a tough time because except for visits to my aunt's house in Ohio, my grandma and Mom were inseparable. The loss hit Mom harder. Caregivers understand this. Nan died right in our home after a long illness. The funeral home hearse arrived to remove her body.

"Mom, Aunt Patty, go upstairs," I said. "I'll come get you when it's over. Don't watch." Saying the words made me look at my mother and I saw for the very first time her frightened inner child. I knew someday her face would be mine when loss would eventually come knocking a third time, bearing another body bag, making *me* motherless.

I was directing a show and stressed to the nines when Death took Nan. Post-funeral I went back to work.

Someone knocked on the door of our little block building at Family Connections. I opened the panic bar; no one was there. In a few minutes, another rap, rap. I again opened the door, looking down this time. In an Easter basket with multi-colored grass sat a blondie-blonde cocker spaniel puppy, a dusty pink lace bow around her neck and a card by her side. Her little face was straight-up staring at me. "I'm your Easter gift," she seemed to be telling me.

No one was there. I took the dog inside, of course, and began to cry. Was this the cutest face I had ever put my eyes on? Yes, it was. Who had done this? I hesitated, then opened that envelope with baby in my lap. It read:

Dear Miss P.,
I know you are heartbroken, losing your grandma. And I also know that nothing or no one can take her place. But I'm hoping you'll open your heart to this puppy and let her love you. Take her home. If it doesn't work out for any reason, I will happily take her back.

Love and prayers,
Brenda

I had to sit down. *No one* had ever done that for me, much less a student. This wasn't a Snickerdoodle, or a droopy rose. It was a precious, peeing puppy. But I worked, and Mom's arthritis would make it impossible to walk a puppy, no matter how tiny its kidneys were. On cue, Brenda came in the building and explained that there were these wonderful piddle blotters that no longer discouraged working folks from pet adoptions.

"They're called Puppy Pads, Miss P," Brenda smiled that incredible high cheek-boned smile. I jumped off my seat at our lunch table and hugged her.

"Bless that inventor," I sang. "I had no idea there were paper commodes!"

"Look!" Brenda's son, Perry, said with those beautiful brown eyes of his burning with discovery. "The puppy's nose matches Miss Ana's lips!"

Sure enough, my pinky-brown lipstick matched the puppy's nose. In a split screen from a magazine fashion feature, "Who Wore it Better," I knew who would win that color way for blush brown lips, and she walked on four legs, not two.

"Look!" Brenda's daughter, Johnna, added with her own observation. "Miss Ana's top matches the pink bow around the puppy's neck, Mom!" And it did. It was a sign.

That baby with those stunning, naturally curly long ears, laid in my lap the entire trip home. I knew one thing. She was going *home* with me. *Forever.* It felt like my child was riding on my lap, except she wasn't crying in a car seat. I hopelessly loved that baby already. Soft Kleenex would no longer be what I needed when days at work were less than stellar. Those long lamb-soft ears were everything. Just cascading my fingertips over the satiny dog-ear blankies nearly made my thumb go automatically in my mouth. But it didn't. I was driving.

"I hope that dog is stuffed. You know we can't have a dog, Lexsana," my mother cautioned. "Take her back. You know I can't walk. I certainly can't walk a dog."

"I won't take her back, Mom. She'll go on these things for dogs called Puppy Pads. Trust me."

Puppy knew her future depended on where she piddled. I bought the pads. She delivered the goods. At forty-one, I finally owned a dog, the kind of daughter who would never ask me for a phone or need an eight hundred-dollar prom dress.

She fit in our home fast, queen of all. Her sensitivity was astonishing. Dogs get the tears of humans. Without a psychology degree, Pipka knew the right thing to do when she sniffed a splintered heart.

I named her "Pipka," because my Auntie Jane, Dad's loving older sister, had called her own children, cousins Donna and Danny, that same tag of ethnic endearment. Pipka did everything I did. If I applied lip gloss, she cried until I put some on her lips. She had her own, Burt's Bees, and it was nicer than my cheaper brand. If I set my hair, she barked until I put small-sized Velcro rollers in her ears. When the dryer cycle stopped, she barked until I opened the door. She loved to pull out the towels and sit on them to fold them Pipka style.

How many less times might my Pennsylvania aunties have come for vacation had they seen that 4 x 6 laundry day picture reveal?

Time passes too quickly, especially for loving pet owners. I watched the revealing white fur circle her nose and eyebrows. Pipka developed cataracts and a retinal problem, requiring many trips to Columbus Ohio Veterinary Hospital. The scales were lifted from her beautiful brown eyes, like Saul of Tarsus. She was made whole again and lived her last years sighted, delighted, able to run with her beloved squeaky toys. But, no matter how youthful her face, her little body was quietly aging, like Cher, whom I also love. Soon, Miss Emmy Lou joined our family. As a Humane Society Board member, I showed her on Channel 5 to find her a good home on the noon news. She got one, because I took her home. We had her for sixteen years, and Pipka had a loyal sister.

Pippi died just before turning thirteen. Part of me died and that dog-child piece of my being has *never* regenerated. I loved her

that much, without apology. But when Brenda's husband, Perry, died followed by now-grown-up daughter, Johnna, something else happened. A year later Brenda passed, and three more pieces of me broke away. I had lost the triumvirate of the dog connection they brought to my world when I didn't realize I needed a dog connection.

When Brenda and Perry's daughter Johnna was a sixth grader, she won a county poster/essay contest for the Humane Society of Harrison County and was to be honored at the state capital in Charleston, West Virginia.

"Lexsana, I have good news I want to share," Brenda said one spring night over the phone. "Johnna just won a contest and I need to ask a special favor." Brenda could not attend the award ceremony at the capital. I did not need to know why. I just knew there was some major scheduling conflict she had to honor.

"Absolutely, I'll go with her and Big Perry." (Brenda's husband was also a former student from my first teaching post. The coincidences along my career path intersected in strange formations, like LA freeways.)

Johnna received her award from Teri Campbell, then Humane Society director, and Governor Cecil Underwood. The governor happened to be an alum of Salem College.

My job at SC (between teaching positions) was alumni director. Mr. Underwood certainly needed no directing. He had a suave persona and the softest lips in politics, because every time he visited Salem College, he pasted one right on my kisser, a public relations buss known as "the gubernatorial graze." "Cecil always took his duties seriously," said the grazed goob to no one, until now.

If any student saved me, it was Mike, as fabulously finessed as any celebrity I never taught. Freshly graduated from Parsons School of Design, he stayed in touch, visiting, writing. Losing my father made me do something ugly. I quit. I stopped the suffering I found in teaching. I could not tolerate students, staff, mankind. Dad's death motivated me to quit doing what he always dreamed I would do. I had no Plan B. Scarlett was out in the field, fist raised, swearing to God as her witness, she would never go teach again because teaching and administrating may have robbed her of her father. But, like always, she lied to herself.

The phone rang. "Lexsana? It's Mike, from your favorite place, New York, New York! I am so sorry about your father. I remember him coming from the county office to school to eat lunch with us. I know how much he meant to you, but now is your time. I want you to hop a plane and come visit me. We'll storm Manhattan!"

Though I resisted because I was so sad a year after Dad's death I wanted to fall into a canal, I ended the call suddenly agreeing to go storm Manhattan. How bad could it be? We'd see *Singin' in the Rain* and everything else I'd ever dreamed about doing in the city. Screw a tour group. I had a transplanted local-turned-metropolitan to show me a few of NYC's truer colors. I decided to start spreadin' the news that I was leavin'----

"---*New York?*" my mother said, looking like I'd asked her to lick the television screen clean. "You're going by yourself (I was thirty-one) to New *YORK?*"

I had lost my father. It made me lose my long, tucked-under tail and grow a flexible-to-firm spine.

"Well, *yeah*, I want to go, and I can stay at Mike's apartment. I deserve a little time away. *He says it's the chance of a lifetime.*"

This was my go-to line, the one Donna Reed uses to hook Jimmy Stewart, who is two inches from her face, while she's on the phone with plastics boyfriend Sam Wainwright (*It's a Wonderful Life*). Though it never worked for me where Mom was concerned, I kept the gravy quotes when I needed a little hope poured out. Because, to the dreamer trampolinist, "hope springs eternal." (Alexander Pope, *Essay on Man*)

"Sounds to me like a chance to get raped or robbed or ripped---" (Kitty Pilewski, *No To You Always*). She kept me restrained emotionally. If I put my hand on the Lumina door, I got a light zap of guilt. It took many friend-analysts to remind me what I already knew but kept avoiding, like laser vein surgery.

"Lexsana, if you go, then you might not come back. That's what your mom is afraid of. That's why you will always get 'no.' Sure, your mother pops your plans. You're the real pet in your house. She doesn't want you to run away."

That was hard to hear. The wag had gone out of my tail stub. How many times I wanted to tell my students that in order to finish growing up, you had to jerk your head out of the leash and run like hell. Sometimes, what we need to teach secondary students we cannot because: A) we aren't allowed to teach real life skills, instead pursuing absurd, imaginary higher state testing scores and B) no one listens these days, as proven by the mandated guidelines of reason #1.

Would my students ever guess that I envied their age, that stage in life when determined feet dig in and desires take flight? If I were their age, I wouldn't be miserable at my current age. I had GERD. Every night I belched up some inhuman stomach cocktail that tasted like beet juice and kerosene. I was Stomach Acid Queen, trapped in wondering what life on the outside was about, guilted enough not to go indulge myself and find out. I, like Buddy's simple elderly cousin in Truman Capote's *A Christmas Memory*, lived off the stories of others. If this continued, how would I ever not become my mother, a hidden poetry-penning absent member of society?

And here was the mistake that I made "over and over and over again..." (Dave Clark Five, *Over and Over*). "----Okay! Enough! SICK of this same old song, Mom!" I yelled at her. "I won't go. Forgive me for even mentioning it. When will I ever learn?"

Surprisingly, I did go ahead with my Big Apple trip. Briefly, I learned that it's fun to fly.

Actually, it wasn't. As the pilot circled the Hudson for a solid hour, I felt Mom's words kicking me right in the rump roast. Our pilot announced that the plane had lost ground contact. After a big dip down below the clouds, we jerked violently back up (Fifth Dimension, *Up, Up and Away*), into the clouds. This Kennywood-ish coaster performed The Whip on us riders twice. Too bad this was before the era of The Cloud. Perhaps it might have retrieved our instrument panel. Then, Mike and I could have made that *Singin' in the Rain* curtain and not been a half hour late. I felt like a bird with amnesia, flying through clouds with no sense of direction, which was my trademark. We circled another half hour.

"My God! We're burning off the fuel," the man seated next to me suddenly said in what some crash sensers identify as a "flat outcome." And, further (joy unspeakable), he was an airline pilot. The look on his blanched face told me he was not playing. "They circle and do that in case of a hard landing."

"How hard?" I asked. "As in *crash*?" I gripped the arm rests. That thick, strong hand on my former journeys was not there to squeeze. My eyes started welling up. Damn! My mother always won the argument because it was a matter of life and death -- that she always be right. She often ruined movies and shows guessing the outcome, always predicting the endings. She'd always predicted mine. She had writing chops, and so much more.

Hearing may intensify and hold on during and after death. Maybe that accounted for the deafening engines taking one last swoop down. I pictured Mom standing by my closed coffin, my god-awful senior picture holding down the lid. Naturally she would be sobbing, telling every mourner, "I just couldn't have the casket lid up. She had really, *really* bad dark circles."

All the suited souls on board who disregarded the flight attendants' mini lesson on emergencies made zero eye contact like some students in my classes who disdained stupid directions. But here those very passengers were, sudden students of aerodynamics, bursting to learn.

The entire cabin seemed to darken, revealing only our softly-lit eyes, 1940s movie style. Joan Crawford's face always darkened while the lighting designer cast this sleep mask of soft lighting around her eyes. The lit eyes were the true storytellers. As we bounced over cloud bumps, there were just wild, rolling marbles of lit-up eyes gauging the fear level in other eyes. It is the way scared little childuts (children-adults) prepare themselves for what they should feel next.

Damn! And I didn't have pen and paper to write that jewel down!

When we finally landed, passengers in that iffy cabin, meaning lots of squealing men and women, clapped and carried either purses or carry-on luggage awkwardly at the tailbone to conceal the potential brown spots on the backs of pants.

At the Gershwin Theater, I kept my program in my fingers, hands folded securely behind my back, posing like one of the *Declaration* signers, just in case. I was ready to declare myself a free New Yorker (furthering the fruit curse from father), and make myself a literal and a figurative apple head. I was done flying. I heard engines in my head throughout the show-with-no-beginning musical. Mike made up for all the near-death stuff. When the rain poured down onto that big stage set, I felt a little bit of dampness, just as I always did.

After I retired, I had time to make lists. I put together some magnanimous acts my students had done for me:

Christmas ornaments (not a macaroni one in the bunch); homemade cards; iconic cakes from Miss Piggy to Woody to Broadway's Cats; *a cocker spaniel; hugs; flowers; Quarter Pounders; a surprise reception for the biggest loser of West Virginia Teacher of the Year; supportive faces showing up at my parents' visitations; Mother's Day cards from Noelle every May; the young man in uniform who was a pallbearer at*

274

my mom's funeral; an at-home brake repair service by Jesse;
a hulking blue spruce live Christmas tree chopped down for
me from Buckhannon, (crashing down on new carpeting after
I mega-loaded it in fine Griswold fashion); Christmas cookies
(especially David's Fastnacht Kuechle); repairing vintage
Christmas lights that my mother desperately wanted to work
(merci, dear Greg); Dereck and Donnie and Zach digging the
graves for two of my dear elder statesmen dogs; Karl and Co.
building me fancy wall shelves I brought home when I retired;
Christmas luncheons; a student escort to the prom (thank you,
Pedro) and a twenty-years-later thank you card from Beth,
inviting me to a twentieth-year class reunion. Great students
like Kelly, Janice, Shalayna, Mike, Jay, Marissa, Gary, Carla,
Olivia, Sharmin, Bethany, Ann, Anabel, Jessica, Aaliyah, Ryan,
Mark, John, Bre, Josh, Barbara Jo, Amy, Donnie, Kim, Moose,
Ida, Heather, Alicia, Becca, the Media Crew, Dena, Zondra,
Bill, Adam, Jocelyn, Justin, Morgan, Dear Britty, Meagan,
Ally, Rhea, Julie, Michelle, Tammy, Patty, Brooke, Thea, Dear
Shirley, Marsha, Courtney, Isaac, Joel, Kevin, Greg, Amanda,
Travis, James, Shareen, Piedad, Shay, Haleigh, Ashley, Kathy,
Addie, Deb, Tiffany, Trista, Tianna, Gabe, Braeden, Bre, Kelsie,
Annette, Abby, Jason, Abe, Todd, Gregg, Wesley, Glen, Rezin,
Susan, Carlie, Erin, Erica, Molly, Heather, Steve, Amber,
Danny, William, Chip, Nancy, Nicole, Sammi, Lacey, Charlie,
Joanie, Monte, Virgil, Thomas, Christian, Angel, Teacher/
Coach A.J., Mark, Stephen, Rachel, Mary, Peyton, Tonya,
Clyde, Shawn, Andy, and so many more, who went above and
beyond their student duties to assist with yearbook, school plays,
room decorating, junior humane projects, creative writing, even
my spirituality. I wish I had space to name you all.

Two of my former favorite old boys, now bank
president and veep in the same lending facility, valued my
graduation speech help eons ago, but that admiration has
never translated into what all dedicated teachers deserve-
--a Hallmark with gratitude cash, conveniently from right

there at the work site (kidding, kidding...but only about the Hallmark card. I have plenty of those).

Then there were Steve and Anna, from the same family. They were so good to me when I barely knew what I was doing as a youngster-educator. I ended up teaching Steve's daughter, Michelle. Steve's wife, Star, was our volunteer cateress for Veteran's Day honor celebrations. My husband and I attended Steve's fortieth class reunion. We had a grand time, with a few surprises.

"Miss P., do you remember how I didn't have money for my senior things?" Steve asked me. "You bought my yearbook for me." Truly I couldn't remember doing it, but it was another reminder how much kindnesses count to students. To anyone.

Then a familiar blonde approached our dinner table and asked if I remembered her and something I'd done for her when she was a senior. Fortunately, that chair had no wheels or recline mode.

"Marcia!" I said, remembering her immediately. She looked youthful and appreciative for some reason.

Here comes the BOOM!

"Do you remember what you did for me in high school? I was having trouble with Mike and sobbing and you reached into your purse and pulled out your keys and said, 'Here, take my car. Just be careful. I'll be here when you get back.' Remember?"

I put my hand to my mouth and let out a scraugh (shock scream/laugh). I did remember it! *Why* did I give an upset blonde seventeen-year-old the keys to my baby? My 1971 apple red Nova was my everything. She was just so sad I wanted to help her. I loved my ride so much I believe I put up temporary fencing around my car-baby every morning at that first teaching job in the teacher-designated Shawshank parking lot. But as much as I loved my car, I loved Marcia more and she had always been one of the most mature students I ever taught... Notice how I keep justifying my actions when I had the reasoning skills of a chair?

Apparently I did the right thing. Marcia and Mike married, had a family, and are still together.

Then along came Julie L-G, who had invited me to that fortieth reunion. We had stayed in touch many years. Julie always let her heart speak. She was forthright as a sword, witty, and always wound up tightly. Some teachers did not like this, but part of me envied personality traits in her. When my father visited our high school, Julie and other seniors ate lunch with the two of us. And when Dad was very sick, Julie sat down and wrote him a beautiful letter, sharing why she thought so much of him and all his kind encouragement. He cherished her letter.

And Piedad (not pronounced Pie-Dad), one of the sweetest, best intellects to grace a public high school. She wrote my student support letter for the T.O.Y. Pageant application. It could have gotten me into Harvard. You couldn't buy a letter like that for $100,000.00, except in Hollywood.

It doesn't truly matter where we land or what we endure, so long as others remember us for something. I thought my list of students boasted more names than Chapter 10 of Genesis (minus the begatting). Impressive? Not really. Most any caring teacher with a few years of loyal service could make my list skinny in comparison. Every retired teacher (or any retired individual), should list how he/she impacted somebody. It fills a void during that emotional life transition from a speeding locomotive back to a drifting row boat with private citizen status.

Though there were no cash and prizes, it kind of was a wonderful work life. Sometimes it escapes me how my mostly-dutiful students put up with me, the oldest kid in the class.

"It's okay, Miss P, we don't mind if you cry. We cry, too. But...s-o-o-o...will there be snack this week?"

I said something most teachers and most colleagues would not have said, because they had higher standards, principles.

"Yes, kids, yes there will be. And if you tell or throw a wrapper on my class floor, that is the end of it. Got it?" They were fueled by food, and I was careful to check for food allergies. They got it, literally and figuratively.

Students know when adults look tired. Teachers take hits. They saw I was struggling and at just the right times, they mothered and fathered me. Sometimes they felt a move of the spirit. "Who do we need to beat up, Miss P.?" Andrew P. always asked me.

And then, there is Sarah, "mini me," who visited the library after school my final teaching years and shared all her days and thoughts with me. I watched her grow up on our high school's stage as a budding actress, starting in the fourth grade. We shared some rough fourth grade stories. How quickly her classmates discovered that she was talented, focused, fierce. Once I told her, "I want to be alive and see you accept your Tony someday." She replied, "You will." She was so convincing I think I shall ---wait. Was she just acting when she said that about my longevity? After all, she is that talented.

Those times when students tried to be extra good and give me more peace and quiet, it felt like they were pulling that extra seat up to the table for me, like family opening its door to a stranger at holiday time. School, after all, is a big, crazy unrelated family where you stay a while and exit, hopefully with some of what it takes to exist. Sometimes, the components get radical achievements and soar like eagles. At the Hotel Academia, you can't check out any time you like, but you can always leave.

Early on I had assigned a visual aid speech at employment site #1. I got a senior (Matt G.) with a pet raccoon that did tricks. He wouldn't have been able to step foot in a school building today with a "potentially rabid, wild animal" that way. That raccoon's behavior pleasantly exceeded most of my seniors. He should have taken that pet on *Star Search*! I could have made a bundle as that masked mammal's agent.

Another senior in that high school brought the mother of all visual aids for his speech. I was seated at my desk and heard a huge horn blast outside. Class got up and went to the windows, just as I had done as a third-grader seeing snow in early May. There stood Harold V. in full fire gear waving. What a sight for my often-sad eyes! It was a Bill Murray movie moment, empowering! My class and I went out to the parking lot. I felt many classroom eyes on me and my latest coup d'etat. There was likely a great foot traffic to the office by teachers crazed with disgust at the disruptive spectacle outside. At least a few old-schoolers were gathering their plants and old semester exam keys, convinced the school had caught fire.

I can say it now. I was the Lindsay Lohan of misguided young educators. Today, my antics would yield one odd arrest record for which Dr. Phil McGraw would invite me on his show just to say to me: "You're a school teacher? You got subpoenaed...you had wildlife in your classroom doing tricks, you had the entire county administration clamoring to your high school thinking a fire truck was being used as a weapon of destruction, you exposed drug runners and got threatened, the assistant principal chased you all over the building, you rubbed

279

elbows with a president and squired a famous senator to fast food joints, you gave your car to an emotionally-wrought teen-aged girl just so she could check on her boyfriend? And, more impressively, you got it for county teacher of the year? Wow! Well done! Write that book! You leave even me speechless, almost."

"Harold! What's this?" I asked smiling. "And, second question: Did you steal it, because I don't have tenure yet and I don't want to be arrested. I already had my brush with one deputy."

"Well, that would be a fire truck, Miss P. You didn't say the visual aid had to fit inside a room. And no, we won't be arrested. I got permission to bring it to school. It's okay; I'm a volunteer fireman. It's my speech!" Harold exclaimed, pushing up his glasses with authority.

Class got a complete schema of the fire truck and gear. I had no clue just how heavy all that fire suiting was. My appreciation immediately grew for fire and rescue organizations. I knew what my class was thinking: "*Damn*, Harold and Matt! You just screwed the rest of us out of A's!"

Harold and Matt certainly got their A's. Those guys were two regular Joes who taught me if you are good to kids, they respond, and nothing will be too small or grand for them to do in order to please. Even though a few possible rules were bent, I felt like a real teacher in those moments, at the very least, an inspirer.

Too bad the student-gifted cakes didn't arrive on my desk daily with uplifting quotes in pinks and purples right before I retired. That would be job Nirvana to a sugar addict like I was. Being known as a giving human, I could have ruled the school. After all, poorer people (meaning teachers, for one) are often the most generous.

A Note from the Teacher's Desk...

Parents, this is the list most teachers wish they could share with you. I understand if you're thinking *Who's she think she is shootin' that memo off to parents like that!?* Teaching and parenting connect. They hold society's launch codes. I admit it! I was never one-hundred percent sure of what I was doing. In fact, I think I was the extra name on the student roster, learning about human nature while teaching English. I felt more like a pinch hitter, a relief pitcher, trying to bring home a student win, helping a few young hearts cope, improve, unleash a little self-confidence. I often marveled at how many kids shared their innermost thoughts and problems with teachers. Full disclosure: We did not have all the answers. We're better at asking the questions.

The Education-Home Connection Wish List

1)   You are your child's first teacher. Nothing can change that. That means your home is your child's first classroom. Children are keener than any monitoring devices, for they see and hear all and naturally take their cues from all they record.

2)   A wise teacher once told me about writing, "Don't tell---show." Regardless of her personal life, Princess Diana was a wonderful mother and produced two inspiring adult sons. They were shown the way to a compassionate life by a mother who demonstrated all it meant to be

human. Children love to feel they are helping. Allow your child that privilege of giving. Attend something with your child that is not party based or trophy attaining. Reach down with your child and pull someone else up.

3) Could we all just put the phones away and concentrate more on family than social media? I don't use a cell phone and somehow, my life is rich, calm, and fulfilled.

4) Teach your child how to talk to another person. Eye contact has gone old-school antiquated. People now speak through their thumbs. Wouldn't Mark Twain howl at that? Most youngsters have never experienced the introductory bond felt in a simple handshake.

5) Read! Read! Read to your child! It's where *Jeopardy* contestants initially got their smarts! If you have time for gaming, then you have time to read to your child. Being read to is a powerful bonding activity, the portal to untapped imagination.

6) Show up! Studies reveal big declines in the number of parents who attend parent-teacher conferences at schools. No matter where I taught, those statistics were true. Part of success is showing up, whether a student or parent. If we make time for the things we love, then...

7) Many teachers welcome parents who volunteer. However, a hypercritical attitude is not welcome. It is not necessary to the volunteer's role. We're all learning what works in life and on the job. Be an encourager. We all need that. Plus two extra hands once in a while.

8) Character still counts. The number one character trait that seems lost is responsibility for one's own actions. Plus dependability. Teach The Golden Rule.

9) Faith and believing are still our national foundation. I took subtle opportunities to work in a little dose of spirituality when I could. If I got fired, I figured I would

rather serve my Master than the school board anyway. When I taught *Beowulf,* most of my students could not even tell me about the allusion to Cain and Abel, or who they were, several assuming they were a nightclub act or a seventies band. And that is just sad.

10)   Make good on your warnings. Spell it out for children the way teachers have to spell it out at school. Behavior problems begin when children are not given choices and consequences ahead of time. Just as teachers must hand out review sheets before semester exams, review behavior choices with children. They know that if they choose to be unkind or unwilling to listen, there will be consequences. Tell them this ahead of the event, but above all else, stick to the consequences. It makes standing in a long line or shopping a lot more pleasant.

11)   Lucille Ball said, "If you fail at being a parent, then you're a failure at life."

12)   Less rewards and materialism and more humility and compassion. (This also applies to the entire world.)

13)   Children really don't like yelling. We all need a subject filter and a volume button. Society is going deaf from human amplification. I tested my theory by making calls to students' homes. Some houses were so loud I held the school phone way out, like a trombone slide.

14)   Teaching a child that helping someone else is the best way to happiness is essential. He who misses the opportunity to do a good deed misses the opportunity to connect with self-fulfillment and purpose.

15)   The best people in this world are caring and kind to animals. Students I had who are now incarcerated began their chosen pathway by hurting animals. Teach that there is NO place on earth where cruelty should live. Teach this to your child early, please, because it would be wonderful to see all schools have active junior humane

society clubs. Millions of unwanted animals end up with tragic outcomes due to a lack of humane education.

I'm just an observer of children's behaviors for twenty-eight crazy years. Like parents, I felt inadequate and overwhelmed many times at my job, and I was also exhausted every single day. My classroom looked worse than your living room ever will. It was a place of messy creativity, not sterility. Most kids liked that lived-in look. We lit up our little corner of the school with holiday decorations, lights, and their creative projects. Students said they felt safe there. I liked hearing it because, after all, don't safety and feeling loved keep our hearts beating?

Sadly, the extreme, worst part of my job was attending the funeral of a student. I chose not to write about that sadness and not deepen the pain of surviving families. Many of those kids came from excellent homes, but many had struggles no one quite saw. I always wonder what I might have done at school, if anything, to reverse a child's decision not to go on in the world. My heart aches for the wonderful parents I know who feel that hurt every day, forever. Home and school have profound, shared responsibilities.

Yes, yes.....Parents think teachers deserve the same sort of "helpful list." Some truly do deserve one, but for my money, the majority of educators are still at least secondary heroes. Just ask Tony Danza. He got the lesson.

Which brings me to my ultimate educational "Game of Tomes". Hey, Hollywood! Why not take my *Chalkboard Challenge*? Do as Tony did. If you have a teaching degree, bring it, book it, get dirty in the trenches. Teaching...the toughest role you'll ever love! (Right behind parenting).

A Funeral Awakening -- The Circle Closes

When I moved away from Salem after marrying, I continued to miss my old money pit house. More than that, I missed my neighbors of forever: Phyl and Jimmy, Winnie and Ken, Bonnie and "Shorty," Betty and Bob, and across the street, Johnnie and Warner Matthey. Phyl and Jim held apple head as a baby. They are still in my life, as is Betty, a nurse, who always came over when one of us was sick. Winnie was like a second mother. Bonnie and Shorty were generous to our family, growing spectacular floral rainbows around their home. Our memories are a very huge, fragrant bouquet. Once upon an era, long, l-o-n-g ago, neighbors knew each other. They talked and visited and did amazing, selfless things for others, without being asked. Warner knew amazing things that only come from long life and honest, hard work. Growing up, I had those dear hearts in my life for extra guidance. I love them up to God and back. But this story revolves around Warner, for he deserves another eulogy for his wonderful listening skills alone, letting me rattle on about all my school problems, patiently taking it all in, maybe quietly planning his supper menu in his head.

Warner was the kind of next-door emergency kit you always reached for, like a kitchen fire extinguisher. He didn't wait until you were out of town to bring your paper over on a rainy day when it might get soaked. He didn't need you to be gone on a trip to keep a watchful eye on your property, his presence a little bit like the billboard eyes of Dr. T.J. Eckleburg in *The Great Gatsby*. He was a fixer, a sharp gardener, a homemade soup deliverer. Sitting in his famous summer porch swing, we looked out on the town below us, hanging plants swaying above our heads, updating each other about the citizenry and my pets' antics. He had such a happy, moderate personality, the kind of man for whom God wished he'd made duplicates. He was part of that neighborhood network of God-fearing folks, and he was loved by all of us. On my birthday and on Mom's birthday, he gift wrapped our Russel Stover chocolates, his signature treat.

The last time I saw my friend he had been moved to a facility, finally incapable of living alone. He was closer to his devoted daughter now. I was no longer teaching, so God said (still sounding suspiciously like Mel Brooks): "Here's the time you always wanted. So…what do you intend to do with it? Remember, it's a gift and I like thank you expressions. Get back to me in ten. I'll be waiting…"

I responded by making the trip to Parkersburg to visit Warner. Driving down streets looking for the care sign denoting the facility, I remembered that I hadn't been in a nursing home since my mother's death four years earlier. If I passed a continuous care facility on a drive going anywhere, I turned my head. Mom's end was devastating, not what I had promised my dad. I had given up things and still failed, letting down---my mother. She was no longer happy.

I hated teaching even more because I had to choose working until sixty for retirement benefits over caring for her, a point driven home by a rude hospital representative after Mom's last stay in the hospital. "You could be arrested if you aren't with her all day, all night…And another thing, we're not a permanent care facility, you know. She's been here three weeks. If you take her home then leave her for even a half hour, you could be arrested." She made her point. Twice.

Take a breath, you baracuda! A stay-at-home daughter instantly turned felon. "You promised your father I'd never go to a nursing home." The words were imbedded under my skin, tick-like. I would have gladly taken Lyme Disease over the involuntary replay of her words. I believe my mother died hating me; I was her greatest disappointment. That's sufficient novacaine to deaden any meaning to the rest of your life. "If you sell this house," one of her last warnings, "I will come back and haunt you." There are nights I find myself waiting...

We hide from Death, and we shy from Death, and we pretend there is no Death. We work to live, but in the lower, waning years of a career, there is a predilection to keep on working, maybe to convince God we still count, that we are still vital. That filled time creates a distance between our lives and our own transport in the special Uber, Death. In the nursing home, Death is a constant visitor, calling as often as the mood hits.

But today, I would attempt to blot out all that past thinking and be with my friend, be in that moment with him. Maybe I could get to Warner's room without condemning myself. Wasn't it normally a positive to face a private demon and walk right over it?

I couldn't. I stood outside the building, at winter's mercy. Maybe I would step inside, pass out, and wake up strapped to one of those beds of pain, "Pit and Pendulum"-style, starring again in a new *Twilight Zone* episode, just as I had during weight roulette death in fourth grade.

Freezing, I opened the door and marched dutifully in, looking down the corridor to Warner's room, as if I were to be punished there. In furtive glancing left to right, I saw seconds of long, exhausted lives in holding patterns:

287

fetal positions, unused slippers facing out along bedsides, murmurings to deceased spouses, slightly-deflated bobbing birthday balloons, reminders of the eventual slow leak in every last one of us, someday. Mom's face could have been on any of those women. Actually, it was on every once-youthful rusted face I saw.

"Warner was my first little boyfriend," Mom would tell us, sometimes, in front of Dad. She arrived from the cotton fields of Louisiana, a pretty pre-teen, "carried" (proper southern expression) to North Central West Virginia in the Davis family's Model A truck. My mother and Warner had lived so long that the reminiscence of their first simple date seemed an ancient time capsule picture to me----black and white smiles captured on brittle Kodak paper during one sweet pony ride in Warner's wagon, *right down main street.*

"Dear God," I whispered, almost to Warner's door. "Please let me accept whatever the day brings. Get me through this without tears." I sucked in my lips until they were not there, the precursor to my weep face.

The last thing Kitty Pilewski ever spoke on her death bed was to me. She looked at me, the color of her green-hazel eyes fading, hair damp, her voice erratic and slurred: "Am I going to die?"

"No...no, Mom, I don't think so," I lied. T*o my mother.* She was dying with gangrene in her gall bladder and eventually, every place else. It would be the last thing she said. I *lied to encourage her, but I lied, an affront to the parent who never permitted me that character deficit.* "All liars have their place in hell," Mom and Nan warned like clockwork. They were full-on, arm-locked Christian soldiers, marching to the saving tune of Billy Graham

Crusades. Deep down, I think I may have been, too.

An hour after my stinging perjure to Mom, the evening shift nurse tenderly explained the clean and dirty effects of morphine to me. "When you feel your mother is struggling to breathe, you can touch this button and increase her morphine, which will increase her comfort level. But realize that doing so makes the end come more quickly. I know it's an awful decision."

Again, with the awful decision making! No one wants that assignment. I'd been there like an emergency squad unit with every dying member of my immediate family. The sound of final breaths and accompanying throat rattles always struck back at me when I was exceedingly tired or mashed under the devil's hoof. I cannot say it enough, even today, to my mother...I...am...*sorry*. I stand at attention under God's sovereign sky, up on our peaceful country hillside, and ask Him to tell my parents how much they mean, how sorry I am for my many mistakes and flaws. I pray until I can take a calm, measured step again and believe forgiveness comes in daily contrition.

There are abhorrent things that outdistance the worst days of teaching, or of any other job. Caregiving family is chief among them. The serrated fileting of my soul was seeing in each fading loved one, not one life, but two, going backwards in time, full circle, to near infancy.

Life sometimes appears to me like a mature wheat field that has been thrashed down to sprouts and stubble, full-grown sheafs together with baby sprouts. Shakespeare had that twice-a-child thing succinct and spot on. In fact, I believe he must have traversed a full-to-capacity nursing home when he wrote *The Seven Ages of Man*, armed with a yellow legal tablet and his grand plumed pen, taking plentiful notes, so afflicted by what he saw that he hoped to die from an actual cerebral writer's blockage rather than linger to dust in long-term care.

He knew me! Warner smiled! I had not visited him enough. This visit would be brief, as he was uncomfortable. He wanted to be up and working. There were white oak baskets to weave, wood to whittle, plants to tend, corn to pick and shuck for supper, cattle to feed, historic coffee table books to read. Missing the sweet labor of work of any kind was The Greatest Generation's lament when failing health became permanent. My God! How we forget that our legs are our two freedoms. Dorothy always said it.

"I'm going home soon," he said to me weakly but determined, lying on his back. I had heard that double meaning from other people right before death. I clenched my teeth tightly, until I could put my face to his ear and not cry. "That is great news, Warner. Now you rest. We'll be back to see you soon," I said. "Hang in there, my dear friend."

I left, thinking about what hapless goodniks we are, those of us visiting hospitals and nursing homes. We try and bring aspirations, wrapped in a little get-well token, like the angel figurine presiding over Jamie's sick bed in Pittsburgh. But our words all sound rather artificial, trite dialogue in a bad play, with weak exit lines. And we leave after visiting, and reward our good deed by eating out, heading to our own homes to smaller concerns we pray consume us, busy us beyond the sad shape of things to come.

When I found out my friend had passed, I cried for days. It was yet another "good cry" (whatever that is). I'd lost three of my closest friends: Frances, then her sister, Roselle (my annual beach buddies/friend-sisters), then Warner. Death put a spigot through my chest and drained out every person I held there.

My husband and I attended my neighbor's crowded funeral and could barely see the front of the funeral chapel from the last row. We did some serious neck preening, trying to catch glimpses of faces we had not seen in some time. There were some lovely backs of heads, completely, totally anonymous to us.

The minister stood up and turned towards us, so tall, baby-faced, readily familiar to me. It was Kevin Lough, a former senior English student from my first teaching assignment. He was still as adorable as he was formerly ornery. His face was still cute as Mr. Peabody's boy, Sherman, a face to which only his high school principal could yell corrective commands. He was lively, a piece of comedy film sped up to increase his audience's laughter. A cancer survivor, Kevin had married well---and, into the Matthey clan. He accepted the call, and traversed many miles and places as a servant of his Savior. There were teachers who likely thought it would be a cold day in hell when the likes of Kevin Lough converted to The Reverend Kevin. I state unequivocally that cold days in hell occur every day in some pocket of the earth. I was glad to be part of this one.

As he began an opening prayer, then some wonderful recollections of Warner, he spotted me in the last row, possibly since I'd stretched my neck so high for a vantage point I had locked it there, like a curious periscope.

"I just saw my high school English teacher [curious periscope] Miss Pilewski, sitting back there, so I want to make sure I use good grammar today during the service." He was smiling broadly, like the Kevin I remembered, doling out his upbeat quips, happy as a puppy retrieving a stick over and over. He badgered me every day with his fervor, and I never once grew weary of him. One of the

291

unusual perks of a full-scale teaching career is the delight that comes from seeing what our students become. And seeing him there, masterfully conducting this important funeral, coming through many personal challenges, was one amazing full-circle chapter for me.

At the conclusion of a moving tribute in music and memories, the crowd stood outside in a hallway, waiting in line to retrieve winter coats. It was a few days after Valentine's Day and suddenly, I felt a cold reality shiver. Even in mourning, whatever life threw my way, I had a wicked arsenal of plot lines from classic literature in my head, my directory of consolation and understanding.

Warner was about to rejoin his wife. My mind drifted to the cemetery scenes in *Our Town*. I tried in vain not to think about another distant vault being lowered into the cold, selfish ground, under a Thornton Wilder black umbrella grave mound, because doing so would remind me of my first awful date with Death, my father's funeral. I swallowed that lump away, because the Bible advises "weep at a birth, rejoice at a death." That King James verse was speaking to me, hushing me like a calming mother applying a Band-Aid to a child's barely-scraped elbow.

"Lexsana..."

Oh! Another shiver hit! Did someone just say my name? No, I imagined it. Sometimes I thought I heard things being spoken to me, but they were not, like taking the hand of a stranger while picking out grapes, not looking back to make sure the hand was attached to my husband and not a stranger eyeing the Bing cherries. "Oops, so sorry, thought you were my husband. But boy! Are your hands soft! So, so soft!" Then I'd double-step it clear over to the feminine aisle of necessary evils and lose that cherry picker.

Again, I heard my name softly spoken, "Lexsana..."

The tender calling a second time assured me I was not mistaken. *Hallelujah!* It was a live male, whoever he was. There was no more reason to look backwards or feel frightened.

The voice was familiar to me, and not the voice of Death (which would suspiciously sound raspy and snarky like Joan Rivers): "Move it, chunky! I gotta get to the casket and make sure I took the right guy. Who picked *that* bunch of flowers out? It belongs at the prom! I got my Porsche hearse double-parked out front and it's frigging freezing in here! It's February, and it's warmer out there! Did the mortician not pay the gas bill again, or is all that ice coming off of you?"

I *had* heard him, even above the hum of soft conversations. I moved forward with the phalanx and there he stood, the handsome cad, still with the inimitable wicked-pretty eyes, his hand stretched out to shake mine.

It was Mr. Bill Matthey, who I hadn't seen in over four decades since high school graduation. I was still drawn to that flameburst of a smile, out-squeezing his grip. We stood face to face, the elite two who owned separate but equally unbelievable sagas of our senior English teacher. I felt like I'd suddenly seen a celebrity, because in his prime time he had all the right stuff to host a late-night talk show. I felt old all of a sudden. Fortunately, neither of us looked remotely decrepit. Bill was there because Warner was his uncle.

"Lexsana," he said a third time.

"Bill Matthey! Oh my God! It's you! I knew I heard you call to me...well, I heard *someone*."

More of that same---though aging--- burn of a smile, like the happy sun on the Raisin Bran box, with even happier teeth. It was a face that could still sunburn your own. I needed some color. I just missed hearing about my paleness from Mom. We continued to shake hands.

"Dorothy Belle would be so proud of you," he suddenly said, completely out of the blue, still smiling. Of all the things he might have said after forty-four years, this was surprising. He had no idea what sort of a teacher I really was, and yet, he was telling me that Dorothy "would be so proud." The urge to break out a good cry was stifled by an involuntary catch in my breath, redirecting me. We'd moved a long way from the "old Pollack" taunts he'd tossed at me a few times in junior high. (Dad cornered Bill one day after school, helping him see the errors of his ways.) Yet, here I was, floored by our momentary reunion and those choice words of his, as if scripted. I wondered if his shin still bore the dents of Dorothy Belle's awakening punts during English class, in the great class of 1972. My God! 1972!----Did numbers actually go back *that far*?

"My God! You have no idea what that means, hearing you say it," I said, after taking my hand from my mouth as if it had fed me his compliment and was holding it there until the right words could form a reply. I suddenly loved him more than cake! More than double rainbows. Decidedly more than avocados or arthritis.

Was it odd (and vainly satisfying), that a former favorite student-now-minister I hadn't seen in decades singled me out during a funeral? Yes. Was it strange seeing a classmate who had done alright (and done some hearty maturing like the rest of us), delivering that one-sentence wow in a hot minute, to my face, up close and sincerely? Yes...yes, it was.

Somehow it seemed to indicate I was standing at the beginning of my closing full circle. Something was about to happen.

294

My husband reached for our wraps, the word my mother used for outerwear, the word I still used just to preserve her memory, her Louisiana heritage. I put my coat over my arm, lost in thought.

Forty-four years of living behind us, and I had just been Billy Matthey'd in a direct face-to-face, an unthinkable compliment straight from the master class clown. As Twain noted, I could live on that compliment a good thirty days! It suddenly struck me that Bill was the student an intrigued Dorothy Belle could not leave alone--- asleep, awake, even at his uncle's funeral. For some reason, I kept hearing her old caution to "make haste slowly." Apparently, Bill was hearing her cautionary wisdom, too, because his compliment was impromptu, directed right out of him by a funereal teacher-ghost, nearly a half-century later.

We began to move again like stalled traffic, all of us inching towards the funeral home's glass doors. I got ahead of my classmate, choosing not to look backward, spilling outside under February's deep amethyst gray sky.

This was the calendar time when the Heavens are stalled between frigid, unmovable cold and thawed sun glints, promising the slow return of warmth, of change. Dorothy Belle was dancing at the soon-budding of her favorite season. Dad was in the ultimate Emerald City perhaps planting, no longer having to mark time in scrawls on calendars and appointment books. At least, that's what I felt was happening in an unseen place, where maybe we continue what was important to us, if given that precious privilege.

Striding back to the car, reviewing the morning's untenable events, I almost smiled. Another erratic day for Big Blonde. The crowded funeral morning was a dial sweep --- saying a difficult goodbye to Warner; flashing back with Kevin, then Bill, to separate generations, both part of me; walking outside into a climactic view between seasons; springing forward with a lesson, an end to stalling and self-doubt.

Even though my watch had stopped, a ticking clock was audible, its hands moving upward. My steps reminded me of time's tempo. We set that tempo, because the choices we make move the dial.

Then a host of lovely words and chronicles began crystallizing above my head, where all my life dreams started.

Time had been patiently waiting on me.

The earth appeared to be greener, softer, and the midpoint of winter inconsequential. My spirit felt warmed, clothed in new confidence.

I kept moving, and just then, I didn't need a coat.

Epilogue

So, that one sincere sentence spoken by my former nemesis, Bill, the comedic heckler, propelled me straight to my writing desk. The words and chronicles over my head outside the funeral home that brisk February pelted like sleet and I hurried to the car because I did not want the story to melt away. After ten years of failed attempts, I wrote as if I actually knew what I was doing. I fully did not. Completing personal objectives was never my strong point. Everyone else always came first. What fueled me this time was a little vocalized belief in me, gifted in a single random sentence. I wanted to tell a story, hopefully help someone, anyone struggling with a career, a crisis, a close relative, a health issue. It's oddly healthy to read about the monstrous fail of someone else's life. It helps us calm down and revisit our determination, if not our full purpose.

When I was crying all those years, asking God why all the calamity was happening to me, I was looking in a mirror at myself *while crying*. I'm finding out that other women do this, too! Instead of reviewing my own crying skills for self-indulgence, I should have been looking *up*, should have been listen-*ING to God's whispered answer* to my calamity question. He was saying: "I'm giving you your dream. Without all the messy parts and lessons, tell me ----**what would you have to write about**?"

...But, I wasn't listen-*ING* until that last bad hospital stay. Apparently, a prayer chain started because someone who worked at the hospital leaked "Miss Pilewski may not live through the night." *Wh-a-a-a-t?* Is NOTHING private any more? (of course not). Texts of my demise were greatly exaggerated!* I survived, then died to education, because it no longer completed me, and for that, I am most proud. Quitting saved me, but Bill's comment *propelled* me.

Then, this happened...

November 29, 2018.

I sent this book, my first child, out into the world, wrapped in a funny flat coat. That letting go was nearly as scary as sending a real child off to school to be evaluated, criticized, perhaps made fun of, maybe accepted, eventually, well read, helpful and serving.

Guess what happened! My child disappeared. Vanished on that same night. I believed it was on its way to be proofed. It practically took NCIS to investigate and track down the box containing my book proof. The popular shipping company, so secure, so trustworthy, told me "There was no ticket ever showing delivery. It's still at Staples somewhere."

December 5, 2018.

But it was NOT at Staples. Where was it? In Oklahoma, according to a message on Facebook with a picture of a shipping label, sent to my husband's son!

My updated, technologically-chic version of Mark Twain's famous quote about reports of <u>his</u> death being exaggerated. Just SO proud we have that one moribund thing in common. However, my brief stint as a Missouri riverboat captain was not as stellar as Twain's. There was no future in it; so, I omitted that whole wet episode from my book.

It matched the number on the receipt we had. Clearly (and incorrectly) delivered by world-renowned delivery service! --- What "ups" with that? The picture initially seemed like a type of ransom note. But it was not.

Further, Oklahoma was not where my publisher is located! So ---- not "OK." Once more, the mention of that tornado of a musical I directed, jinxed the entire manuscript. I also heard it landed in Ontario, seeing the world, just like Flat Stanley. (If you happen to be an elementary teacher, you'll get the reference.) That reveal turned out to be incorrect. Flat Stanley stayed in the states on a western round-up before heading back home to Almost Heaven. My own manuscript, taunting me! I was furious!

He (Stanley) was finally returned by a woman right before Christmas who expected presents for her kids from an aunt in West Virginia and got a goofy book proof parcel mix-up by a no-name career complainer instead. I am sure she was furious as well. She didn't want my baby. She wanted her presents, and I wanted Stanlcy back. Maybe it was some sort of shadowy sign, or maybe some eerie modern take on *The Gift of the Magi*. To clarify, I did *not* have her kids' presents. They may have landed at NASA's Space Station, because apparently, that lady's aunt sent her niece's children's presents from *the same location, the same way, the same night* I did. Merry Christmas to all!

January 3, 2019.

And where is my husband in all this? Hiding under the bed, perhaps? A former teacher, trucker, and mail carrier, he combined his career experiences into one manly mission: deliver his wife's baby straight into the hands of Mrs. Michelle McKinnie for editing before final proof. He would not rely on the kindness of any transit service again. My delivery man is already en route with the manuscript whether it wants a printer's proofing or not. Everything I saw in Mr. Carr's eyes at prom that night in April was correct. Everything. He has never let me down.

On another Christmas---a deep dip back in time when Dad began to sense that teaching was not a religious experience for his daughter, he made a grand gesture without words. Leo went to James and Law Office Supplies in Clarksburg, West Virginia, and bought that big little girl a Smith-Corona electric typewriter, the writer's equivalent of the sleek and powerful black Trans-Am (Burt Reynolds' *Smokey and the Bandit* hot ride) of the late seventies. He slapped a bow on the case and hid it behind the by-now, artificial tree in our hallway. Maybe Dad bought it as a thank you for not making him put up the sacrificial blue spruce, because it seemed, coincidentally, that Dad was finding his Christmas joy and religion all at the same time.

That automated, ink-ribboned wonder was in my top four best-gifts-from-family of all time. The other three were: my 71 red Nova, which I still have; a Louis Vuitton purse straight from my brother's visit to Vietnam, which I still have; and my wedding rings, which I will always have.

But Dad's gift is still my favorite. I believe that he knew I would use that typewriter somehow, someday, as a heart link between his career as a typing/business teacher and my own, allowing me to see my life more clearly and positively. He was recognizing my love of words over teaching, sensing that writing reveals answers.

Dad told me one time never to write things down I didn't want to perpetuate. "Words," he cautioned, "live forever. Never write even one in anger."

Maybe he saw potential he could not express directly; he wanted me to plant my own garden, my way, with words.

In time, that typewriter started to clunk and sputter like Dad's old '48 Fleetline Chevy. It still does, but it is long since retired, like its owner. I had to shift to odt's and Open Office Writer and a new printer and monitor to finish my story.

The moral of my story is Dad's moral: *Words count. Choose them wisely, have a purpose, then share them.*

Couldn't the world use some well-chosen, supportive words with purpose right about now? Did someone change your world, inspire you forever, make your burdens lighter? I believe we could all raise an affirmative hand there and say, yep, sure did. One question, and I assure you, it is not a quiz: *Did you ever tell that person how he/she made you become a better human being?* We all owe a debt of gratitude to someone. Don't let busyness supersede conveying your thanks. Life gets a little better for someone who reads an unsolicited tribute or hears an unexpected sentence spoken that refreshes, renews, saves.

Make that effort.

One short, spoken observation framed my dream. At a funeral! Think what your words might mean to that one extraordinary person who has never heard them from you. Maybe he or she needs to be reminded that no act of kindness is *ever* forgotten.

Finally....if you purchased my apple head story, thank you. I assure you as a former failure on the Humane Society Board who had the fundraising skills of a preschooler, that one dollar from every book sale will go to the local Humane Society here in Harrison County, West Virginia. You will have helped a pet who needs extra care and adopting, and in doing so, I will feel a little redeemed.

You have your assignment. Find a pen. Speak your good on paper...*Let's go, people!*

About the Author

Lexsana Kay Pilewski-Carr has eight pedantic syllables in her name. She lives with her unbelievably-patient spouse on the top of a baby mountain where it will never flood. When she moved to the lovely country, staff had one burning question: "Now, will all your dogs continue to live in the house with you? Why don't you put them outside, where they'll be happier?" Those loving, happy dogs are very much inside, which explains why company is not an issue for the Carrs.

JC and Lex enjoy nut gathering in fall, holiday decorating, shoveling their long drive in the winter, planting flowers for pups to water every spring, and cleaning seasonal décor out the Amish barn every summer, sending it to the Humane Society Thrift Store so Lex can buy more seasonal décor! She calls it her "new circle of life."

Lexsana still talks to the squirrels about her mom's fabulous food as they steal black walnuts and hickory nuts around the property. The deer appreciate their Carr refuge.

Her most enjoyable moments are now lengthy lunches of all types, several of them with former students, with zero interruptions and no more irritating, joy-ending bells!

"Jean Dixon" - Carr predicts a few more provocative books to come.